Furniture
Repair
and
Refinishing

Furniture Repair and Refinishing

L. Donald Meyers
Richard Demske

RESTON PUBLISHING COMPANY, INC., Reston, Virginia 22090

A Prentice-Hall Company

Library of Congress Cataloging in Publication Data

Meyers, L   Donald, 1929-
  Furniture repair and refinishing.

  1. Furniture—Repairing. 2. Furniture finishing.
I. Demske, Richard, 1930-   joint author.
II. Title.
TT199.M45   684.1'044   74-8485
ISBN 0-87909-273-4

© 1974 by
Reston Publishing Company, Inc.
A Prentice-Hall Company
Box 547
Reston, Virginia 22090

10 9 8 7 6 5 4

Printed in the United States of America.

Contents

Preface

Believe it or not, it was the ecology movement that gave impetus to this book. Waste is not confined to energy, food, and Lake Erie. We throw away all kinds of things, among them some great articles of furniture.

Drive around any town on rubbish day, and notice the old chairs, sofas, desks, etc., all laying there worn and broken. As a matter of fact, pick a few of them up and put them in your back seat. All it takes is a little tender, loving care to make some of these pieces useful—even beautiful—again. Instead, they wind up in the dump. (And that's another good place to look for treasures.)

But it isn't only that these pieces are good for restoration. It's the misuse and neglect that could have been avoided. With a little care, the furniture on the junk heap might have lasted forever. One small repair, effected in time, could have saved a chair from completely falling apart.

There are lots of good reasons for learning the art of furniture repair and refinishing. They're outlined in the first chapter of the book. But you can't repair everything. Some are beyond hope, and when you think of the work that went into each piece, all the mighty striving Nature did to produce the tree it came from—well, it's sad, and that's another, better reason to learn how to preserve furniture.

Thanks for help in preparing this book must go to the Cooperative Extension of Cornell University, The Seng Company, the American Plywood Association, the Hardwood Plywood Manufacturers Association, the Forest Service of the U.S. Department of Agriculture, and that old pro, Howard E. Noble.

L. Donald Meyers
Richard Demske

Before
You
Begin

Someday a songwriter will compose a classic called "An American Lament," and one of the lines will be "I'm paying more money and it won't last as long"—not great poetry, but an accurate appraisal of many of today's manufactured items. There are exceptions to every rule and, happily, furniture is an exception. Sure, maybe new pieces cost more than they used to (but not much, relatively speaking), but good furniture will, as it always has, last forever.

Well, almost. "Forever" is relative, and wood eventually decays, but with proper care there is no reason why a good piece of furniture should not be kept usable as far into the future as anyone can foresee.

"Care" means maintenance methods such as periodic waxing, polishing, regluing of loose joints, and the like. But even when this *is* done properly (rarely), the best piece of furniture reaches a point where cosmetics can no longer hide its fatigue. Furniture is not, after all, designed primarily as art. It is meant to be sat in, dined upon, leaned against, and stored in.

It is at this crucial point—when the once-proud possession gets a little creaky in the joints, wrinkly in the skin, and dowdy in its dotage—that furniture often gets tossed aside, betrayed in favor of something younger and more zestful.

1

FIG. 1-1 • Good furniture will maintain its beauty and strength with proper care.

Fortunately, a complete rejuvenation is possible. The knowledgeable restorer is a veritable fountain of youth, able to do to wood what medical science and medieval explorers fail to do for mankind.

Not only is the restored blessed in getting another go at life, but the restorer shares in the good fortune. He has taken a discarded piece of "junk," which he acquired for little or nothing, and turned it into a useful and decorative piece of furniture. If he is skilled at buying and restoring, he may even have a truly valuable antique that is worth many times the expense and effort.

THE CRITICAL DIFFERENCE

When is a piece worth saving—or buying—and when is it not worth the effort of restoration? At one level, it is true that anything is worth saving. At the very least, a restored piece is one less on the massive garbage dump that mankind has been erecting for centuries. Furthermore, we become attached to certain things in our lives, and an old chair or desk can have a sentimental value far beyond its real worth. Another coat of paint can keep "Grandpa's chair" in the family for a few more years. Also, the restoration of the old dining room set means that you don't have to go out and pay three or four times more for a new one than you paid when you were first married.

    If your goal, however, is more than just ecology or sentiment or saving money (not that there is anything wrong with any of those motives), professional restorers find certain criteria useful in making a decision about whether to scrape or scrap. The same guidelines are generally true, as well, when deciding whether to buy an "antique" with restoration in mind. Is it of genuine

FIG. 1-2 • Complete rejuvenation of furniture is possible by mastering the skills discussed here.

use to you? Pretty, valuable, family heirloom, or whatever, if you haven't got a place for it, get rid of it. There are some styles of furniture that just don't mix. Many old pieces are just too heavy and ponderous for modern decors. Maybe there isn't room for it.

What kind of shape is it in? Is it sturdy? Loose joints can usually be fixed, but if it's poorly designed, can't hold its weight, is too spindly or coarse, maybe it isn't worth restoring. Look for signs of quality, such as dovetailed joints and easily opened drawers. Are there missing parts that can't be replaced easily? How much work will it take to get it into shape again? Maybe it just needs cleaning.

What is it made of? What kind of wood is used? If it's burl walnut, rosewood, or any of the other valuable woods, you should certainly not throw the piece out, no matter how ugly. Turn it into something else, shorten it, do *something* (Fig. 1-3). Or take it to a professional cabinetmaker and have him do it for you. Or sell it. But don't throw out valuable woods (not that wood has the same value, say, as an old coin or painting, but some woods have a priceless beauty all their own which just shouldn't be wasted).

Perhaps the most important question is: Do you like it—or, better—can you live with it? You may see something at an auction, antique shop or flea market that looks as if it might be a "valuable antique once it's fixed up." And well it might, but it's not worth a penny to you if you don't like it. Even when it's restored to its former beauty, you may hate it. Or it may clash horribly with the rest of your things. Sure, you can sell it (maybe) for more than you paid for it (maybe), but that isn't enough to justify all the work you're going to have to go through to restore it.

Ultimately, the answers to all these questions will depend on experience. It's like finding a job. The employer wants someone with experience, and the only way you can get experience is by working there. But you can find your way by keeping the criteria in mind and by depending on good old trial and error.

DO IT YOURSELF?

It is not difficult to restore furniture when you know how. The same, of course, applies to brain surgery, although it takes a little longer to learn "how." Facetiousness aside, brain surgery requires a great deal of skill and deftness, which not everyone can muster, but you don't need special talents to be able to restore furniture. You do need a certain respect for hard work, a little know-how, and a "feel" for what will work. But you can acquire these things. What you cannot learn is perhaps the most vital consideration of all—a real affection for and appreciation of good furniture. In particular, you need a deep respect for the craftsmanship and talent that produced the piece in the first place.

If you didn't want to do at least some restoration yourself, you wouldn't

(a)

(b)

FIG. 1-3 • Save the good parts of a piece of furniture by turning it into something else. The new desk (b) was made by removing the mirror and casters from the old vanity (a) and then refinishing.

5

be reading this book. But there are times when you should turn the job over to professionals. One of these times is when you stumble across what is truly a valuable antique. How you can tell that is another question, but if you have good reason to think that something is rare and old, take it to a reputable antique dealer for an appraisal. (He may charge you, but it'll be worth it.)

Chances are that the piece isn't worth as much as you thought it was, but if it does prove to be valuable, don't touch it at all unless you are quite experienced (even then, it may be wiser to pay a pro to do the job).

Whom do you contact? If you know someone in the field, fine. If not, a search of the Yellow Pages is the quickest way to locate people. For appraisals, look under "Antiques—Dealers" for a person who advertises that he does that type of work. Professional restorers and refinishers can be found in two places: right after the antique dealers under "Antiques—Repairing and Restoring" and under "Furniture—Repairing and Refinishing." (Maybe you can figure out why one "restores" and the other "refinishes." We can't.) Remember that not all the listees are qualified to do this type of work but a careful reading of the listings, plus a phone call or two, should ferret out someone who can help you.

Chances are very great that the piece you have in mind is not a valuable antique. That doesn't mean, however, that it isn't worth restoring. If it isn't a rare antique but is a nice-looking piece that would enhance the looks of your home, then this is a job that you can do.

Formidable though the job may look, it really isn't that bad. Remember that the beauty of old furniture lies in the rich patina of the wood, which has mellowed through the years. It isn't necessary (or desirable) to scrape the wood down to a point where it looks like new, raw material. All you have to do is get rid of the old, worn-out finish.

Upholstered furniture may require little or lots of work, depending on how complicated the job was originally. Dining-room-chair seats are a cinch; ornate sofas can be brutal. Tufted work should not be undertaken by an amateur. Here, the rule of thumb is, "try it." You can't really wreck anything (except the material). If the job looks easy, give it a whirl. If it's obviously a complex operation, you can do the refinishing and then send it to an upholsterer for that end of it. Also, before you buy an upholstered piece, look for the tag, required in most states, certifying that the object has been sanitized. (See Chapter 9 for more on upholstery.)

Furniture repair is another of those "iffy" problems. Minor repairs are fairly easy to make. Loose rungs and arms can be glued. Missing parts are sometimes easily duplicated, usually not. In this instance, you *can* ruin the piece by improper repair. If you're at all unsure, try the same Yellow Pages fellow you looked up under "Furniture Repair and Refinishing." (Repairs are more completely covered in Chapters 5 and 6.)

Before you do any of the above, however, you should check out the possibility of reviving the old finish with primitive materials such as a cleaner-conditioner or a little warm water and lots of elbow grease. Many pretty miserable-looking finishes are startlingly metamorphosed with polish alone (see Chapter 6). There are effective ways to remove scratches and stains which almost anyone can utilize with a little practice and patience.

LOOKING FOR A VICTIM

You aren't the only person interested in collecting old furniture for refinishing. As a matter of fact, the competition for old pieces is quite stiff and getting stiffer, driving prices up as a result of operation of the age-old law of supply and demand.

An antique shop is the obvious place to look for an unsuspecting chair or table on which to start working. Most of these shops contain a wide range of pieces, from very good to horrible. You can spot the dogs by their bargain price. If you're completely green at refinishing and are afraid you'll screw up your first job, it may be wise to choose one of the smaller pieces from the Early Awful or American Outhouse collections. Otherwise, pick out something you can use when you finish it (assuming that it turns out all right).

Antique shops are poor places for bargains, though. A good antique dealer knows his stuff and isn't going to part with anything decent at a discount price. If you have the time and stamina to devote to the art of acquisition, attend such homespun functions as garage sales, basement sales, flea markets, and auctions. Shop Goodwill, Salvation Army, and St. Vincent de Paul stores. Better yet, search the recesses of your attic and basement and those of friends and relatives. You can have their "junk" free or for nominal cost. Even junkyards and town dumps have been known to contain treasures.

Unfortunately, even these tried-and-true sources are becoming more competitive. Antique dealers, wholesalers, or "scouts" will be outbidding you at auctions, and Salvation Army smarties are taking a closer look at donations in order to discover hidden treasures.

WHEN AN ANTIQUE ISN'T

If you have real confidence in your ability to tackle a restoration job, or when you've had some experience in the art and are ready for something "big," it's time to go back to that antique shop. You will pay a premium for shopping there, but most antique dealers are reliable and knowledgeable. They'll be happy to sell or steer you to a piece that needs renovation. Even though you will pay more for expert advice, you'll be reasonably sure of getting something decent and not just somebody's castoff. Think about what you pay for expert advice from a lawyer, M.D., or dentist and the dealer's premium won't seem so bad.

If you're shopping in the no-man's land of auctions, flea markets, and garage sales, you're taking a real chance of being skinned. That "country bumpkin" you're buying from knows a lot more about his stuff than you do. You may well pick up a bargain. More often, it will be pure junk.

Remember that according to the U.S. Customs Department, antiques are those items (officially) made before 1830 or (unofficially) over 100 years old. (They're duty free.) Some experts would say that "antique" can mean something as young as 50 years. If it's younger than that, it simply doesn't qualify, no matter how it looks.

In our sense of the word, "antique" has been defined as "any work of art, piece of furniture, decorative object, or the like, created or produced in a former period, usually over 100 years ago" and, alternatively, as "a piece of furniture, tableware, or the like, made at a *much earlier* period than the present." The emphasis is added, but note the insistence on "much earlier."

Many of the guidelines as to whether or not a piece is worth restoring (p. 2) apply also to buying antiques. No matter how old something is, it isn't worth very much if it is poorly constructed, unattractive, or in unrepairable shape. It is possible, of course, for something to be an authentic antique but not fit in with your decorating scheme. If you can't use it, there isn't much point in finishing it—unless, of course, you're in this to make a profit.

For the novice refinisher, it is much more practical to restore a good, serviceable piece than to try to make money by buying and selling antiques. Once you get good enough (and fast enough) you might consider going into the business of buying, restoring, and reselling, but learn the fundamentals on something more modest.

WHY BOTHER?

With all the caveats involved, why should anyone bother with a messy and thankless job such as furniture refinishing? You shouldn't, really, unless you like it. And there's the "rub," you should pardon the pun. It really is—not fun exactly—but rewarding and satisfying to watch an old piece of "junk" turned into a lovely, glowing work of art, and to realize that you did it all by yourself (with maybe a few tips from us).

Don't, whatever you do, go into this with the idea that it's going to be a great big party. Expect to work, rework, and start over a couple of times. Trial and error is the keystone. For those who rejoice in the creation of the good and beautiful, it will be well worth their while. If you like easy pleasures and evanescent thrills, put this book down.

2

Knowing
Woods and
Why You
Should

If you know anything at all about furniture, you know that almost any material imaginable is used in modern design—from glass to metal to plastics (derived, in turn, from coal and chemicals).

When talking about repair and refinishing, however, the discussion generally concerns wood furniture. Wood lends itself easily to effective restoration, and it is virtually the only material furniture makers have had until recently.

Even if it weren't for the above considerations, wood would still be the material of choice for the vast majority of people. This old standby is our most versatile building material. It is easily cut, shaped, fitted, and joined, and it can be finished to a rich warmth that cannot be matched by any other product.

It is imperative for the budding restorer to know as much as possible about wood. The characteristics of wood, as given in Table 2-2 at the end of the chapter, are vital guideposts in knowing how to repair and refinish. Some woods are porous, some are dense; some are soft, some are hard; some are light, some are dark. All these qualities are important in determining the type of finish and degree of workability.

─────────── **TREES IN THEIR NATURAL STATE** ───────────

The two general classifications of lumber are softwood and hardwood. **Softwood** comes from evergreen trees (conifers) such as pine, cedar, spruce, and fir. These trees keep their needlelike foliage the year round, and they also produce cones. **Hardwood** is cut from broad-leaved trees (deciduous); ash, oak, walnut, birch, and elm are common varieties. These trees lose their foliage in the winter.

Fundamentally, both types of woods are made up of the same substances. The difference is in the arrangement of these elements. The millions of tiny hollow cells in a tree are packed tightly together in a honeycomb formation. In hardwoods, the cell walls are thicker, which makes the wood denser, heavier, and stronger. Softwoods have thin-walled cells, making them lighter and more porous.

A tree is a complex structure of roots, trunk, limbs and leaves. Only the larger portion of the trunk, the **bole**, is used for lumber. This portion is first crosscut into logs (Figs. 2-1 and 2-2).

In most species, wood at the center of the trunk **(heartwood)** is darker than wood in the outer part **(sapwood)** and varies from it slightly in physical properties. The relative proportion of heartwood and sapwood in a tree varies with species and environment. Sapwood normally can be seasoned more easily than heartwood. It is more easily impregnated with wood preservations. There is no difference in strength.

When tree growth is interrupted or slowed each year by cold weather or drought, the structure of the cells formed at the end of the growing season is different enough from that formed at the beginning to define sharply the annual layers or growth rings (Fig. 2-3). In many species, each annual ring is divided more or less distinctly into two layers. The inner layer, the **springwood**, consists of cells that have relatively large cavities and thin walls. The outer layer, the **summerwood**, is composed of smaller cells. The transition from springwood to summerwood may be abrupt or gradual, depending on the kind of wood and growing conditions at the time the wood was formed. In most species, springwood differs from summerwood in physical properties, being lighter in weight, softer, and weaker. Species such as the maples, gums, and poplars do not show much difference in the structure and properties of the wood formed early or later in the season.

Strength of wood depends on the species, growth rate, specific gravity, and moisture content. An extremely slow growth produces a weaker wood. Softwoods also are weakened by extremely rapid growth. Wood with low specific gravity or high moisture content is generally weaker. Defects such as grain deviation caused by spiral growth, knots, and burls also result in weaker wood.

Yet these structural defects frequently enhance the appearance of wood. **Spiral growth** results in a winding stripe on turnings. **Butt wood** shows the assembly of root branches, and **crotch wood** has a merging or diverging pattern.

FIG. 2-1 • Here is where it all starts. Lumberjacks fell a tree that will wind up in somebody's table, chair, or other furniture.

A **burl** produces attractive boards that show tissue distortion. **Bird's-eye** figures result from the elliptical arrangement of wood fibers around a series of central spots. Some quartersawed woods show pronounced whitish flakes where the wood rays are exposed. This forms an interesting pattern, especially in oak and sycamore.

TREE INTO LUMBER

Lumber is sawed from a log in two different ways, with the plane of the cut either radial or tangential to the annual rings (Fig. 2-4). When the cut is tangent

FIG. 2-2 • Lumber on the hoof—a lumber train wends its way from the mountain wilderness to the saw mill.

FIG. 2-3 • Cross-section of a log showing annual growth rings. Light rings are springwood; darker areas are summerwood.

to the annual rings, the lumber is called **plainsawed** (hardwoods) or **flat-grain lumber** (softwoods). When the cut is in a radial plane (parallel to the wood rays), the lumber is called **quartersawed** (hardwoods) or **edge-** or **vertical-grain lumber** (softwoods). Generally, lumber with annual rings at angles from 45 to 90 degrees is considered quartersawed, whereas lumber with rings at angles from 0 to 45 degrees with the surface is considered plainsawed.

The relative advantages of the two types of cuts are as follows. **Plainsawed** is usually cheaper because it can be cut from the log faster and with less waste. It is less likely to collapse from drying. Shakes and pitch pockets extend through fewer boards. Round or oval knots affect surface appearance and strength less than the spike knots in quartersawed boards. Figures formed by annual rings and other grain deviations are more conspicuous. On the other hand, **quartersawed** shrinks and swells less in width than plainsawed lumber. It cups and twists less and does not surface-check or split as badly in seasoning and use. It also wears more evenly, and raised grain caused by the annual rings is not as pronounced. Quartersawed wood is less pervious to liquids and most species hold paint better. Figures that result from pronounced rays, interlocked grain, and wavy grain are more conspicuous. The width of the sapwood appearing in a board is no greater than that of the sapwood ring in the log.

As it comes from the sawmill, lumber has a high moisture content and is unsuited for use in furniture (or anything else). It is important that lumber be

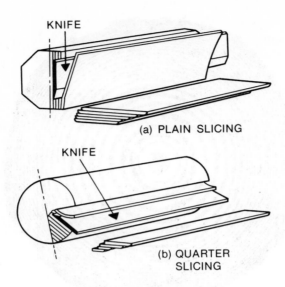

FIG. 2-4 • Two ways of sawing dimension lumber: (a) Plainsawn lumber is cheaper and less wasteful of the wood. (b) Quartersawn lumber has better grain and is less prone to warping and shrinkage.

seasoned until the moisture content is in equilibrium with the conditions under which the wood will be in service. When a condition of equilibrium moisture content is reached, the lumber has no tendency to shrink, expand, or warp. Because of normal changes in atmospheric moisture, this condition never holds constant. It is desirable, however, than an approximate equilibrium moisture content be reached.

Lumber can be seasoned by natural air drying or kiln drying or by use of various chemicals (common salt, urea, etc.) in combination with the other methods. The time available for drying, the species of wood, and the ultimate use of the wood are important factors in determining the method of seasoning. Kiln drying is the common commercial practice. Chemical seasoning in combination with air or kiln drying is used for seasoning some high-quality lumber.

FURNITURE WOODS

Certain characteristics are particularly desirable in wood used to make furniture:

* **Stability**, or the ability to maintain shape without shrinking, swelling, or warping

- **Ease of fabricating, surfacing, and finishing**
- **Pleasing appearance** (which may actually include some surface defects in the lumber)
- **Suitable strength and grain characteristics**
- **Availability**

Invariably, the best furniture is made of hardwoods, although some fine colonial-style furniture has been constructed from white pine and other softwoods. Hardwoods contain all the qualities listed to a greater or lesser degree. Softwoods ordinarily lack the desired degree of stability, strength, and grain characteristics. Furthermore, its appearance is suitable only for the specific rustic look of primitive furniture, such as Early American. Softwoods are, however, perfectly acceptable for painted furniture.

PLYWOOD

Most people think of **plywood** as the big 4- by 8-foot sheets used for home building or in do-it-yourself projects. These are, indeed, the primary uses for this product. This softwood plywood, however, is only one type. In furniture, rather extensive use is made of hardwood plywood.

For some people, the highest mark of quality in furniture is that it is made of "solid" mahogany, oak, or whatever. Actually, solid wood is used only for legs, rungs, and similar parts, and would not only be wasteful but not nearly as attractive as veneered hardwood (or plywood) for flat surfaces. Veneer is able to take advantage of the best methods of cutting the wood while retaining the strength that plywood has (Fig. 2-5). An increasingly important virtue of the veneering process is the efficient utilization of rare and valuable species of wood. Low-grade veneers can be used on the interior (and usually the back) without affecting the appearance of the final product.

Plywood is composed of thin plies or veneers that are glued together with the grains at right angles. Three-ply plywood has a center core faced with two veneers. Five-ply plywood has a core, two inner plies or crossbands, and a veneer facing. Plywood provides strength in both length and width and has good resistance to splitting and moisture changes. (Certain plywood varieties are put together with waterproof glue and are suitable for exterior use.) Plywood can also be bent or formed.

The most common types of hardwood plywood are:

1. **Veneer core** — All inner plies are of wood veneer, cut from a less expensive grade than the exterior plies [Fig. 2-6(a)].

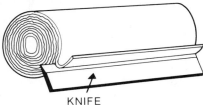

KNIFE

FIG. 2-5 • Plywood is made by slicing logs lengthwise on the huge veneer mill. A single "slice" or ply can be less than 1/16 inch thick. (*Courtesy of Georgia-Pacific*)

2.   **Particleboard core** — The interior is made of chips or pieces of wood combined with an adhesive binder. Also referred to as **chipboard** or **chipcore**. Used for kitchen cabinetry and similar work [Fig. 2-6(b)].

3.   **Lumber core** — The center consists of strips of wood several inches wide, bonded together, with a layer of cheaper veneer on both sides of that and the back and face veneers outside those [Fig. 2-6(c)].

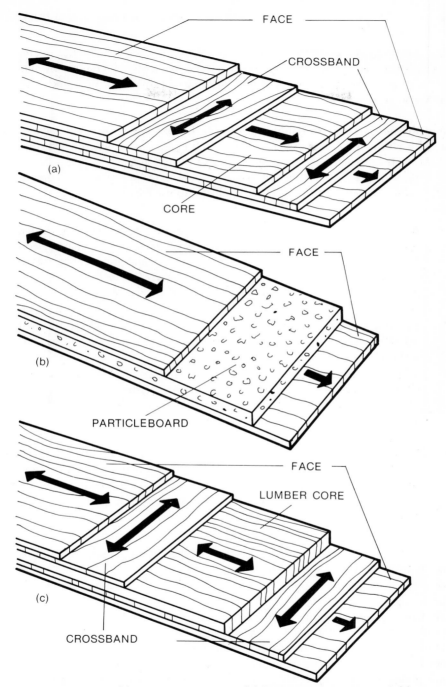

FIG. 2-6 • (a) Veneer core plywood. (b) Particleboard core plywood. (c) Lumber core plywood.

There are many other combinations of wood veneers and other exotic materials such as hardboard, kraft paper, plastic foam, and aluminum foil, but the best and mostly commonly used material for furniture is lumber-core hardwood plywood.

How plywood is made • Hardwood logs can be cut in four different ways to produce plywood. Of these, the first three result in no sawdust whatever, further increasing the efficient, maximum utilization of the cut logs.

Prior to use, most hardwood logs are heated to make cutting easier and to help ensure a smooth-cut veneer. The four methods used are these:

1.   **Rotary lathe** — The log is chucked in the center of each end and the log rotates against a knife, producing veneer very much like unwinding a roll of paper. A bold, variegated grain pattern is generally evident in rotary cutting. Eighty to 90 percent of all veneer is cut by this method.

2.   **Slicing** — Most slicers consist of a stationary knife. The **flitch** or section to be cut is attached to a log bed which moves up and down; on each downward stroke a slice of veneer is cut by the knife. Slicers are used primarily for cutting decorative face veneers from woods such as walnut, mahogany, cherry, and oak.

3.   **Stay-log cutting** — The stay-log method produces veneers intermediate between rotary cut and sliced veneer. A rotary lathe is used; a flitch is attached to a **stay log** or metal beam, mounted off center in the lathe. The stay-log method produces half-round veneer, which is generally used for faces.

4.   **Sawn veneer** — A very small quantity of veneer is cut in this manner. A circular-type saw called a **segment saw**, which has a thin, interrupted blade, turns on an arbor. The thin blade reduces saw kerf. This method generally is used only for certain species and to achieve special effects. Oak and Spanish cedar are often cut by this process.

After rotary veneers are cut, they may go directly to a **clipper**, which cuts the veneers into manageable rectangular sections, or they may be stored temporarily on a series of horizontal storage decks or on reels. From the clippers the veneer goes to the dryers—large chambers equipped with heating elements and fans and having automatic conveying systems on which the veneer moves. Some mills now use high-speed dryers located behind the rotary lathe, which allows the veneer to be dried in a continuous sheet after it is cut. Veneers are generally dried to moisture contents of less than 10 percent—a level compatible with gluing and consistent with the moisture content that hardwood plywood products will be exposed to in service. After drying, sheets smaller than full size are dry-clipped and joined together to form full-sized sheets. Taping machines and tapeless splicers are used in this joining process. Any necessary patching or repairing is done at this time.

The veneers are now ready to be glued. Alternate ply veneers are fed through a glue spreader, which coats both sides of the sheets with liquid glue. The spreader rollers control the amount of glue transferred to the veneer. Now comes the most important step in the process, the pressing together of the veneers. Heat (around 250°F) and pressure (150 to 300 pounds per square inch) are applied by means of a hot press. Presses have as many as 35 or more openings, each capable of pressing one thick panel or two thin panels. After pressing, the panels are stacked for conditioning, sawed to dimension, and sanded. They are then ready for inspection, grading, strapping, and shipping. Grading and inspection usually are done at intermediate steps in the manufacturing process.

Types of hardwood plywood • Table 2-1 was prepared by the American Plywood Association to denote the various types and grades of softwood plywood (primarily Douglas fir). (The Hardwood Plywood Manufacturers Association uses a similar grading system, with numbers rather than specific descriptions and letters.) Interior hardwood plywood, designated **Type II** plywood, is used most commonly in furniture. It is made using urea–resin adhesives and is resistant to water but not waterproof. It should not be used outside.

Type I hardwood plywood is designated for outdoor use, with a glue bond consisting of phenol, resorcinol, phenol–resorcinol, melamine, or melamine–urea waterproof adhesives. There is also a **Type III** hardwood plywood, used in some containers and for other rare usages, which has a urea–resin base mixed with more water and/or extenders than Type II.

Grades of plywood • If you examine the softwood plywood chart, you will notice that the grading system refers to whether one or both sides are suitable for the job in mind. Hardwood grading is a little more complicated, since more than one piece of wood may be used in each veneer (Fig. 2-7), and the patterns, color, etc., are taken into consideration. The most important of the many grades are the following:

Premium grade (A) ○ In *Premium Grade* the face veneer may be made from more than one piece. With most species, multipiece faces must be book-matched, or slip-matched (see Fig. 2-7). The quality of veneer is high; only a few small burls, occasional pin knots, slight color streaks, and inconspicuous small patches are allowed.

Good grade (1) ○ In *Good Grade* the faces are similar to that of Premium Grade faces except that matching is not required. Sharp contrasts in color and great dissimilarity in grain and figure of two adjacent pieces of veneer in

TABLE 2-1 • Grade-Use Guide for Appearance Grades of Plywood[1]

	Use these symbols when you specify plywood	Description and Most Common Uses	Typical Grade-trademarks (2)	Veneer Grade			Most Common Thickness (inch) (3)				
				Face	Back	Inner Plys					
Interior Type	N-N, N-A, N-B, N-D INT-DFPA	Natural finish cabinet quality. One or both sides, select all heartwood or all sapwood veneer. For furniture having a natural finish, cabinet doors, built-ins. Use N-D for natural finish paneling. Special order items.	N·N · G·1 · INT·DFPA · PS 1·66 N·A · G·2 · INT·DFPA · PS 1·66	N	N,A, B or D	C or D	1/4				3/4
	A-A INT-DFPA	For interior applications where both sides will be on view. Built-ins, cabinets, furniture and partitions. Face is smooth and suitable for painting.	A·A · G·3 · INT·DFPA · PS 1·66	A	A	D	1/4	3/8	1/2	5/8	3/4
	A-B INT-DFPA	For uses similar to Interior A-A but where the appearance of one side is less important and two smooth solid surfaces are necessary.	A·B · G·4 · INT·DFPA · PS 1·66	A	B	D	1/4	3/8	1/2	5/8	3/4
	A-D INT-DFPA	For interior uses where the appearance of only one side is important. Paneling, built-ins, shelving, partitions.	A-D GROUP 1 INTERIOR DFPA	A	D	D	1/4	3/8	1/2	5/8	3/4
	B-B INT-DFPA	Interior utility panel used where two smooth sides are desired. Permits circular plugs. Paintable.	B·B · G·3 · INT·DFPA · PS 1·66	B	B	D	1/4	3/8	1/2	5/8	3/4
	B-D INT-DFPA	Interior utility panel for use where one smooth side is required. Good for backing, sides of built-ins.	B-D GROUP 3 INTERIOR DFPA	B	D	D	1/4	3/8	1/2	5/8	3/4
	DECORATIVE PANELS	Rough-sawn, brushed, grooved or striated faces. Good for paneling, interior accent walls, built-ins, counter facing.	DECORATIVE · B·D · G·1 · INT·DFPA	C or btr.	D	D	5/16	3/8	5/8		
	PLYRON INT-DFPA	Hardboard face on both sides. For counter tops, shelving, cabinet doors, flooring. Hardboard faces may be tempered, untempered, smooth or screened.	PLYRON · INT·DFPA			C & D			1/2	5/8	3/4
Exterior Type	A-A EXT-DFPA (4)	For use in exterior applications where the appearance of both sides is important. Fencing, wind screens, outdoor storage units, cabinet work exposed to the weather.	A·A · G·4 · EXT·DFPA · PS 1·66	A	A	C	1/4	3/8	1/2	5/8	3/4
	A-B EXT-DFPA (4)	For use similar to A-A EXT panels but where the appearance of one side is less important.	A·B · G·1 · EXT·DFPA · PS 1·66	A	B	C	1/4	3/8	1/2	5/8	3/4
	A-C EXT-DFPA (4)	Exterior use where the appearance of only one side is important. Sidings, soffits, fences, structural uses, privacy screens.	A-C GROUP 2 EXTERIOR DFPA	A	C	C	1/4	3/8	1/2	5/8	3/4
	B-B EXT-DFPA (4)	An outdoor utility panel with solid paintable faces.	B·B · G·1 · EXT·DFPA · PS 1·66	B	B	C	1/4	3/8	1/2	5/8	3/4
	B-C EXT-DFPA (4)	An outdoor utility panel for farm service and work buildings.	B-C GROUP 3 EXTERIOR DFPA	B	C	C	1/4	3/8	1/2	5/8	3/4
	HDO EXT-DFPA (4)	Exterior type High Density Overlay plywood with hard, semi-opaque resin-fiber overlay. Abrasion resistant. Painting not ordinarily required. For concrete forms, cabinets, counter tops.	HDO · A·A · G·1 · EXT·DFPA · PS 1·66	A or B	A or B	C plgd		3/8	1/2	5/8	3/4
	MDO EXT-DFPA (4)	Exterior type Medium Density Overlay with smooth, opaque, resin-fiber overlay heat-fused to one or both panel faces. Ideal base for paint. Highly recommended for siding and other outdoor applications. Also good for built-ins.	MDO · B·B · G·2 · EXT·DFPA · PS 1·66	B	B or C	C (5)		3/8	1/2	5/8	3/4
	303 SPECIAL SIDING EXT-DFPA	Grade designation covers proprietary plywood products for exterior siding, fencing, etc., with special surface treatment such as V-groove, channel groove, striated, brushed, rough-sawn.	303 SIDING 16 o c GROUP 4 EXTERIOR DFPA	C Plgd. or btr.	C	C		3/8		5/8	
	T 1-11 EXT-DFPA	Exterior type, sanded or unsanded, shiplapped edges with parallel grooves 1/4" deep, 3/8" wide. Grooves 2" or 4" o.c. Available in 8' and 10' lengths and MD Overlay. For siding and accent paneling.	T-1-11 GROUP 1 EXTERIOR DFPA	C or btr.	C	C				5/8	
	PLYRON EXT-DFPA	Exterior panel surfaced both sides with hardboard for use in exterior applications. Faces are tempered, smooth or screened.	PLYRON · EXT·DFPA			C			1/2	5/8	3/4
	MARINE EXT-DFPA	Exterior type plywood made only with Douglas fir or Western larch. Special solid jointed core construction. Subject to special limitations on core gaps and number of face repairs. Ideal for boat hulls. Also available with overlaid faces.	MARINE · A·A · EXT·DFPA · PS 1·66	A or B	A or B	B		3/8	1/2	5/8	3/4

NOTES:

(1) Sanded both sides except where decorative or other surfaces specified.

(2) Available in Group 1, 2, 3 or 4 unless otherwise noted.

(3) Standard 4x8 panel sizes, other sizes available.

(4) Also available in STRUCTURAL I (face, back and inner plys limited to Group 1 species).

(5) Or C plugged.

(a) BOOK MATCHING

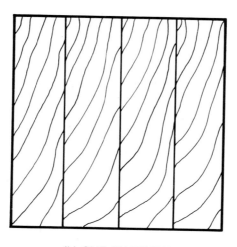

(b) SLIP MATCHING

FIG. 2-7 • Veneer patterns.

multipiece are not allowed. In this grade of veneer only a few small burls, occasional knots, slight color streaks, and inconspicuous small patches are permitted.

Sound grade (2) ○ *Sound Grade* plywood provides a smooth surface. The veneer need not be matched for grain or color but must be free of open defects.

Utility grade (3) ○ In *Utility Grade* open defects are allowed; there may be knotholes up to 1 inch in diameter, and wormholes and splits not exceeding 3/16 inch in width and not extending half the length of the panel are permitted.

Backing grade (4) ○ *Backing Grade* is similar to Utility Grade except that larger-sized open defects are permitted; knotholes not greater than 3 inches are allowed, and splits may be up to 1 inch wide, depending on the length of the split.

Plywood not conforming to any of the foregoing grades is called *Specialty Grade*, the characteristics of which must be agreed on by the buyer and seller.

Size and thickness • Hardwood plywood can be made in many sizes and thicknesses. Aircraft plywood and other specialty-use plywoods as thin as 3/64 inch are not uncommon. One of the standard thicknesses for flush doors is 2¼ inches.

The size of the plywood panel depends largely on its intended use. A standard panel is 4 feet wide and 8 feet long. A number of producers are capable of making plywood 5, 6, or 7 feet wide by 12 feet long. With special scarfing equipment, panels can be made as long as 40 feet or more; the maximum size depends largely on transportation and handling limitations.

History of veneering • The art of **veneering** has been known for many centuries. One of the earliest records is a pictorial mural that archaeologists unearthed in Egypt and have dated at 1500 B.C. This mural pictures workmen cutting veneer by means of a tool much like the modern-day hatchet; the glue pot over a fire suggests that the adhesive used in that period was some type of animal glue. The thin sheets of veneers were spread with glue, and pressure was applied by sandbag weights. Artifacts of Egyptian furniture taken from sealed tombs in the past century show that the first plywood manufactured by man was used in overlaid and inlaid furniture.

One historian describes how the Greeks decorated with wood veneers. Also, the Romans were early users of veneer and plywood. Most historians believe that the primary use of plywood in these two cultures was to achieve beautiful decorative effects by the use of highly figured veneer. Articles of furniture overlaid with veneer in these times were highly treasured articles. There is little reference to the use of veneer in the years that followed until the seventeenth and eighteenth centuries, when a revival of this art occurred in western Europe. In 1830, the piano industry became the first industry to use plywood. The earliest veneer-cutting lathe is described by Jon Dresser's American patent of 1840; however, it was not until some 35 years later that the veneer slicer was developed. The second half of the nineteenth century saw plywood being used to make chairs, desk tops, sewing machines, organs, and other articles of furniture. The stock panel idea was conceived of during the early years of the twentieth century. A panel was made in a standard size (originally 3 by 6 feet), which could be cut into smaller sizes as desired.

HARDBOARD

Hardboard is not ordinarily a component of fine furniture, but it is used often for snag-proof drawer bottoms, case and mirror backs, and for other uses where strength is more important than looks. (Specially finished hardboard panels, however, are in wide use for room paneling and may someday be perfected for use in better furniture.) Since you may encounter hardboard in your work, you should know what it is.

To make hardboard, logs are chipped down, and the chips are reduced mechanically into fiber bundles. These are then separated into individual fibers and formed into a mat, or thick, wet blanket of loose fibers. When compressed in giant hot presses, the result is a grainless, dense, uniform panel ready to be humidified and trimmed to size.

Hardboard, by definition, is more dense than wood and other composition panels and is therefore stronger and more durable, better able to resist dents, abrasion, scuffing, and hard use. It has excellent natural water resistance, but with tempering additives or other special processing it attains further improved moisture resistance, increased strength, and extra durability. Because it has no grain, it is equally strong in all directions. Like the wood from which it is made, hardboard is easily sawed, shaped, routed, drilled, bent and die-cut. Hardboard is free of slivers and splinters. Its smooth, hard surface is an ideal base for most types of opaque finishes or decorative surfacing materials, and it has no grain to raise or check the surface.

Hardboard is also used in cabinet building and can be shaped or molded into chair backs and seats. Perforated hardboard is often used for specialty purposes such as hanging tools or display items. Many people refer to hardboard as Masonite, which is the name of a large (but not the exclusive) manufacturer of hardboard.

TABLE 2-2 • Common Furniture Woods

Wood	Color of heartwood	Color of sapwood	Pattern figure	Strength	Uses
Alder, red (*Alnus rubra*)	Light pinkish brown to white	Same	Obscure	Medium	Panel cores, table tops, sides, drawer fronts, exposed parts of kitchen furniture. Stains readily in imitation of mahogany or walnut.
Ash, green, black, white (*Fraxinus*)	Light grayish brown	White	Pronounced	High in bending	Solid tables, dressers, wardrobes.
Beech (*Fagus grandifolia*)	White to slightly reddish	Same	Obscure	High	Chairs and exterior parts of painted furniture. Bends easily and is well adapted for curved parts such as chair backs. Also used for sides, guides, and backs of drawers, and for other substantial interior parts.
Birch, yellow and black (*Betula*)	Light to dark reddish brown	White	Varying from a stripe to curly	High	Solid and veneered furniture. Same uses as hard maple.
Cherry, black (*Prunus serotina*)	Light to dark reddish brown	White	Obscure	Medium	Solid furniture. Relative scarcity causes it to be quite expensive.
Chestnut (*Castanea dentata*)	Grayish brown	White	Conspicuous	Medium	Cores of tables and dresser tops, drawer fronts, and other veneered panels. Used with oak in solid furniture.

24

Wood	Color of heartwood	Color of sapwood	Pattern figure	Strength	Uses
Elm, American and rock (*Ulmus*)	Light grayish brown, often tinted with red	White	Conspicuous	High	Used to some extent for exposed parts of high-grade upholstered furniture. Easily bent to curved shapes such as chair backs.
Gum, red (*Liquidambar styraciflua*)	Reddish brown	Pinkish white	Obscure to figured	Medium	Gum furniture may be stained to resemble walnut or mahogany. Also used in combination with these woods.
Gum, tupelo (*Nyssa aquatica*)	Pale brownish gray	White	Obscure to striped	Medium	Cores of veneered panels, interior parts, framework of upholstered articles.
Mahogany (*Swietenia, Khaya*)	Pale to deep reddish brown	White to light brown	Ribbon or striped	Medium	All solid and veneered high-grade furniture, boat construction, and cabinet work.
Maple, hard (*Acer saccharum*)	Light reddish brown	White	Obscure to figured	High	Bedroom, kitchen, dining, and living room solid furniture. Some veneer (highly figured) is used. Most furniture is given a natural finish.
Oak, red and white (*Quercus*)	Grayish brown	White	Conspicuous	High	Solid and veneered furniture of all types. Quartered-oak furniture compares favorably with walnut and mahogany pieces.

TABLE 2-2 • Common Furniture Woods (continued)

Wood	Color of heartwood	Color of sapwood	Pattern figure	Strength	Uses
Pine, ponderosa (*Pinus ponderosa*)	Light reddish	White	Obscure	Medium	Painted furniture.
Poplar, yellow (*Liriodendron tulipifera*)	Light yellow to dark olive	White	Obscure	Medium	Crossbanding of veneers, inexpensive painted furniture, interior portions of more expensive furniture, frames of upholstered articles.
Rosewood (*Dalbergia nigra*)	Dark reddish brown with black	White	Obscure, streaked	High	Piano cases, inlays, musical instruments, handles, etc.
Sycamore (*Platanus occidentalis*)	Reddish brown	Pale reddish brown	Obscure to flake	High	Drawer sides, interior parts, framework of upholstered articles.
Tanquile (*Shorea*)	Pale to dark reddish brown	Pale grayish to reddish brown	Ribbon or stripe	Medium	Similar to mahogany.
Walnut, black (*Juglans nigra*)	Light to dark chocolate brown	Pale brown	Varying from a stripe to a wave	High	All types of solid and veneered furniture.

TABLE 2-3 • Selected Face Woods Categorized by Color

Light-colored woods: ash, birch, cativo, hackberry, limba, maple, pine

Medium-colored woods: butternut, cherry, chestnut, elm, hickory, lauan, mahogany, oak, pecan, persimmon, sycamore, teak

Dark-colored woods: ebony, paldao, red gum (heartwood), rosewood, walnut

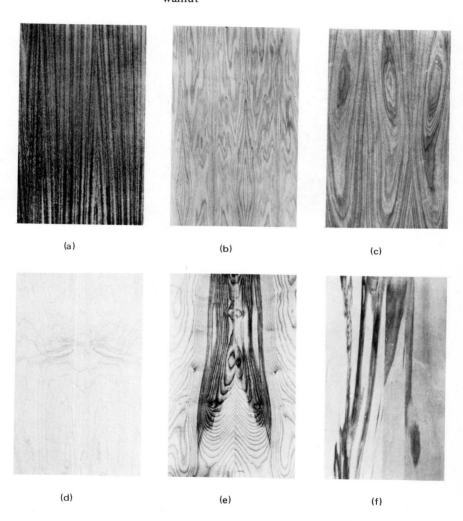

(a)   (b)   (c)

(d)   (e)   (f)

FIG. 2-8 • Illustrated are (a) mahogany, (b) oak, (c) walnut, (d) maple, (e) birch, and (f) gum.

TABLE 2-4 • Selected Face Woods Listed by Specific Gravity

Ebony	.90	Birch	.62	Sycamore	.49
Rosewood	.78	Ash	.60	Limba	.48
Persimmon	.75	Maple (hard)	.60	Mahogany	.47
Hickory	.72	Walnut	.55	Chestnut	.43
Oak	.68	Hackberry	.53	Lauan	.43
Pecan	.66	Red gum	.52	Cativo	.42
Teak	.66	Maple	.50	Pine (white)	.39
Paldao	.65	Elm	.50	Butternut	.38
		Cherry	.50		

FIG. 2-9 • Various plies are set across grains for strength (left edge). The finished edge at the right has been given a thin strip of wood edging for more stability and a better-looking side view.

TABLE 2-5 • Cores for Hardwood Plywood Panels

Core type	Panel thickness	Advantages	Disadvantages
Veneer (all inner plies of wood veneers)	¼ inch (3-ply) or less 5/16–½ inch (5-ply) Over ½ inch (7-ply)	Inexpensive Inexpensive Best screw-holding power	Difficult to machine; exposed edge shows core voids and imperfections; most susceptible to warping (doors)
Particleboard	¼ inch (infrequent) through 2 inches (usually 3 plies)	Most stable; least expensive (generally)	Poor edge screw-holding; heaviest core
Lumber core (consists of strips of lumber 1½ to 4 inches wide)	5/8–2 inches (usually 5 plies)	Easiest machined; exposed edges are solid; stable construction	Most expensive; worst overall screw-holding

Tools
and
Materials

Did you ever see a serious fisherman with a cheap reel? Or an experienced hunter with a bargain-store shotgun? Or a gourmet cook with low-quality utensils? Yet it is all too common for these same people to try something as time-consuming and delicate as furniture restoration with inadequate tools and materials. To save a dollar or less on a tool, they take the chance of negating hours of precious work spent on a restoration project.

Furniture is expensive; so is your time. If you intend to work with both of these precious commodities, it is foolhardy to jeopardize them by using inferior equipment. This doesn't mean that you should throw away your money by buying every expensive tool in town. It does mean that you should determine what tools you will need and buy the best possible tool for the best bargain. It means not picking up cheap imported hammers and screwdrivers from bargain counters in supermarkets. It means putting out some money for some power equipment such as an orbital sander and ¼-inch drill.

You don't have to do this all at once, though. Take one project at a time, figure your needs for this job, then buy what you need (and if something that you'll need for your next project happens to be on sale, pick that up, too.) If you have to, charge, go into hock, or whatever.

IT DEPENDS ON THE JOB

There are very few people in this world who do not own some kind of hammer, screwdriver, and a saw. And some sort of measuring device (if only a tape measure) is present in every home.

In addition to these common household tools, there are several tools that are a must for any job—and a host of special ones that you may or may not want to buy. It all depends on the type of restoring you want to do. Do you, for example, want to get involved with seat caning, gold leaf, and all the many special finishing techniques used in painted furniture? If so, fine, but you'll need special tools and materials. We shall divide the tools and materials, then, into three categories: essential, nice-to-have, and specialty.

ESSENTIAL TOOLS AND MATERIALS

No matter what you're finishing, you'll need certain tools to repair the structure and prepare the finish. A bare minimum repertory is set down below.

REPAIRING

- **Electric ¼-inch or 3/8-inch drill** — with large set of bits (Fig. 3-1). Works better than a bit and brace and costs less overall.
- **Clamps** — lots of them and in varying sizes. Get a pair of each kind you can find. Wood or hand-screw clamps (Fig. 3-2) will be vital and C clamps the most versatile. For long stretches you'll need pipe or bar clamps. (See p. 92 for more on clamps.)
- **Glue** — lots of it and different types. Glue is the major material for holding furniture together; screws, nails, or other devices are used primarily to hold the wood together until the glue sets. Be sure to have some animal or fish glue, plus "white," plastic resin, and casein glues around. (See the special section on adhesives, p. 49, also p. 88.)
- **Rope** — nylon best, but almost any kind will do, even a piece of old clothesline. This will be used in making tourniquets around legs, arms, etc.—often the only way to apply the proper type of pressure.
- **Knife** — a well-sharpened Boy Scout or "stockman's" knife fine (Fig. 3-3). Also have an old dull knife around for scraping off old glue, cleaning out holes, and other assorted tasks.
- **Wooden mallet** — just the thing for banging things in and out of place (Fig. 3-2). A rubber, leather, or soft plastic mallet can substitute.
- **Dowels** — in addition to glue, the best way to hold two pieces of wood together. Dowels come in the form of sticks that you cut yourself, or

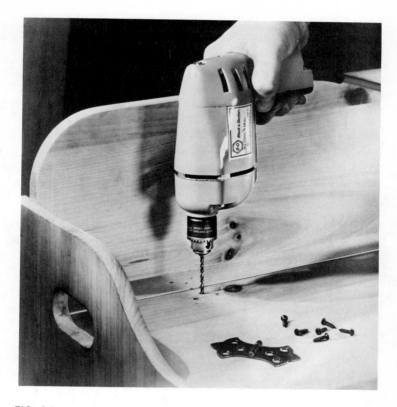

FIG. 3-1 • An electric drill is almost a necessity in today's home—and a great asset in furniture work. A 1/4-inch drill is shown, but 3/8-inch drills are becoming less expensive, and thus more common. (*Courtesy of Black and Decker*)

sometimes you can buy a package of precut, different-sized dowels from a lumber or hardware store. Dowel sticks also make good rung replacements.

- **Screw assortment** — not as good as glue for holding wood together, but sometimes the only way. Have some around, if only to hold the joint until the glue dries.

- **Wooden toothpicks and matches** — handy to fill up loose joints (in conjunction with glue, of course).

- **Razor blades (single edge)** — not really an essential tool but cheap enough so that you can afford to invest in a few. Used for cutting veneers.

- **Wood dough** — often referred to by one of its most popular brand names, Plastic Wood (Fig. 3-4). Used to fill in missing wood areas where surface appearance is not important. Strong, workable, and can be cut, sawed, screwed, and nailed into.

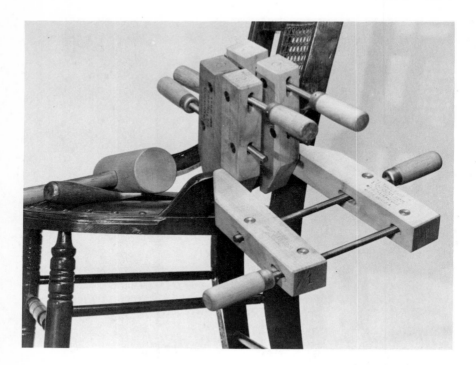

FIG. 3-2 • Three different tools illustrated here will be needed in your work. A handscrew or wood clamps hold the chair together. A wooden mallet and wood chisel are on the seat. (*Courtesy of Adjustable Clamp Co.*)

- **Angle irons, braces, etc.** — purists will tell you not to use these metal braces, and they shouldn't be used unless all other forms of bracing have been exhausted. They are useful, though, when all else fails.
- **Backsaws** — so named because of reinforcing rib along the back. They come in various sizes, but there is no need to get all of them at once. Start with the largest one, about 12 teeth to the inch (miter-box saw). Others range up to 20 teeth per inch and are called dovetail saws, veneer saws, and razor saws (largest to smallest). You can add these as you go along, if you wish.
- **Sandpaper, files, rasps (assortment)** — some of each, for cutting wood down to size. Start small and add to your collection as you go along. Don't skimp on the sandpaper, though. It's not expensive. (See Table 3-1 at the end of the chapter for sizes and types of abrasive paper.)
- **Smoothing plane** — the basic plane, essential for cutting large boards evenly, especially on the edges (Fig. 3-5).
- **Sanding block** — preferably with a small pad (Fig. 3-6). Makes sanding so

FIG. 3-3 • Some items you will become more familiar with are a good knife, a clear sealer (one of many finishing materials), tinting colors, and a 2-inch natural bristle brush. (*Courtesy of Sherwin-Williams*)

much easier you'll wonder why anyone does without it. You can make a serviceable one easily enough out of a piece of 2 by 4.

• **Scratch awl** — you wouldn't think you'd use it much, but once you've got it, you wonder how you got along without it. Great for marking for saw cuts, starting screw holes, etc.

• **Wood-marking gage** — a necessity for marking boards lengthwise. Scribes lines equidistant from the designated side.

• **Nail set** — not so much for driving nails as for knocking out dowels, plugs, etc. You could buy a center punch and be fancy, but you can also use the nail set for setting nails.

• **General tools** — those found already in most homes: crosscut saw, hammer, screwdriver, pliers, folding and steel rules, pencil, etc.

FINISHING

• **Brushes, old** — used, cheap paint brushes, for applying paint removers and similar substances.

FIG. 3-4 • Two more essentials—wood dough is a must for filling holes, and, of course, a screwdriver. (*Courtesy of American Plywood Association*)

- **Brushes, new** — used for applying paint, varnish, and shellac. Two-inch brushes are the best for nonspecialized work (Fig. 3-3).
- **Brushes, artist** — a few varying sizes, for touchups and special effects.
- **Putty knife** — for applying wood dough, lifting off old paint and varnish after it has been softened by removers, and assorted tasks. Use the oldest one, with rounded corners for scraping.
- **Scrapers** — wide-bladed knives for large areas. If you haven't got an old one, file down the sharp corners for scraping.
- **Toothbrushes, old** — for scrubbing off old paint and varnish after a remover has been applied.
- **Orange sticks (or meat skewers)** — for digging into moldings, etc., to remove old paint and varnish.

FIG. 3-5 • Shown here are a number of necessary things for the wood-worker. A smoothing plane is used on wood held in a vise. (Use smooth jaws for fine woodwork.) A good workbench is a must, as are the crosscut saw and level hanging on the Peg-Board wall behind the workbench. (*Courtesy of Masonite Corp.*)

• **Steel wool** — pads, starting with a package of mixed grades 1/0 to 3/0, if available. Used for mopping up and cleaning off the messy residue left by paint and varnish removers, as well as other fine abrasive jobs throughout the finishing process.

• **Chemical paint removers** — the jellylike removers are the best for all-round use (Fig. 3-7). (See p. 129 for details in selection and use.)

• **Linseed oil** — for various uses, including color restoration. Have at least one small can each of raw and boiled oil.

• **Denatured alcohol** — many uses in reviving and removing old finishes, notably shellac.

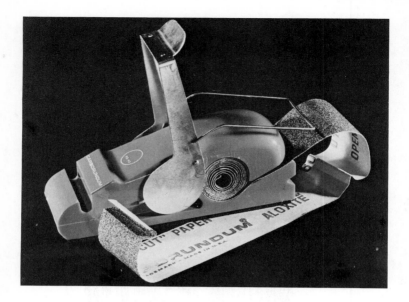

FIG. 3-6 • This professional sanding block also has a backing pad. (*Courtesy of Carborundum Co.*)

- **Rottenstone and pumice** — two fine powders used in hand-rubbing finishes and reviving old ones. Rottenstone is a little finer than pumice. (Use 3/F or 4/F pumice.)
- **Turpentine** — used for reviving old finishes, as well as paint cleaning and removing.
- **Shellac sticks, wax sticks, and/or a box of crayons** — for filling in scratches and gouges.
- **Stains, fillers, bleaches, varnishes, shellac, paints, and other finishing materials** — specifics not included here because of the wide variety, but you will need some of them all the time and all of them some of the time. They are discussed in Chapters 7 and 8.

OPTIONAL TOOLS AND MATERIALS

These are the items that are nice to have around, if you can afford them, and can pick them up one at a time at your leisure. Some are just time-savers; others will be absolutely essential if and when you need them. It depends on the job at hand.

FIG. 3-7 • You will be using a lot of paint and varnish remover. See pages 129-31 for a discussion of the pros and cons of liquid and semi-paste removers, such as the ones shown here.

REPAIRING

- **Bit and brace** — for some, this old-fashioned drill offers more control than an electric drill. It also works better with the larger-sized augers. If you are used to one, continue to use it. If not, an electric drill is really better.

- **Center punch** — useful when working with dowels or other items that require exact centers. Essential for starting holes in metal.

- **Dowel pins** — grooved pins for use when inserting dowels in matching pieces. More for new or reconstructed work than for old work.

- **Dowel jig** — useful when fabricating new pieces (Fig. 3-8).

- **Drill press** — great for the kind of intricate work involved in dowelmaking and joinery (Fig. 3-9). (See Chapter 5 for a discussion of joinery.)

- **Power sander** — as you progress, you'll probably want both a straight-line and an orbital sander. Start with the orbital (Fig. 3-10). (Rotary sanders are not good for furniture.)

- **Lathe** — terrific for forming new legs, etc. Get one of these only after you've mastered the more primitive steps in this book.

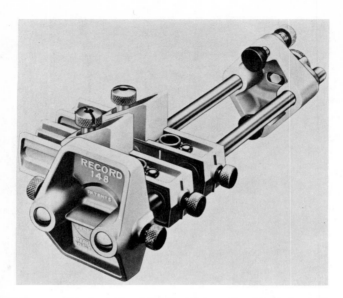

FIG. 3-8 • This new type of doweling jig is made in England and available in the United States. (*Courtesy of Record Tools, Inc.*)

- **Planes, block and jack** — for new work, mostly, but useful when forming new parts that have flat surfaces. The block is for small work, the jack for long, straight cuts.
- **"Surform" plane** — a sort of combination plane and rasp that is useful on curved surfaces (Fig. 3-11).
- **Radial-arm or table saw** — for new work, mostly, but extremely handy when you need one (Fig. 3-9). Particularly good for joinery, multiple cuts, moldings, or other fancy designs with special cutters.
- **Hand saws** — an infinite variety, depending on how your need and budget correspond. After buying ones we have listed as being essential, get a ripsaw, a keyhole saw, and a coping saw, then maybe a hacksaw, a crosscut saw of varying teeth per inch, and whatever else you can find. Many of these, however, will be superfluous if you have a good power saw.
- **Miter box** — the steel kind with the capacity for an infinite number of angles is best, but the wooden type is fine for 90 and 45 degrees, the most common angles used.
- **Glue injector** — actually a syringe made of metal or plastic which forces glue into difficult places (Fig. 3-12). Great for loose veneer, un-pull-apart-able joints, etc.
- **Electric grinder** — mainly for keeping tools sharp, an important requirement for fine furniture work (Fig. 3-13).

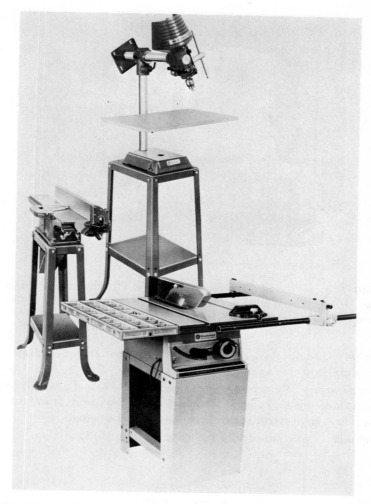

FIG. 3-9 • Three tools for the serious woodworker are a drill press (top), a jointer (middle), and a table saw (bottom). (*Courtesy of Rockwell Mfg. Co., Power Tool Div.*)

- **Spoke shave** — a small plane with ears, which works by being drawn toward you. Indispensable for close work.
- **Chisels** — wood, of course (Fig. 3-2). Necessary items if you want to fool around with joinery.
- **X-Acto knife** — if you're handy with a razor blade, you won't need these, but there are lots of uses for the different-shaped blades.

FIG. 3-10 • An orbital sander can be very useful for fast wood removal or for smoothing large surfaces. (*Courtesy of Rockwell Mfg. Co., Power Tool Div.*)

- **Vise** — woodworking or with woodworking jaws (Fig. 3-5). Holds things steadier than even a third hand can do.
- **Saber saw** — if you have one of these (Fig. 3-14) and a ¼-inch drill, you can throw the keyhole, compass, and coping saws away. It will cut almost any line, but it is particularly good for curves and cutouts.
- **Router** — great for edgings, moldings, etc. (Fig. 3-15).

FINISHING

- **Tack rags** — you can make your own (see p. 153), but it's easier to buy a few at the paint store or auto shop (Fig. 3-16). Used for final wiping of a piece before varnishing to remove lint, dust, and other foreign bodies.
- **Swab sticks** — sold in drug stores as Q-Tips or under other brand names. Used to make pick sticks, which remove small pieces of dirt and other offending specks from a newly varnished surface. (See p. 154 for further details on making pick sticks.)
- **Rubbing blocks** — like a sanding block, only a little more flexible.
- **Rubbing pads** — hard felt about 1 inch thick, used for the final finish with abrasive powders.

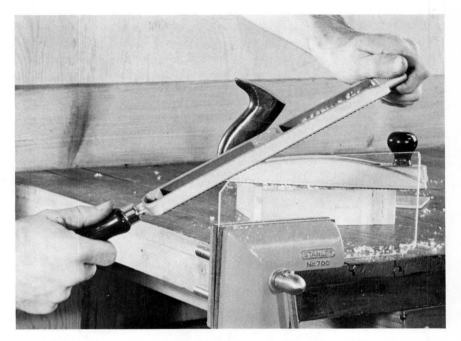

FIG. 3-11 • This "Surform" plane is handy for making odd shapes with all types of materials. Two varieties are shown. Also note the wood fiber jaws in the vise to avoid scratching the acrylic plastic. (*Courtesy of Stanley Tool Co.*)

FIG. 3-12 • This glue "injector" is actually a hot glue gun, especially made for some of the newer, solid, hot-melt glues. (*Courtesy of USM Corp.*)

FIG. 3-13 • An electric tool grinder will keep a sharp edge on chisels and other cutting tools—an important factor in fine work. Safety goggles are advised whenever using this type of tool or any other that could injure the eyes.

- **Spatula** — for applying patching materials and stick shellac.
- **Alcohol lamp** — for heating spatula and putty knives without leaving soot on the blades.
- **Varnishes, stains, etc.** — same comments as under "essential" materials; just add to the supply as you go along.

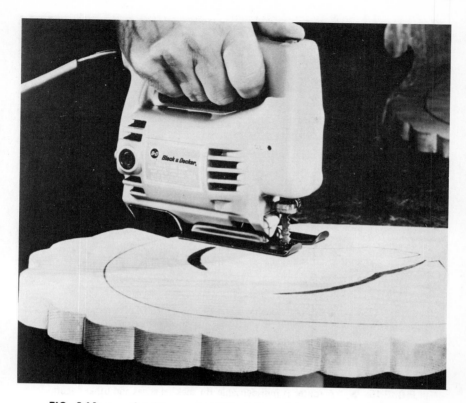

FIG. 3-14 • A saber saw is particularly useful when making freehand ornamental or curved cuts in wood. (*Courtesy of Black and Decker*)

SPECIALTY TOOLS AND MATERIALS

Some specialty tools may be essential for your use, some may not. If you do even minor upholstery jobs, for example, you'll need a tack hammer. On the other hand, if you stick purely to repair and refinishing of wood, you really don't need any of the tools or materials listed. Tools listed for repair and refinishing that are also used for upholstery are not repeated here.

UPHOLSTERY

- **Tack hammer** — a must for an assortment of jobs.
- **Staple gun** — sometimes used instead of a tack hammer, but you'll find ample use for both. (Do not try to use an office-type stapler.)

FIG. 3-15 • A router is indispensable for making edges and other decorative touches, as well as good glue joints. (*Courtesy of Black and Decker*)

- **Shears** — good quality, sturdy enough for cutting through heavy materials. It's not a bad idea to have another small pair for lighter material. (Southpaws should get a special left-hand pair.)
- **Webbing stretcher** — for pulling the webbing (and sometimes the fabric) tight.
- **Webbing** — a roll of burlap or plastic material used for seat and back reinforcement, holding springs, and similar tasks.
- **Assorted tacks and nails** — all sizes of plain and fancy tacks, common nails, and staples, for tying cords and things to the wood.
- **Manila or hemp string—tying twine** — oddly enough, for tying strings.
- **Heavy flax cord (1/8 inch in diameter)** — for fastening springs, webbing, and other parts. You may also need other specialized cords, such as mattress twine.
- **Small metal straps** — for fastening springs to wood.
- **Padding** — foam, cotton, and any other kind you like.

FIG. 3-16 • You can buy tack rags or make them yourself as described on
p. 153 (*Courtesy of Bond Chemical Products*)

- **Muslin** — for the underside of chairs and sofas.
- **Upholstery needles** — some standard sewing needles can be used, but large needles, straight and curved, are necessary to sew through heavy upholstery fabric.
- **Fabric** — this is expensive stuff and is usually bought when and as needed. If you intend to follow upholstery in a big way, you may want to have a few bolts of your favorite cloths on hand (but ordinarily not).

CANE, RUSH, SPLINT, ETC.

Techniques for replacing chair seats require no special tools except for pegs and clamp clothespins (if, in fact, they are tools). You will, of course, need materials. But other than the seating materials themselves, the only tool you will really need is a strong pair of hands. All the following materials are available at chair-seating and specialty stores.

- **Caning material** — the best and only material for a long period was **rattan**, a plant bark from India, Ceylon, Malaysia, and the People's Republic of

China. The best cane comes in long, select lengths up to 20 feet. Sugar or bamboo cane, although suitable for some jobs, is not strong enough for chair seating. Plastic cane is also acceptable, if not as authentic in appearance.

- **Rush** — can be bought at supply houses that specialize in these things, but you can also get your own rush by raiding the nearest swamp during August or the few weeks on either side of that month. (See p. 210 for details on preparing your own rush.)

- **Fiber rush** — the same as the rush described above except that it is made from a very tough grade of paper into rushlike form. It comes in varying widths and colors.

- **Splint** — long, superthin strips of native ash and hickory or tropical palm trees. The tropical palm strips are cut from the same tree as rattan. Here, the center or core material is split into strips and called **reed**. Both are used similarly, except that reed is a little easier to bend, and true splint makes a better-looking seat.

- **Macramé cord** — this can be almost anything that's knottable: polished cotton, sisal rope, India twine, Hong Kong grass, etc.

PAINTED AND DECORATIVE FINISHES

As used here, this type of finish is a highly specialized, difficult art that takes more natural talent and a keener eye than the finishes described elsewhere. Some of the effects are stunningly effective, however. The basic materials are listed here, with some of the techniques summarized in Chapter 10. Those seriously interested in this type of art should procure a copy of *The Art of the Painted Finish for Furniture and Decoration* by Isabel O'Neil, William Morrow & Company, Inc., New York. It's not an inexpensive book, but it does cover all these more esoteric finishes in great detail.

- **Japan colors** — available at some art-supply stores but often difficult to find. These paints are manufactured by T. J. Ronan, 749 East 135th St., Bronx, N.Y. 10451. Basic colors are as follows:

liberty red medium	burnt umber
signcraft red	raw sienna
chrome yellow light	burnt sienna
green medium (coach paint)	French yellow ochre
green light (coach paint)	lampblack
raw umber	

- **White poster paint** — mixed with the japan colors to provide lighter shades.
- **Solvent and diluents** — some will be the same as those recommended under refinishing, but you should also add "flatting" or soybean oil, japan drier, and liquid detergent Triton X100.
- **Brushes** — most will be same as those used for refinishing, except that you'll need more and better artist brushes. Numbers 3 and 6 long-haired point sable are the basic decorating brushes.
- **Palette knife** — used to blend colors.
- All kinds of other ingredients are used to effect the many decorative effects possible for painted furniture. Lacquers, casein paste, ox gall, kaolin powder, india ink, aniline powders, and other obscure materials will be needed as the art progresses (see Chapter 10). One subdivision of decorative furniture art is gilding, which employs pure gold leaf. At one time the most popular and attractive of the techniques, this art threatens to die a rapid death with the current price of gold.

THE IMPORTANCE OF ADHESIVES

There is no factor more important in the repair process than the proper selection and correct application of adhesives. As you progress in furniture repair, you will find that certain adhesives are more to your liking than others. No matter how beautiful your repair job is, that finely finished coffee table isn't worth much if it collapses under the weight of a half-empty glass. And what do you say to a visitor who ends up on the floor amid the scraps of the Kennedy rocker you so lovingly reconstructed? Good glue and gluing techniques can spare you this type of trouble and embarrassment.

GENERAL CATEGORIES

Because there are so many trade and brand names for the various glue products, selection of the proper glue is often difficult. Consequently, a knowledge of the generic types is usually helpful.

In general, there are two types of glue: (1) those formulated from materials of **natural origin** and (2) **synthetic-resin** glues, developed over the past four decades by the chemical industry. Ordinarily, furniture does not require a water*proof* glue, although it is helpful if the glue is water-*resistant*, as many are. If of course the furniture is to be used outside, then the glue *must* be waterproof.

EFFECT OF PRODUCT CONSTRUCTION

The choice of glue depends, first, on the conditions intended for the glued product. These are generally either normally dry interior use or service under damp or wet conditions, with direct exposure to the weather.

Wood shrinks and swells with changes in moisture content—an appreciable amount across the grain but generally only an extremely small amount along the grain. These dimensional changes across the grain are almost twice as large for flat-grain stock as for vertical-grain stock. Consequently, the stresses on the glue joint between two flat-grain pieces of lumber glued together with the grain at right angles (cross-laminated) will be very large with appreciable changes in moisture content. The stresses are cut almost in half if the pieces are vertical grain; and if the grain in the two pieces is parallel (laminated construction), the stresses are generally insignificant in comparison to cross-laminated construction.

If the layers of wood are thin (veneers), such as in plywood, the stresses exerted are greatly reduced, and glue bonds can be made that will perform satisfactorily even under severe moisture changes. As an example of the effect of veneer thickness, a flush door having 1/8-inch-oak face veneers is more apt to develop glue failure between faces and crossbands than one having 1/24-inch faces of oak, because the magnitude of the stresses on the joints will be greatly reduced when the thinner veneer is used.

It is very important, therefore, to design a joint so that the stresses will be minimum under changing environmental conditions. If this is not possible, a glue that suffers the least damage under continued or repeated stress must be selected.

WOOD SPECIES

There is a wide variation both in density and shrinkage characteristics between different species of wood. A combination of high density and high shrinkage results in the greatest stress on the glue joints. Conversely, a low-density species having small shrinkage develops low stresses on the joints.

A criterion for a good glue joint in which side grain is bonded to side grain is that it should be as strong as the wood (fail in the wood when the joint is tested). A weaker glue bond that would suffice for a weak- or low-density species might not do for a higher-density species. For example, a glue that performs well on a medium-density softwood might not be adequate for a high-density hardwood.

SURFACE PROTECTION OR FINISH

Deterioration or weakening of glue bonds may be caused by a variety of factors. Exposure to moisture, heat, and shrinking and swelling stresses are all known to cause degradation of certain types of glues. A good finish (having high moisture-excluding effect) can significantly retard moisture changes in the wood, reducing shrinking and swelling stresses. At the same time, it provides appreciable protection for the glue bonds. The benefit from good finishes in reducing the rate of moisture changes of glued wood products is often overlooked as a means of prolonging the useful life of glue joints. In selecting the proper glue, the type and durability of the finish is an important consideration.

USE CHARACTERISTICS OF GLUE

The temperature at which glue sets (room, lower than room, or elevated) is an important factor in the proper selection of glue. Pot use (usable life after mixing), storage life, ease of spreading, and ease of equipment cleanup are other factors that must be considered. Permissible assembly period (time between spreading and pressing) and the length of time the joint must be under pressure are other factors that generally play an important role in the selection of a glue.

HOW IMPORTANT IS COST?

Since prices of glue are continually changing, it is impractical to list exact figures. The cost increases, however, from the relatively low-cost soybean and vegetable glues to the animal, casein, and synthetic-resin glues, and finally to the straight resorcinol–resin glues, which are the most expensive. Cost must be considered, however, in terms of actual cost per pound of mixed glue and of the amount of glue spread required, that is, the cost to spread a certain joint area. Waste due to short pot life and cost of equipment needed must also be weighed in comparing glue costs.

But the most important consideration in the selection of a glue is: *Will it give satisfactory performance for the intended use*? Considering the time spent on this type of project, the cost factor of even the most expensive glue is negligible.

GLUES OF NATURAL ORIGIN

The glues formulated from materials of natural origin include animal, vegetable, casein, soybean, and blood glues.

Animal glues • **Animal glues**, also called **hide glues**, or **hot glues**, are probably the oldest known type of wood glue. They are made from the hides, bones, sinews, and hide fleshings of cattle. Most animal glues come in a dry form and are prepared for use by soaking in water, after which they are melted and applied while hot. Liquid animal glues, ready to use at room temperature, are also available (see below).

Animal glues come in different grades. The higher grades are preferred for joint work, the lower grades are suitable for veneering. Hot animal glues develop strength first by cooling and jelling and later by drying. They are preferred for hand spreading on irregularly shaped joints and for assembly work. The chief disadvantages of these glues are their low moisture resistance, the importance of temperature control in their use, and their relatively high cost.

Vegetable glues • **Vegetable (starch) glues** are usually made from cassava starch. They are sold in powder form and may be mixed cold with water and alkali, although heat is commonly applied in their preparation. These glues are relatively cheap and remain in good working condition for many days. The normal vegetable glues prepared from powder are extremely viscous, and it is not practical to spread them by hand. Special liquid glues, although easier to spread, are more expensive and are somewhat unpredictable.

Vegetable glues set relatively slowly, mainly by loss of water to the wood. In the past, vegetable glues were widely used, particularly for veneering, because the time between spreading and pressing could be varied without affecting the quality of the joint. The use of vegetable glues is limited today because, like the animal glues, they lack resistance to moisture and cause staining in thin veneer. These glues have not been used extensively for joint work.

Casein glues • **Casein glues** are made from casein curd (protein) precipitated from milk either by natural souring or by the addition of acids or enzymes. Lime and other chemical ingredients are added to the casein to prepare the glue for use. Formulas are available for compounding your own glue from raw casein, but it is generally more convenient to use the prepared glues supplied in powder form, which require only the addition of water before use. The prepared glues are available in small retail packages. The many casein glues available include glues with long pot life but relatively low moisture resistance, and glues with good moisture resistance but definitely limited pot life.

Casein glues have sufficient strength for either veneer or joint work, although with high-density wood species, the glue bonds are not as strong as the wood. They are used cold (although they may be hot pressed), and when properly mixed can be spread with a brush. The moisture-resistant casein glues are intermediate in moisture resistance, superior to vegetable and animal glues but poorer than most synthetic-resin glues. Disadvantages of casein glues are their tendency to stain veneers, the relatively short working life of some types, and the dulling effect of the glue lines on tools. Each of these limitations may be minimized separately by special formulations, but generally at the sacrifice of some other property.

Soybean glues • **Soybean (vegetable protein) glues,** which are similar in general composition and characteristics to casein glue, are formulated from dried protein of soybeans. They are cheaper and generally produce lower-strength joints than do casein glues and are therefore mainly used for veneering, primarily of the softwood species. Soybean glues are not normally suitable for hand work or small shop operations. Their moisture resistance is generally somewhat lower than that of casein glues.

Liquid glues • **Liquid glues** originally were made from heads, skins, bones, and swimming bladders of fish (Fig. 3-17), but most recently they have also been prepared from animal-glue bases by special treatments. The liquid glues tend to vary considerably in quality from sample to sample, but the better types produce joints comparable to those of hot animal glues. Liquid glues are more expensive than other nonresin glues and are primarily used in small-scale operations, such as assembly or hobby work.

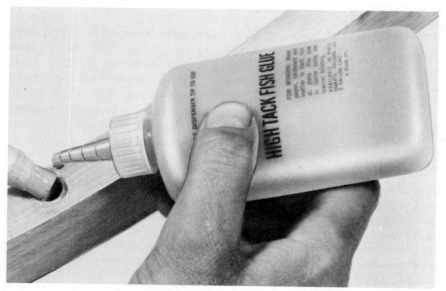

FIG. 3-17 • Fish glue is similar to hide glue in performance. (*Courtesy of Edmund Scientific Co.*)

SYNTHETIC-RESIN GLUES

Synthetic-resin, or simply resin, glues of various types have been introduced as woodworking glues since the early 1930s, but the greatest progress in their development began during World War II and is still increasing. These resin glues are products of the chemical industry and originate from raw materials as are derived from coal, air, petroleum, natural gas, and water.

All resin glues described here, except the conventional polyvinyl-resin emulsion glues, are thermosetting types. They undergo irreversible chemical curing reactions to produce insoluble, infusible glue films in the joint. The polyvinyl-resin emulsion glues are thermoplastic; that is, they do not undergo any chemical curing during the gluing process but remain in a reversible state and soften on subsequent heating.

Some resin glues are sold in a single package ready to use or as a powder to be mixed only with water. Many others, however, must be prepared for use by mixing resin, catalyst, fillers, extenders, and water or other solvent at the time of use. In any case, the manufacturer's instructions should be followed closely.

Plastic-resin glues • **Plastic (urea)-resin glues** are available in powder and liquid forms to be used with or without added catalysts, fillers, and extenders. These glues are formulated for curing at room temperature (usually considered as about 70°F) or at hot-press temperatures of 240 to 260°F (not for the do-it-yourselfer). The glue lines are colorless to light tan and have only a moderate dulling effect on tools.

Urea-resin glues have high water and moisture resistance at normal room temperatures but are sensitive to elevated temperatures and degrade more rapidly as the temperature increases, particularly with high humidity. These glues are not for exterior use. Resistance to elevated temperatures and exterior conditions can be somewhat improved, however, by modification with special fortifiers. When properly formulated, the unmodified urea-resin glues give high initial strength and are suitable for both veneering and joint work. They are generally not recommended where poorly fitted joints and thick glue lines are involved.

Resorcinol glues • **Resorcinol and phenol-resorcinol resin glues** are dark reddish in color and are generally supplied as liquids to which a liquid or powdered curing agent is added before use. These glues have much the same performance characteristics, including high durability, as resin glues. They have the added advantage of curing sufficiently for many applications at low room temperatures. They are, however, among the more expensive of the current woodworking glues.

Recent formulations of phenol-resorcinol resin glues are much lower in price than straight resorcinol-resin glues and appear to retain most of the desirable characteristics of the resorcinol resins. They are formulated for different rates of setting, the faster ones for use in cool weather and the slower setting for use in hot weather. Intermediate setting types are also available. They are all used for laminating or assembly of articles where a high degree of durability to exterior and other severe service is required. Their relatively high cost prevents their use as a veneering glue except for special applications. Several brands of resorcinol-resin glue are available for small-scale shop work and are of particular interest to the amateur boat builder.

Polyvinyl-resin emulsion glues • Polyvinyl-resin emulsion glues (the familiar "white glues"–Fig. 3-18) are available in a ready-to-use liquid form that sets at room temperature to a colorless glue line. Unlike the other resin glues described, these glues do not cure by a chemical reaction, but set by losing water to the wood. They remain somewhat elastic and thermoplastic after setting, which makes their use in highly stressed joints inadvisable. The polyvinyl-resin

FIG. 3-18 • One of the most versatile and popular glues on today's market is the familiar "white" glue. Technically a polyvinyl-resin emulsion glue, this adhesive is good for most furniture work. (*Courtesy of Duro Plastic*)

emulsion glues are useful, however, for certain types of assembly joints, where their greater elasticity is an advantage over the conventional rigid woodworking glues. Within recent years special vinyl copolymers have been introduced. These have some thermosetting properties and greater durability than conventional polyvinyl-resin emulsions.

Aliphatic-resin glues • **Aliphatic-resin glues** are cream-colored liquids that harden to a tone similar to that of animal glues. They are high-tack types that set up very quickly. Since they do not "creep" under pressure, they can be used on load-bearing joints. (Some resin glues can be used on such joints only if the joint itself actually carries the load.) Aliphatics can also be used to fill gaps in poorly fitted joints, since they do not crystallize or powder out. Aliphatics can be applied and will set at temperatures as low as 50°F (no need to worry about a chilly workshop). Aliphatic resins are water-resistant but not waterproof.

Epoxy-resin glues • **Epoxy-resin glues** set by chemical action and, since there is no problem of trapped solvent, can be used to join nonporous materials. Originally developed for bonding other materials than wood, they have been found useful in woodworking. Because they do not shrink appreciably on curing, they can be used in thick glue lines. Their "anything" qualities make them the choice in building those projects utilizing different materials, such as wood and metal or glass.

Epoxies are among the strongest wood glues available, but they are in the higher price range. They come in a two-part formulation and must be mixed before use (Fig. 3-19). At normal room temperatures, the mixture has a working life of about 2 hours. Total setting time is about 18 hours, but this can be accelerated by the application of moderate heat, such as from a lamp.

FIG. 3-19 • Epoxy glues come in two tubes, ordinarily: one, a resin and the other, a hardener. They are best for those areas where all else fails; they are not the easiest adhesives to use for furniture (*Courtesy of Duro Plastic*)

That about covers the sticky scene. All the types mentioned are available under various names; your supplier should have at least one of each type. Whichever you use, there is one final point that must be stressed: *Read the manufacturer's directions, and follow them to the letter*! Even the strongest glue won't affix a postage stamp if not used the way it was intended to be. (See p. 89 for tips on using specific adhesives.)

THE PLACE WHERE YOU WORK

It is important in furniture work to have a warm, dust-free place to work. Glue, in particular, needs warm conditions; also, constantly varied temperatures and moisture conditions will cause a lot of trouble. Many varnishes, shellacs, etc., just won't perform except within a certain temperature range. So shoot for a heated basement first; a heated garage, second. But settle, of course, for what you can get.

FIG. 3-20 • Professional woodworkers know the value of a work platform. It keeps the work at a comfortable height. Note the use of a wood block for sanding. (*Courtesy of Brown-Saltman Furniture Mfg. Co.*)

WORKBENCH

A big, old-fashioned **workbench** is not only a great place for working on chairs upside down, but it also gives you a place to store all those tools and things. Perforated hardboard in back of the bench is terrific for the storage of hammers, saws, etc., and a few shelves will hold the finishing materials (Fig. 3-5). Also put a 2 by 4 strip at the back of the bench for two excellent reasons: (1) it keeps things from falling off the back, and (2) you can drill holes in it to hold bits, brushes, screwdrivers, or almost anything else.

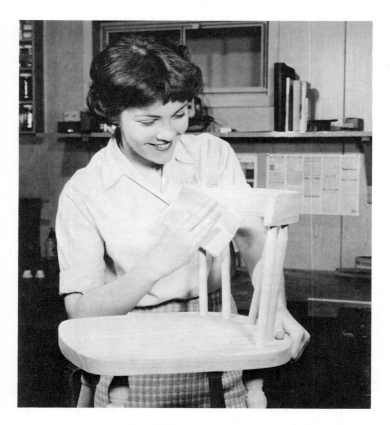

FIG. 3-21 • When working on curved surfaces, the sanding block only hinders the work. Use abrasive paper alone for this work.

WORK PLATFORM

A work platform is a great idea, for a couple of reasons. It raises the piece you're working on to a manageable height, and it provides a completely level area (if you build it right) for checking chair legs, or whatever, for evenness (Fig. 3-20). (Never trust a floor.) Furthermore, the rug it's covered with prevents your work from being scratched or dented.

To make a work platform, make a frame about 4 by 3 feet and 2 feet or a little less off the floor. Make sure it's level. It's a good idea to place the back next to a wall so that you can have something to push things against when you need pressure. A good example is when using homemade wedges (see p. 94).

The 2 by 4 frame is covered with a sheet of 3/4-inch plywood (or you can cheat a little with something a little thinner if the price is too high). You can also use boards if you prefer. The plywood is covered with a piece of carpeting tacked around and under the outside of the frame.

The platform is a convenient place to use for stripping the furniture and also for refinishing. But cover the rug or floor covering with newspapers when using such materials as paint remover.

TABLE 3-1 • Selection Chart for Abrasive Paper[a]

Grit	Grade	Description	Use
20	3	Very coarse	Floor sanding by machine
24	3½	Very coarse	
30	2½	Coarse	Not used for furniture
36	2	Coarse	
40	1½	Coarse	
50	1	Medium	Occasionally used for rough
60	½	Medium	wood and paint removal
80[b]	**1/0**	**Medium**	Paint removal and rough shaping
100	**2/0**	**Fine**	Preparatory softwood sanding
120	**3/0**	**Fine**	
150	4/0	Fine	Preparatory hardwood sanding
180	5/0	Fine	
220	**6/0**	**Very fine**	Finish softwood sanding
240	**7/0**	**Extra fine**	Finish hardwood sanding
280	**8/0**	**Extra fine**	
320	—	Superfine	Polishing finishes
360	**9/0**	**Superfine**	between coats;
400	**10/0**	**Superfine**	often used wet
500	—	Superfine	Used rarely for furniture
600	—	Superfine	work, mostly for plastics, ceramics, stone, and metals; used wet

[a]Silicon carbide (Carborundum) or aluminum oxide papers are recommended for furniture work, although garnet paper is acceptable.

[b]Boldface indicates those papers most commonly used in furniture work.

Furniture Styles and Their History

It isn't necessary to know that a certain piece of furniture is early Chippendale or late, or even that it's Chippendale. A chair can give just as much pleasure whether or not you know that it's a cornucopia-back Hitchcock. But as you "get into" furniture, you naturally develop a curiosity and interest in the types and styles of furniture, how they were constructed, when, etc. Knowledge increases and sharpens our enjoyment of things, and it is in the interest of pursuance of pure knowledge that this chapter is written.

It would be a serious mistake to assume that such knowledge is necessary to produce a good-looking repair and refinishing job (although it's helpful if you're interested in "restoring" a piece in the original sense of that word—making it look like it was in the beginning). You can take any old piece and make something nice out of it without having the foggiest notion of furniture style. So, if you're bored with styles and designs and want to get to the meat of the work, skip this chapter and turn to the next one. That concerns furniture construction, which is something you *must* know. The rest of you read on.

FIG. 4-1 • Recognizing furniture styles is an interesting, though not essential, offshoot of furniture repair and refinishing.

THE FICKLENESS OF STYLE

Another word for **style** is **fashion** and fashions change from year to year. Furniture styles are like clothes fashions, except that the cycles of change are a lot more durable. As we write, the current fashion is **eclectic**, which means (as far as anyone can figure out) that anything goes—as long as you like it. Theoretically, you can mix anything with anything, which sounds a little grotesque. Would you put an Early American chair next to an ornate sofa, or mix a Spanish table with modern chairs? Bad as it sounds, it works out, apparently, in practice.

But eclecticism is new, and was preceded by a Spanish or Mediterranean craze, which in turn was preceded by both Modern and Colonial preferences. Yet, while all these fads were going on, furniture manufacturers were making other styles as well, which goes to show that not everyone follows the mob. You can't afford to with furniture. It's something you expect to have a long time, through numerous fads.

THE OLDER STYLES

In the last few centuries, it was a reigning monarch who dictated furniture styles. We have the Georgian style (after the early English King Georges) and the various Louis styles, after the French monarchs. In the earliest known days, however, furniture was designed by craftsmen strictly for its utilitarian value, with a little style thrown in if possible (particularly in early Egypt).

It wasn't until the Middle Ages that a conscious attempt was made to create stylized furniture. From the twelfth to the sixteenth centuries there was only one style, and it was called by the general term **Gothic**. Religion was the dominant—often the *only*—theme in their lives, and therefore the furniture style was decidedly ecclesiastical. What was in the church was also in the home. After all, most of it was made in the monasteries. Greatly influenced by current architecture, Gothic furniture was ornate, massive, and much the same throughout the western world (Fig. 4-2).

FIG. 4-2 • Medieval furniture was characterized by heaviness of both style and wood, with wrought iron and elaborate arches.

Most furniture of the period was made of oak and was characterized by deep moldings and pointed arches. Wrought iron locks, hinges, and straps abounded. The universal furniture piece, dictated by the exigencies of the nomadic times, was the coffer, an all-purpose chest used for sleeping, seating, dining, and storing valuables. There were also thronelike chairs, trestle tables, joint stools, and benches, but the few remaining other pieces—hutches, sideboards, and cupboards—were simply variations of the coffer.

Toward the end of this period, however, the Renaissance was coming into full bloom. Having begun in Italy, it had spread to France and Spain. The glories of the ancient cultures of Greece and Rome were admired and imitated. During this remarkable period, the emphasis was on man—humanism—and his glory as an individual. Shakespeare, Galileo, Copernicus, and Chaucer were among the spokesmen. Although there was no revival of classical furniture as such, the Renaissance spirit demanded that furniture designers model their works after what was best for man. New ideas of harmony and beauty required things that were compatible with Renaissance man, furniture that was more elegant and graceful.

As the Renaissance spread to Holland, Germany, and then England, an improved economic climate meant that the new middle class had money to spend on furniture and other amenities of life. In at least its rudimentary form, every type of furniture imaginable was created in this era (1500–1700).

Although there were individual nuances to the various Renaissance pieces, the styles were pretty basically similar, with some differences based on the country of origin.

LATE RENAISSANCE ELABORATIONS

As the Renaissance drew to a close around the end of the eighteenth century, there were several styles that evolved as elaborations of the basic style. On the Continent, the most cherished deviations were the bold, forceful **Baroque** and the more delicate, graceful **Rococo**.

TRADITIONAL, PROVINCIAL, AND ALL THAT

Traditional generally means those styles that were favored by monarchs—hence, society—of their period. **Provincial** refers to the type of furniture that evolved from the "provinces." In some cases, these were crude imitations of the traditional; in others, they were less elaborate, more classically simple. These are named after the country of origin. Contemporary furniture is somewhat of a misnomer, since it means the furniture that is being built today (or in recent years) regardless of what the style is. In other words, the starkly modern acrylic table and the heavy oak chair can both be classed as contemporary if they are manufactured in the present period. **Period**, incidentally, is another confusing word, ordinarily synonymous with "style."

For our purposes, these somewhat arbitrary classifications will be played down and the emphasis placed on the various styles from both country of origin and chronology—more or less ("more or less" because many of the styles overlapped). Virtually all furniture you see today, old or new, dates from one or more of the late and post-Renaissance styles outlined below.

EARLY ENGLISH

There will always be an England, say the British, and it seems like there has always been a distinctly British style of furniture. This was particularly true during the seventeeth to nineteenth centuries, when furniture makers from England gave us a multitude of pleasant styles.

The **Early English** styles date back to the late Renaissance mystique, and reigns of the famous royal families:

Jacobean (1603–1649) • The **Jacobean style**, also known as **Stuart**, covers the reigns of James and Charles I. It is massive and bold. The wood, primarily oak, is extensively carved. Square and rectangular lines are dominant. Decoration is very ornate.

Commonwealth (1649–1660) • The **Commonwealth style**, also known as **Puritan** (which describes it better) was a violent reaction against the "corrupt" Jacobean. Straight and severe lines dominate, with little or no carving or other decoration. Square shapes predominate, with high straight backs and low seats. Stout underbracing (very practical) and somber-hued upholstery were the order of the day.

Carolean (1660–1688) • The **Carolean style** is also known as **late Jacobean** or **Restoration**. "Restoration" comedies were very popular in this period, and the naughty sophisticated style of this type of drama is analogous to the furniture. It was a return to early Jacobean influence and, coincidentally, featured kings of the same names—James and Charles again, each "II" this time. Features were elaborate, deep carvings, spiral turnings or twirls on legs or stretchers, with molded paneling. Oak is still predominant, with some walnut. Cane seats were common, and rich tapestries were used for upholstery.

William and Mary (1689–1702) • The **William and Mary style** is named after Mary Stuart and her Dutch husband, William, who brought to England the craftsmen and styles of the Continent. The more graceful and subtly styled furniture combined straight and curved lines in a harmonious manner that was well suited for home use as well as in the king's castle. Walnut began to take over from oak as the most popular wood, and upholstery was much more extensively used than before. Decorations featured the inverted cup at the top of legs, with flowers, cupids, and wreaths as carvings. Much of this was gilded, painted, and lacquered.

TRADITIONAL ENGLISH

Traditional English is the term usually applied to those furniture styles developed during the great upsurge of the art in Great Britain during the eighteenth century. Many of our most popular styles date from this time.

Queen Anne (1702–1714) • The **Queen Anne period** is often referred to as that of the first modern furniture (Fig. 4-3). The cabriole leg, curved and ending in a foot, was an ever-present feature, as were undulating lines and a trend away from elaborate ornamentation. (Scallop shells were a favorite theme.) Comfort

FIG. 4-3 • The Queen Anne style, as illustrated here by contemporary reproductions, was called the first modern furniture style. (*Courtesy of Bigelow-Sanford, Inc.*)

was beginning to be a factor, with the overstuffed chair coming into its own. Brocades and embossed leather were the favorite materials and walnut the chief wood, with some oak, ash, pine, and mahogany.

Georgian (1714–1795) • The **Georgian period** was marked by the reign of the King Georges, famous in American history as well as English. English furniture making evolved to such a high degree during this time that several of the craftsmen have their name attached to certain styles, for the first time in history. The period is also known as the **Age of Mahogany**, since new tariff laws allowed heavy imports of this reddish tropical wood, and furniture manufacturers used all they could get their hands on. Other general features are the predominance of curves over straight lines and the influence of French and Oriental styles (Fig. 4-4). Rich upholstery and gilding are common. The masters of the period were:

FIG. 4-4 • Curved lines and dark mahogany predominated in the various Georgian styles, as exemplified by this desk.

- **Thomas Chippendale** (1740–1779)–heavily dependent on carved decoration, delicate and intricate or bold and lavish, depending on the piece. Familiar motifs are shells, lions' paws, the leaflike acanthus, acorns, roses, scrolls, and dolphins. Chippendale wrote the first *Directory* of furniture making, which is still consulted today.

- **Adams Brothers** (1760–1792)–primarily architects who went into furniture designing to fill the houses they built. Heavily influenced by the early Greeks and Romans, the style of three brothers Adams was classically simple, restrained, and delicate. Straight, slender lines with flat surfaces are common, with sparse, low-relief ornamentation. Dainty, carved moldings, and urns are the most common features.

- **Thomas Hepplewhite** (1770–1786)–built things on a smaller scale than the others, with graceful, refined, and slender lines. Distinguished by serpentine fronts and concave, cut-in corners. Graceful curves are combined with sturdy construction. Restrained use of dainty carvings, with wheat ears, urns, rosettes, ferns, and other classical motifs.

- **Thomas Sheraton** (1780–1806)–really a designer, writer, teacher, bookseller, and sometime fanatic more than a craftsman. He would create a piece and turn it over to others to produce. His designs were delicate and refined, much sturdier than they appeared. His pieces are well proportioned, with straight lines dominant. Inlays are used more than decoration. Carvings utilized urns, ferns, ovals, and floral swags. Sheraton was fond of mechanical devices such as trick springs and secret locks.

LATER ENGLISH

No master craftmen have approached the fame and beauty of design since the four masters of the eighteenth century. There have been several styles in vogue in England, however, since that time. These are generally referred to as:

English Regency (1793–1830) • **English Regency** is not to be confused with the French Régence period discussed below. This marked a return by the British to simplification and functionalism, with a great deal of foreign influence. The French Directoire and Empire styles (see below) were much admired and copied. The Orient, particularly China, was extensively studied, with most of the pieces being covered with lacquer (a Chinese trademark). Black was the favorite color, with white and ivory as occasional alternates. Gilding was very common. Furniture was scaled down to quite small, intimate sizes. Curves were simple, bold, and combined with straight lines. Chinese motifs were the favorite, carved and in relief.

Victorian (1830–1890) • The long reign of Queen Victoria is well known for solemnity, primness, and sentimentality. Furniture was no exception. **Victorian** designs were heavy, substantial, often clumsy. Both upholstery and wood were dark and usually dreary. "Stuffiness" is a word commonly applied to the era and its furniture. Yet some of the pieces have a quaint charm, and the best examples are very good indeed. Black walnut and rosewood took over the favorite's role from mahogany.

EARLY FRENCH

The French have always had a flair for design and decoration that sets their work apart from the rest of Europe. French furniture is characterized by a delicate sense of balance, attention to fine details, with skill in carving, inlay, and painted techniques:

Louis XIII (1610–1643) • The **Louis XIII style** is marked mostly by straight lines, squares, and symmetrical designs. Prominent decorations are twisted columns, broken pediments, inlays, elaborate carvings, spiral legs, and turned balusters. Ebony, walnut, and oak are the principal woods.

Louis XIV (1643–1715) • The lavish court life of the **Louis XIV period** is reflected in the heavy, massive, baroque furniture encouraged by this luxury-loving and long-reigning king. (Versailles is an example.) Dominated by straight lines, chairs are high-backed, carved, and upholstered. Understructures are elaborately carved and heavy on all pieces. Walnut, oak, and ebony are favorite woods.

French Régence (1715–1723) • The name **French Régence** derives from the fact that the king (Louis XV) was too young to rule and was temporarily replaced by Philip of Orleans (*Régence* = regency). The massive forms of the previous era were supplemented by rococo ornamentation, lighter and more airy. Fantastic curves and elaborate, sometimes eccentric, designs were the rule.

Louis XV (1723–1774) • The ornate and luxurious rococo **Louis XV style** came into full flower during the half-century rule of this king. At the same time, however, Louis XV furniture is smaller and more delicate in scale, as well as more comfortable, than that of earlier styles. Small desks, chaise lounges, and occasional tables came into being during this time. The extremely fancy designs of this period included a multitude of curves, cabriole legs, carved knees, and scroll feet. Louis' personal *bureau du roi* (kings's desk) is reputed to be the most elaborate piece of furniture ever built. Its decoration included carvings, metal inlays, ormulu (goldlike) mounts, painted panels, gilt, and lacquer. Favorite woods of the day were mahogany, oak, walnut, chestnut, and ebony.

Louis XVI (1774–1793) • During the reign of **Louis XVI**, the last monarch before the Revolution, furniture saw a gradual withdrawal from the florid style of Louis XV. The discoveries of classical ruins at Pompeii and Herculaneum prompted a revival of chaste, unadorned simplicity. The furniture of the period exhibited the flair that characterized the prior decades, but toned down just enough to bring out the best of the style. Refinement and elegance were the bywords, with curves giving way to more straight lines and classical motifs emphasizing the authority and beauty of line. Mahogany was the preeminent wood, with some rosewood, ebony, and tulipwood.

Directoire (1795–1804) • The furniture excesses of the Louis's were not unlike the other abuses of the aristocracy. The Revolution changed both life and furniture styles radically. Under the rule of the five directors (**directoires**) following the Revolution, the Jury of Arts and Manufacturers ruled public tastes in furniture, among other matters. The trappings of royalty and aristocracy were eliminated and replaced by classic and military ornaments. Furniture is straight-lined, graceful, elegant, and pure.

French Empire (1804–1815) • In line with the imperial ambitions of Napolean, furniture again became ponderous and ostentatious during the **French Empire period**, but was dignified by classic restraint and simplicity. Furniture finish began to receive new importance, with sheen and high polish replacing some of the more gaudy forms of decoration. Roman eagles, torches, lions, and wreaths were the dominant symbols. These empirelike symbols were surpassed only by the more obvious "N" enclosed in a victor's wreath. Rosewood and ebony were used in addition to the still popular mahogany.

FRENCH PROVINCIAL

The evolving **French Provincial style** covered a period of approximately two and a half centuries, from 1650 to 1900. This style began as a practical and functional art, with the pieces designed simply to meet the needs of the French farmer. During the latter part of the period, however, the peasant styling drew its inspiration more and more from the salons of Paris. The result is that pieces from the diverse areas of Normandy, Provence, Burgundy, and elsewhere began to take on a certain traditional similarity. These designs were far less heavily ornamented than the Louis designs they copied and used local, more readily available woods, such as oak, walnut, ash, poplar, and fruitwood. Later, well-established French Provincial styles are often preferred by experts over the court styles. They are simpler, more comfortable, and less pretentious. The designs and ornamentations varied from province to province, with the common feature being more streamlined versions of the gaudier Parisian creations. Some of the common characteristics were paneling and carving replacing the inlay of Paris traditional with large locks, oversize hinges, and other metal decorations (Fig. 4-5).

(a)

(b)

FIG. 4-5 • (a) Authentic French Provincial furniture decorates a sitting room for film star Lauren Bacall. (*Courtesy of American Cyanamid Co.*) (b) Still popular, French Provincial styling is shown in these reproduction pieces. (*Courtesy of Armstrong Cork Co.*)

AMERICAN COLONIAL

The popular term for furniture of this period is **Early American**, but according to the experts the correct name for the style of furniture in the pre-Revolutionary days is **American Colonial**.

Early Colonial (1620–1700) • **Early colonial** is a hybrid style transported to this country by the early settlers from their homelands. The first New Englanders were Puritans and their furniture was plain and utilitarian, a sturdy, simplified, and more severe version of the Jacobean styles back home (Fig. 4-6). All the early colonial pieces were crude but efficient, and constructed out of whatever wood happened to be around. Pine, birch, maple, and walnut were the most common.

FIG. 4-6 • Early American Colonial furniture utilized rather simple shapes and designs, but as the art progressed, a few curves, rush seats, and other primitive "frills" were added. (*Courtesy of Georgia-Pacific*)

Late Colonial (1700–1790) • Another name for the **late colonial period** is **American provincial**. As the period began, the emerging American colonists were rejecting the designs of local cabinetmakers and importing furniture from England. American craftsmen in the cities began to reproduce Queen Anne, Chippendale, and Sheraton pieces for the well-to-do, and very fine designs developed as the craft progressed. This type of furniture is formal and sophisticated and is really more traditional than provincial. The great cabinet-maker of the day was **Duncan Phyfe**. Phyfe's shop in New York City became famous for lyre-back chairs, pedestal tables, and curved base sofas with flared legs and lion's-paw feet. Phyfe drew his inspiration from the works of Sheraton, Adams, and Hepplewhite (1790–1820) and later from the works of American Empire or Federal. Phyfe used mahogany almost exclusively. His designs are finely proportioned as well as structurally sound. Prominent motifs, in addition to the ubiquitous lyre, were acanthus, cornucopia, lions' heads, medallions, wheat, and leaves of palm, oak, and laurel.

American Empire (1795–1830) • In the **American Empire style**, also known as **Federal**, Duncan Phyfe was again dominant, but there were other themes that this style drew from, mostly French Empire. The American versions of their European counterparts were heavier and sturdier. Motifs are similar to the late colonial except that patriotic motifs such as eagles became more and more popular.

Pennsylvania Dutch (1680–1850) • **Pennsylvania Dutch**, a popular American style, spans several centuries and is traced to the German immigrants (incorrectly called "Dutch" as a perversion of *Deutsch*) of eastern Pennsylvania, New Jersey, and southern New York. These were solid Germanic pieces, simple and plain. Decoration was primarily in the form of colorful painted motifs similar to the hex signs so popular today. Woods were locally available varieties such as maple, walnut, pine, and fruitwood.

Shaker (1776–1850) • The Shakers are a Quaker off-shoot, and share the conviction of such groups against machinery, fancy frills, and almost everything nonreligious. Thus, **Shaker** furniture is severely functional, handmade, and totally lacking in decoration. Paint or a stain was occasionally allowed, but as often as not a light coat of varnish was the only "decoration." By the same token, the Shaker devotion to handwork produced excellent craftsmanship, eye-appealing symmetry, and line. Native pine was the main wood, with some maple and other hardwoods.

ITALIAN PROVINCIAL

Like other provincial styles, **Italian Provincial** spanned roughly a century, from 1700 to 1850. Also like French Provincial, the style originated diversely in scattered rural areas and then began to copy some of the better features of traditional design. Italian Provincial owes more to the early baroque style than some others. Local craftsmen kept the large, bulky scale, while eliminating the lavish decoration. The lines of this style are predominantly rectangular with straight, tapered, square legs and unornamented, sparse curves. The main forms of decoration are paint, enamel, moldings, and brass hardware. Walnut, mahogany, and fruitwood are the popular woods.

BIEDERMEIER

Germany has certainly not been the cradle of furniture design that the countries above have, but there was a brief burst of activity in Germany during the early half of the nineteenth century. The stolid German middle class rejected the baroque and rococo styles that emanated from the rest of the continent. Local designers began producing their own versions of French Empire and Directoire furniture, severely simplified and stripped down. The name **Biedermeier** was humorously attached to the style after a fictional German character named "Papa Biedermeier," supposedly the typical bourgeois German. These pieces are quite varied, again because of various places of origin, but common features are functional design, plainness, and sparseness of ornamentation, with reliance on native fruits, flowers, and painted details. Woods are birch, maple, ash, fruitwood, and mahogany.

OTHER STYLES

There are, of course, many other furniture styles. Those interested in the subject should read many of the fine books on the subject. **Mediterranean**, for example, recently enjoyed a huge burst of popularity (Fig. 4-7). This rather vigorous, heavy style is a throwback to the Moorish domination of the region, of which there are few remaining authentic artifacts outside museums. The more modern styles (usually of pecan) are not usually the subject for refinishing. They just aren't old enough. The same holds true for the many different **modern** and **contemporary styles**. Not only are they too new, but some are made of plastic and other materials that are not really "refinishable" (Figs. 4-8, 4-9, and 4-10).

HOW TO RECOGNIZE STYLES

The descriptions and figures in the previous sections will help you pick out certain styles, but overlapping of styles and periods is bound to cause confusion. The best way to recognize many types of furniture is by the chair and leg shapes.

FIG. 4-7 • The Mediterranean style had a great burst of popularity in the 1960s and is still widely sold.

Figure 4-11 is a guide to some of the more readily identifiable styles. Do not assume, however, that a certain piece is "genuine" because it has the proper characteristics. The best styles have been, and will continue to be, frequently copied.

FIG. 4-8 • New modern furniture makes extensive use of bright colors, plastic, metal, and glass. (*Courtesy of Armstrong Cork Co.*)

FIG. 4-9 • Danish modern is one of the most popular styles in recent years. The walnut wood and the straight, simple, and "soft" architecture of this chair are characteristic of the style. (*Courtesy of Dux, Inc.*)

FIG. 4-10 • Ultra-functional is this futuristic vision of a child's bedroom furniture. Not much work here for the refinisher. (*Courtesy of Armstrong Cork Co.*)

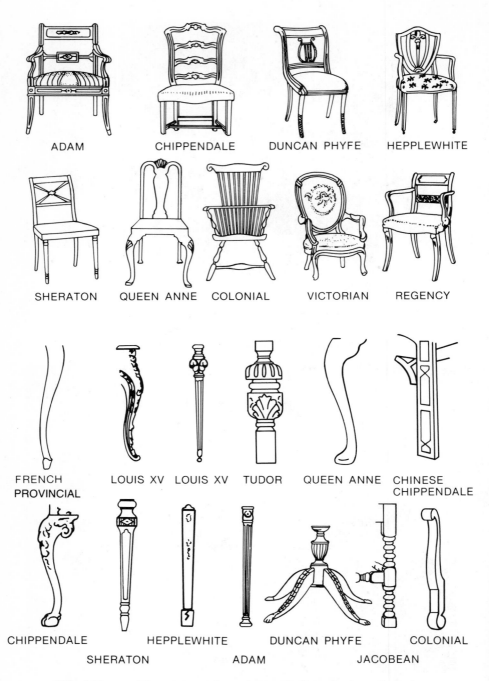

ADAM CHIPPENDALE DUNCAN PHYFE HEPPLEWHITE

SHERATON QUEEN ANNE COLONIAL VICTORIAN REGENCY

FRENCH PROVINCIAL LOUIS XV LOUIS XV TUDOR QUEEN ANNE CHINESE CHIPPENDALE

CHIPPENDALE HEPPLEWHITE DUNCAN PHYFE COLONIAL
SHERATON ADAM JACOBEAN

FIG. 4-11 • The most popular and recognizable styles have distinctive features which are exemplified in chair and leg designs. (*Courtesy of Seng Co.*)

Rudiments of Construction and Structural Repair

If a piece of furniture is in need of repair, you have several choices. You can:

- Throw it away.
- Give it to a pro to fix.
- Convert it to something else.
- Take it apart and fix it up.

The choice is up to you, and depends on how valuable the piece is and how energetic you are, among other considerations.

There's not much anyone can say about the first two choices. You either do or you don't. There's a lot someone *could* say about the third choice, such as how to convert an old round table to a cocktail table, but this is also a very individual thing and depends on the particular piece in question. However, we can—and will—say a bit about the fourth.

Perhaps the first question is whether the piece *has* to be taken apart. Generally, the answer is "yes," remembering now that it is assumed to be in bad repair. Something that just needs a new finish or has a loose rung can be fixed without going to extremes. A chair or table in poor shape, however, is almost impossible to fix without taking it apart to see how it was put together.

BASIC CONSTRUCTION

Fortunately for all of us, furniture making is a simple, if demanding, art. No one would recommend that the average person take a television set apart or strip down the family car. Matter of fact, most of us are thrown for a loss by a power mower. There is something clean and simple about wood, though. Turn a table over and a quick examination will tell you how to take the top and legs apart. There's nothing mysterious about it. The top is attached to a frame and so are the legs. Find the screws and/or glue blocks and remove them.

JOINERY

The key to effective furniture repair is an understanding of the art of **joinery**. Being able to take down and repair the joints of furniture is what separates the expert from the amateur. Before you can do that, however, you should know how the joints are put together.

There is an infinite variety of joints used in furniture building and cabinetmaking (Fig. 5-1). All have the same purpose—to make a joint as strong as possible, able to withstand the stresses and strains of normal usage, while remaining as unobtrusive as possible for esthetic reasons. (It goes without saying that all joints are held together with glue.)

BUTT JOINTS

Plain-edge or butt joints are the simplest of all joints and also the least satisfactory for most purposes. Nails or screws must invariably be used to ensure holding. These joints are rarely used in furniture construction, and when they are, the edges must be carefully checked for square before the pieces are fitted together. It is essential here that all mating surfaces be perfectly joined.

LAP JOINTS

Halved or lap joints of various types are commonly used in such areas as shelves, cabinets, and chair stretchers. They are easily made by first laying one piece of wood on top of the other and accurately marking the width of each cut. A try square is then used to square these lines across both work edges, and to square the shoulder lines of both the face and the edge of the workpieces. A marking edge is ordinarily used to indicate the depth of cut.

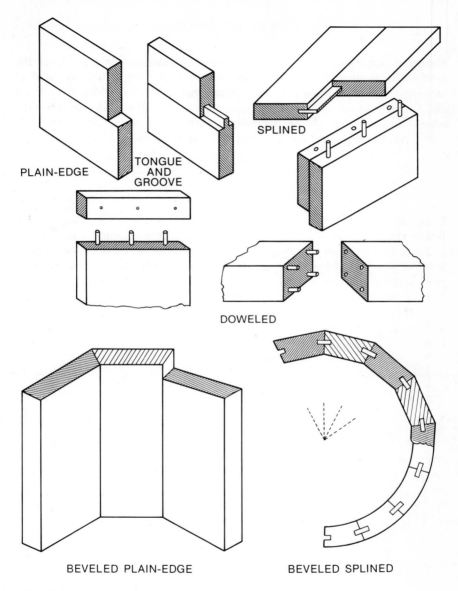

PLAIN-EDGE

TONGUE
AND
GROOVE

SPLINED

DOWELED

BEVELED PLAIN-EDGE

BEVELED SPLINED

FIG. 5-1 • Types of joints.

With the workpieces secured in a vise, a backsaw is used to cut to the required depth. If wood notches more than 1 inch in width must be cut, it is advisable to make several cuts to maintain the accuracy of the depth. A chisel is then used to remove the waste down to the proper depth. The cuts can then be filed to a uniform depth for a perfect fit.

RABBETED JOINTS

Rabbeted joints are formed by cutting recesses (or rabbets) on the edges of the workpieces so that they may be fitted into each other. They are used in cabinetry, tabletops, and other constructions that utilize long joints. The rabbets are cut by marking a squared line across the face of the work and down the edges, corresponding to the thickness of the joining piece. Depth lines are marked on the edges, and the scrap material is then cut out.

DADO JOINTS

Dado joints consist of a groove cut into a board into which another board is fitted. There are several variations (Fig. 5-2), the most commonly used of which is the housed dado. In this joint, the entire end of the piece to be fastened fits into the groove of the main piece. The piece to be fastened is set on the other piece and the width of the cut is marked and squared. The depth of cut is then marked and the cut made with a backsaw. Scrap is removed with a sharp chisel.

Other types of dado joints are the stopped dado, in which the groove does not extend the full width of the board, the dovetailed dado, and the dado and rabbet.

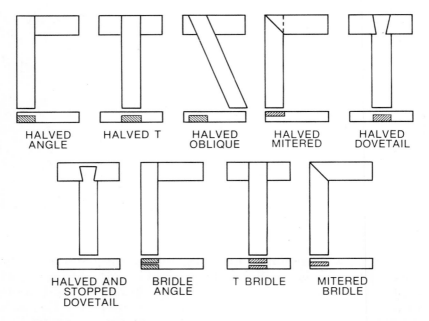

| HALVED ANGLE | HALVED T | HALVED OBLIQUE | HALVED MITERED | HALVED DOVETAIL |

| HALVED AND STOPPED DOVETAIL | BRIDLE ANGLE | T BRIDLE | MITERED BRIDLE |

FIG. 5-2 • Dado joints.

MORTISE-AND-TENON JOINTS

Mortise-and-tenon joints are favorites with skilled cabinetmakers. They are strong and dependable but must be fitted accurately. They are widely used in the construction of desks, tables, chairs, and cabinets of fine quality.

Again, as can be seen from Fig. 5-3, there are several variations of this joint, but all are laid out and fitted in the same general way. The tenon, or male, end is made first. Both work pieces are then cut and squared to the desired dimensions and both faces of each piece are marked for easy identification. The length of the tenon is measured on the appropriate piece, then a square used to mark this shoulder line around the piece. A rule of thumb is that the tenon should be a quarter to half as thick as the entire piece.

The exact center of one edge of the piece is measured and, using this center point, the outline of the tenon is scribed on this edge. The lines across the end of the piece and down the other edge are carefully scribed. The tenon's width is marked in the same way.

The piece is placed in the vise and a backsaw and chisel are used to cut the tenon. The position of the piece is changed around so that all cuts will be made square. The shoulder cuts are made last.

The length of the mortise must equal the width of the tenon. If you are making such a joint yourself, locate the exact center of the piece, and working from there, lay out the mortise. Carefully check the dimensions against those of the tenon.

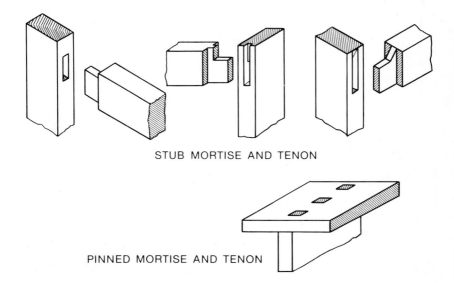

STUB MORTISE AND TENON

PINNED MORTISE AND TENON

FIG. 5-3 • Mortise-and-tenon joints.

When you are satisfied that your layout marks are correct, fix the piece in the vise. Select a drill or auger bit 1/16 inch smaller than the width of the mortise, and adjust the bit gauge to bore 1/8 inch deeper than the length of the tenon. Place the spur of the bit on the center line and bore a series of overlapping holes with the two end holes touching the end lines of the mortise. Make sure that the bit is kept perpendicular to the face of the workpiece. Use a sharp chisel to clean out the scrap in the mortise and to trim the sides and corners, keeping the walls of the mortise perpendicular to the face of the workpiece.

DOVETAILED JOINTS

Dovetailed joints (Fig. 5-4) are also favorites of skilled woodworkers, especially in such applications as drawers and in furniture projects where strength and good appearance are important. The flare of the projections (called **pins**) fitting into matching dovetails provide the strength. However, the angle of the dovetail must not be too acute, as this would defeat the purpose; an acute angle would be weakened by the short grain at the corners of the angle.

Dovetailed joints require a certain skill to make (Fig. 5-5), and it is suggested that the amateur woodworker practice on scrap wood before tackling

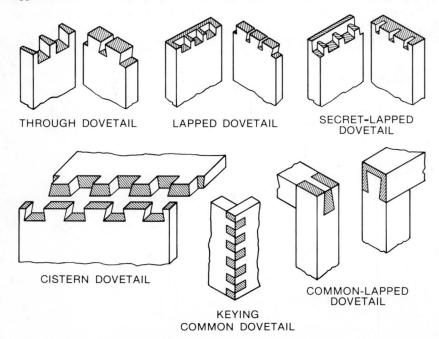

THROUGH DOVETAIL   LAPPED DOVETAIL   SECRET-LAPPED
                                                DOVETAIL

CISTERN DOVETAIL

KEYING
COMMON DOVETAIL

COMMON-LAPPED
DOVETAIL

FIG. 5-4   •   Dovetail joints.

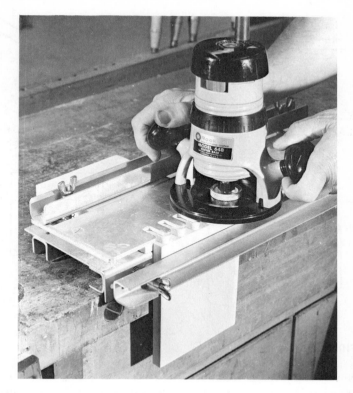

FIG. 5-5 • If you really want to make professional dovetail joints, a router and this dovetail jig will almost do it for you. (*Courtesy of Rockwell Mfg. Co., Power Tool Div.*)

an actual project. (You can also buy a jig for your power saw.) A template of cardboard or thin wood is used to lay out the dovetails after the proper angle has been decided. Cuts are made with a backsaw and sharp chisel. The common-lapped dovetail, through dovetail, and lapped dovetail are the most commonly used. Actually, dovetails are nothing more than more sophisticated mortise-and-tenon joints.

MITER JOINTS

Miter joints (Fig. 5-6) are used primarily for making frames and screens. They are usually cut at an angle of 45 degrees. Although it is a simple matter to mark an angle of 45 degrees, it is usually more satisfactory and safer to use a miter box to cut the workpieces accurately; or else cut the boards on a table saw or radial saw with the gages properly set for the angle.

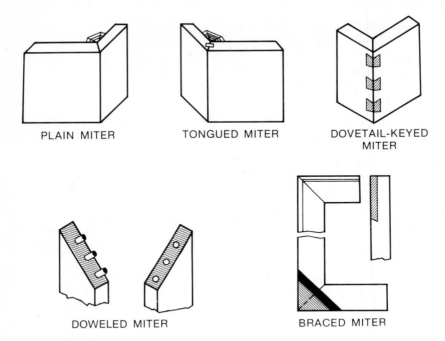

PLAIN MITER   TONGUED MITER   DOVETAIL-KEYED MITER

DOWELED MITER   BRACED MITER

FIG. 5-6 • Miter joints.

Since the miter joint is simply a butt joint cut at an angle, dowels, tongues, or braces are often used to strengthen it. To make a tongued miter joint, grooves are cut in each of the pieces and a wooden tongue is glued into the groove. In addition to strengthening the joint, this also helps to prevent warping.

DOING IT YOURSELF

Making complex mortise-and-tenon and dovetailed joints is fun once you get the hang of it, but it is not an easy art to learn. Patience is required, particularly if the parts are handmade. Power equipment and the appropriate jigs will help, if you have them. Many of these cuts can be made with a circular saw, jointer, drill press, or router. If you buy these tools, the manufacturer's instruction booklet will usually show you how. If you no longer have the book, Rockwell has an excellent series on how to use these various power tools. *Getting the Most Out of Your Circular Saw and Jointer* has a very good chapter on how to make wood joints. Consult your Rockwell dealer or write the company: Rockwell Manufacturing Co., Power Tool Division, 550 N. Lexington Ave., Pittsburgh, PA 15208.

On the other hand, there is no real need to know how to make all these joints yourself. You should know enough about them to be able to take them apart and put them back together again. You should know how to reglue and strengthen them if necessary. Once in awhile, you may have to fabricate a new piece and connect it to an old one. If the joint is a complex one, you can always take it to a cabinetmaker and let him do it, saving your energy for other chores. You're going to need it.

Actually, most joints that will need repairing are simpler ones, where an arm goes into a back or a rung into a leg. The dovetail and other difficult joints rarely fall apart, because they are built to last.

BEFORE YOU START

It's tempting to pick up that wooden mallet and give everything a whack to see what's going to fall apart, but don't do it—not yet. Before you take things apart, take a good look at the piece and see what you're going to have to do. That way you can whack at the right places.

A thorough inspection is the best way to plan your work. Here are some of things to look for:

- Unless the thing looks almost perfect, it's a good idea to make notes as you proceed. Many of those who do a lot of repair work have a platform, which serves several purposes (see p. 59). One purpose is to provide a stable, level surface to see whether the legs are even. It is also a good place to rock the frame and locate any loose joints. Look for any missing parts and, while you're at it, search all surfaces for holes, cracks, gouges, dents, etc. The veneer should be inspected for blisters, cracks, loose edges, or whatever. Note any warped boards.

- Open drawers, doors, and other moving parts. See if slides must be fixed, hardware replaced, joints repaired, or hinges fixed.

- Look at the piece overall with a jaundiced eye. See if any of the parts detract from the overall good looks and consider removing them. Would it look better cut down? Many older chests with high legs might look better a few inches lower. Might some parts look better painted than varnished? Ask yourself all kinds of similar questions. Try to imagine what it is going to look like when it's finished, and make any changes *first*. There's nothing more frustrating than working on a part for hours and then deciding to get rid of it.

TAKING THINGS APART

Now comes the fun part, something you can even talk the kids into doing. Working from your checklist, knock apart all loose joints, remove parts to be discarded or replaced, take off all hardware except hinges (and if they're shot, take them off, too). Put the hardware in a safe place. Use a wooden mallet for whacking or wrap some rags around a claw hammer (Fig. 5-7).

You may find, however, that the old joint won't come loose with normal hammer blows. If so, don't whack harder without looking more closely. It may be that the joint is held together with hidden screws or nails in addition to the glue, or that it is one of those old-fashioned joints wherein a piece of dry wood was fitted with a small knob on the end, then inserted into a piece of green wood, which then dried and shrank. This made a fine, tight joint at the time, but over the years it tends to loosen.

For the chair with the hidden hardware, look for buttons or round plugs that may be hiding the screw head (Fig. 5-8). Remove the button or plug as carefully as you can to get at the screw. As far as the old knob joint is concerned, you really shouldn't remove it all, because you'll have to force it and the knob won't fit right afterward. The best way to fix this is by forcing glue into the loose joint with an oil can, squeeze bottle, or ordinary toothpick. You can also use a **glue injector**, a tool available at specialty shops, and force the glue into the joint through a 1/16-inch hole drilled in an inconspicuous place.

THE RIGHT GLUE

Chapter 2 gave you a complete rundown on the types of glue available, and each of them is best for certain jobs at certain times. However, what you'd like to know is what is the best all-around furniture glue. Well, without hedging, so would we. Talk to a dozen cabinetmakers and you'll get at least a half-dozen answers. Some will use nothing but hot hide glue; others think Elmer's is just great. Casein is popular with many others. Others will tell you, "It depends on the job." Well, we'll only hedge a little. Here's a little chart meant only as a *rough* guide. (For specific jobs, consult the section on glue beginning on p. 49).

- All-purpose indoor glue—hide glue. This is a little old-fashioned, but we have a great fondness for it. It takes a little longer to set, but when clamped and dried properly, nothing can beat if for general use.

- Light-strain areas—white glue like Elmer's (polyvinyl-resin emulsion). Easy and quick.

- Where high strength is needed but the joint's a little loose and needs filling—casein glue.

- Edge-to-edge gluing, other high-strain jobs with tight-fitting joints—plastic resins such as Weldwood.

- Exterior use—resorcinol.

- When all else fails—epoxy resins.

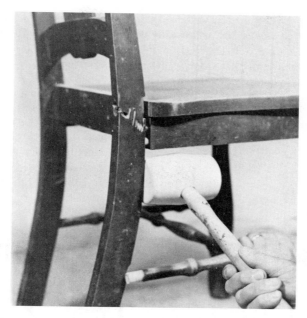

FIG. 5-7 • After all the screws or other fasteners are removed, the chair is knocked apart with a rubber or wooden mallet.

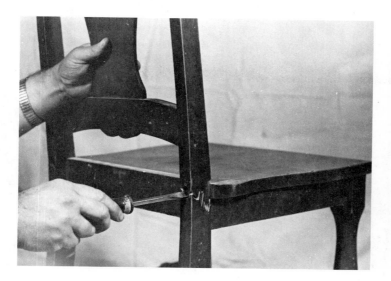

FIG. 5-8 • Always look for hidden screws. The screw in this kitchen chair was covered by a button which was easily pried out with a screwdriver. This screw has to be removed before the chair can be disassembled.

Using glue • With a little persistence, you should be able to determine which glue is best (even second best will usually do). But how to apply it? Whether you have to heat it or mix it depends on the glue, so consult the manufacturer's recommendations. But that's only half the answer. The other half lies in what you do before and after you apply the glue.

Preparation for gluing • The best glue in the world won't stick well at all unless the **surfaces** are **completely clean** before application. This means that all old glue must be scraped or sanded clean before you put the pieces back together again (Fig. 5-9). Your knife and your electric sander will come into good use here. Be careful, though, that in your eagerness to have the piece "come clean," you don't take off too much wood along with the glue. This is particularly true if you use a power sander or a very sharp knife.

You should also be sure to work in a reasonably warm place. There is ordinarily no problem, but if your workshop is an unheated garage (it shouldn't be), you'll be well advised to do your gluing in some warm corner of the house where this sort of work will be tolerated by others in the family—or save the job for summer. Most glues do badly in cold temperatures.

Pressure • In addition to having a clean surface, the other "must" is **pressure**. The type of pressure depends on the job to be done. If you are gluing a chair leg into its socket, or mending a broken one (a risky job at best), you should apply heavy weight downward on the chair seat. This is most easily accomplished by having an elephant hold his foot on it. If you don't have an elephant (and a

FIG. 5-9 • When broken parts have not been glued previously, the pieces should fit together without difficulty. Test them first to see how they fit; then clean out any dirt before gluing.

gentle one at that), you might try a set of books or a piece of lead, rock, or the like.

Tourniquets ○ The downward method of applying pressure works fine on seats and dresser tops that have a nice, flat surface for stacking books upon, but most repairs are more complex than that. Some sort of clamping is necessary for most repairs. That doesn't mean that you need a set of every clamp available. That good old piece of rope will prove to be one of the most valuable tools you'll have in your shop.

For all jobs involving side-to-side pressure, like the common rungs-and-legs repair, it is a simple matter of tying the rope loosely around the legs a couple of times, then inserting a stick between the strands, known in the trade as a *tourniquet* (Fig. 5-10). Twist the stick a couple of times until the rope is good and tight, then rest the end of the stick against one of the rungs or legs to keep it from flying back. Insert some rags or something where the ropes bite into the legs to prevent the rope from chewing up the surface.

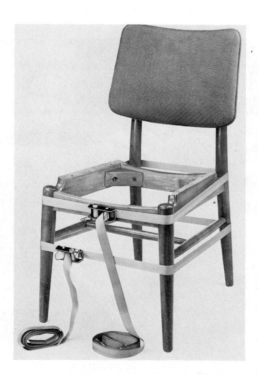

FIG. 5-10 •   For maximum pressure around the underframe of a chair, this tourniquet is unequalled. Actually a belt clamp, it holds all legs and rungs tightly. (*Courtesy of Adjustable Clamp Co.*)

Clamps ○ You will always find situations where one of the commercial *clamps* will be necessary. The more work you do, the more use you'll find for bar clamps, wood clamps, and C clamps. Pipe clamps are also handy to have around for extra-long jobs. For them, you'll also need an assorted set of pipe lengths, threaded on one end to match the clamps. Clamps and pipe are available in either 1/2- or 3/4-inch sizes.

Wood clamps ○ Use *wood clamps* to hold two small pieces together or to clamp one piece of wood to a larger piece where the distance is not great. Although these wood clamps come with jaw openings up to 15 inches, you'll probably use the smaller ones most often, substituting the bar or pipe clamps for longer stretches. The beginner is often puzzled by difficulty opening and closing the hand screws. There is a quick and easy trick for moving the jaws to the proper width. Simply grip one handle in each hand and swing the clamp around until the jaw opens or closes to the desired distance.

To use the wood clamp, open to a width slightly wider than the distance to be spanned, then tighten each screw until the wood grips evenly and firmly. Give the outer screw just a little more final twist for added tension (Fig. 5-11).

FIG. 5-11 • The right and wrong ways to use wood screw clamps are illustrated here. The clamp on the left holds tightly over the whole surface, while the one on the right holds only at the tip of the jaws. (*Courtesy of American Plywood Association*)

There is no need to use any padding between the wooden jaws if you don't apply excess pressure.

C clamps ○ *C clamps* are used mainly for small, spot jobs, such as gluing down a chip or repairing a broken chair rung (Fig. 5-12). They come in many sizes but again, the small ones are the most commonly used. These clamps have harsh metal jaws and a thin piece of wood or other padding is necessary wherever the jaws bear against a finished surface.

Bar and pipe clamps ○ The serious repairman should have at least two *bar clamps* around (Figs. 5-13 and 5-14). These come in very handy when spanning a fairly wide surface like the back of a dresser. The jaws are opened up by sliding the movable section down the bar until it is just a little larger than the span to be bridged. The clamp is attached and the screw tightens the clamp until the proper pressure is applied.

Pipe clamps are not self-contained, as the bar clamps are. When you buy pipe clamps, all you get is the ends. You have to buy the pipe to match, either from a hardware or a plumbing-supply store. One end is threaded to hold the stationary clamp. The other section of the clamp is free to move up and down the pipe to span whatever width you need. The size of a pipe clamp, then, is infinitely variable and limited only by the length of the pipe. If you think you

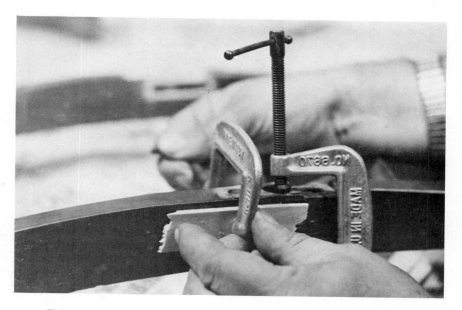

FIG. 5-12 • C clamps are used to hold the broken pieces of chair together. Note the pieces of wood under the clamp jaws to prevent damage to the wood surface.

FIG. 5-13 • Bar clamps can be used for the entire length of the bar. (Pipe clamps are similar and almost unlimited in length.) Note the use of wood blocks, again, to protect the wood's surface. (*Courtesy of Adjustable Clamp Co.*)

have a job for a 100-foot clamp, you can manage it with a pipe clamp. Use wood blocks under both bar and pipe clamping to avoid damage to finished surfaces.

Other clamps ○ There are such things as *corner clamps*, but usually you can improvise with one of the others (Fig. 5-15). The only exception might be picture frames, where corner clamps made for this purpose are helpful in holding the edges firm until the glue dries.

You can also make your own *wedge clamps*, which are very useful for such jobs as binding boards together edge to edge. Wedge clamps are made of a rectangular piece of fairly thick wood (3/4 to 1 inch is best), which is marked 1/2 inch from each edge and cut down the diagonal to form two almost triangular pieces. The pieces to be glued are laid on a wooden surface such as a subfloor or platform. The outside piece is braced against a wall or similar solid vertical surface. Put the two wedge pieces together as they were before cutting, then nail the outside one down, leaving the heads slightly protruding so that you can pull them out later. Then force the remaining wedge between the other wedge and the work by tapping with a hammer. If the wood to be glued is thin,

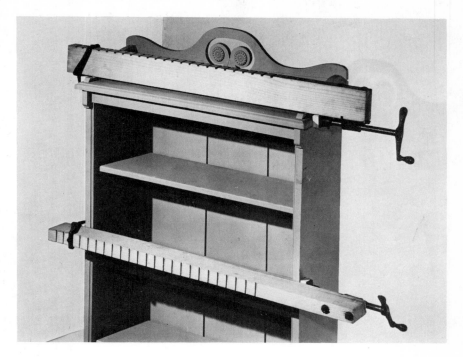

FIG. 5-14 • The wood bar clamp fixtures on the two ends of these clamps can be purchased, but you have to fabricate the wood bars yourself. (*Courtesy of Adjustable Clamp Co.*)

weight it down to keep it from buckling under the pressure. Put waxed paper under the glued area to keep it from sticking.

SPECIFIC JOBS

If you master the primary principles of furniture repair—surface preparation, proper gluing, clamping pressure—you should be able to repair almost any job with a little ingenuity and luck. There are a few tricks, however, that go with every job.

LOOSE CHAIR PARTS (LOWER SECTION)

Once the underpinnings of a chair start to go, everything seems to go with it. One loose joint deserves another, or something like that.

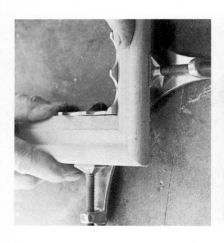

(b)

(c)

(a)

FIG. 5-15 • Corner clamping is the most difficult job of all. Three ways of accomplishing this dual job are shown. (a) Bar clamps are fitted with edge-clamp fixtures that screw onto the bar. (b) Special corner clamps are used for picture frames. (c) The C clamps hold a triangular piece of wood glued to a piece of Kraft paper, which is glued temporarily to the wood. When the joint is solid, the wedges, paper, and clamps are removed. (*Courtesy of Western Wood Moulding and Millwork Producers*)

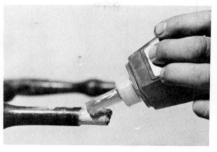

(a)   (b)

FIG. 5-16 • To repair the chair taken apart according to the description on p. 87, (a) all old glue is scraped off the old joints, and (b) new glue is applied to both surfaces.

The first thing to do is take apart all the parts that are loose. Then check to see if the parts will be tight when you glue them back together. The rung-to-leg joints will usually fit all right, but often the joint where the leg is fastened to the seat will have widened due to wobbling of the leg. No amount of glue is going to hold this unless the joint is tightened. Use toothpicks and wood matches to fill the loose space.

Another way to expand a loose joint is by sawing a kerf down the middle of the leg top, filling with a hardwood spline just slightly larger than the kerf, and pounding it in until the spline pushes out the leg enough to fill.

If the thickness of the pieces to be joined allows it, you can insert a dowel between the end of one piece and into the other. Drill the holes carefully with an electric hand drill or drill press and a bit of the same diameter as the dowel. Hold the wood very carefully to make sure that the holes are vertical. Grooved dowels offer the most glue surfaces and a tighter joint, but straight dowels are all right if used properly and roughened with a rasp.

Test the dowels to see if they fit tightly without binding. If the holes are misaligned, you're better off plugging up the old holes and drilling new ones. Once alignment is satisfactory, spread a generous amount of glue (casein is usually preferred here) and clamp the pieces together until dry.

Fancier chairs, like those used in the dining room, will usually have stretchers forming a frame for the seat. This type of chair usually holds together better than the kitchen variety, but there are times when it shows its age, too. In this situation, you'll probably have to remove and reglue corner blocks, and sometimes contend with screws holding the legs to the stretchers.

Dowels are often used, too, in this type of construction and are sometimes broken off. To remove old dowels, use an auger bit. New dowels are a must in

(a)

(b)

(c)

(d)

FIG. 5-17 • (a) Glued surfaces are pounded back together. (b) A rope tourniquet is wrapped around the chair and (c) held in place with a stick. (d) When the chair is safely together, screw and button are replaced and the chair is ready for refinishing.

this situation, as are new corner blocks where ruined. Otherwise, repair techniques are the same as for any other chair.

If nothing else works, wood or metal braces may be added to produce the required strength.

LOOSE CHAIR PARTS (UPPER SECTION)

Wobbly arms are the main offender here, and their repair is a little tricky. Often, the arms are held in place with screws in addition to the glue joint. The biggest problem here is that the novice may not realize that the screws are present and he may wreck the joint by trying to pry it apart without removing the screws.

Screws holding chair arms are countersunk and often covered with little wood buttons, or wood plugs that have been cut off flush with the surface. The older and more skillfully finished the piece, the more these plugs blend in with the finish and are quite difficult to find. If the arms won't come out, however, with the usual whack or tug, don't ruin things by banging it around until it comes apart. You may find the entire chair in pieces.

When you run into this situation, you have to remove the button or plug and get at the screw. The button can be pried off with a knife or similar instrument and saved for replacing later. Removing the plug is a little tougher. Take your knife or a sharp awl and dig the plug out, which will ruin it, of course. You'll have to make a new one out of a dowel. Or simply fill up the resulting hole with colored wax or a shellac stick. (See p. 114 for details of these techniques.)

After you expose the screwhead, the next step is to remove the screw (logically enough). This may not be easy, but your chances are increased if you use a screwdriver that fits the slot perfectly. A good tool for removing stubborn screws is a screwdriver bit in your brace. You can bear down harder and apply more torque. Particularly stubborn screws will often loosen up if you jerk the bit quickly first left, then right.

Once the screw is out, the joint should respond quickly to a rap with your mallet. Clean and reglue as described above, filling the old screw hole with bits of scrap wood (or toothpicks and matches). You won't need clamps for this type of repair, since you will replace the screw, which does the same job.

Backrests of kitchen and Windsor-type chairs are often loosened in the same manner as rungs and legs. The same principles apply as working on the lower part of such chairs. Here, though, the slats or spindles are usually installed with little if any glue, with the main outer rail taking the brunt of the punishment. Devote your energies to strengthening the main members of the back and hope for the best with the spindles. Your toothpicks and matches should prove useful for chair backs as well as legs.

BROKEN ARMS, LEGS, ETC.

Almost any broken piece can be put together again with proper gluing. The only exception might be chair rungs, where the biggest man on the block is sure to rest his foot and break the repaired joint. With a clean break, you don't have to worry about the old glue—but be sure the surfaces to be glued are clean and dry. Usually the break is partially longitudinal so that you have a fairly large surface to clamp together. C clamps are the treatment of choice, one at each end of the break, with more in the center if there is space.

A broken part almost always loosens up the joints at either end of the part, so you may as well reglue these while you're at it. Matter of fact, if you let the break go awhile, you may find that other parts have loosened as well. Tighten up everything at the same time, or your repair is doomed to failure. Don't forget to use thin wood blocks on either side of your clamp jaws. You'll also have to use either a bar clamp or a rope tourniquet to hold the loosened parts together while drying.

If the break is in the same place as an old one, be sure to clean off the old glue. Better yet, don't bother fixing it, since the second glue job will probably be weaker than the first. Chair rungs are easily fabricated from a similar wood dowel, but more complex parts will require a lathe or a cabinetmaker (preferably the latter) for replacement.

New parts are fitted the same way the old ones would be. You may have to shave the ends a little if they are too big or you may have to fill with scraps if the part is a little too small. Finish as any new part.

Chair legs often break right at the top where they join the seat. In most cases, the only realistic answer is a whole new leg, or a new piece scarfed into the old leg. In either case, a cabinetmaker is your best bet—or, again, doing it yourself with a lathe.

MISSING PARTS

When you find or buy an old piece of furniture, some of the parts may be missing. Simple parts like rungs and other underpinnings may be fabricated yourself from wood of the same or similar species (always use hardwood). Decorative parts are another matter entirely. There are several ways to handle this:

- You can leave the part off. If it is not one of a pair, you may not notice that it's gone once you're through with the refinishing.
- You may be able to buy the same or a similar part in a second-hand shop, or find a matching part on another piece of furniture. Large cabinet-makers' shops may stock the part. The best source for those (and lots of

other things) is Albert Constantine & Son, Inc., 2050 Eastchester Rd., Bronx, N.Y. 10461. (Along the same vein, never throw away decorative parts that may be of some use later.)

- This is a pretty drastic step, but one you may want to consider. For parts that come in pairs, you could remove the matching part. On a high-back chair, for example, with a missing "rabbit ear" at the top of the back, it is possible to cut off the one on the other side. This may leave a somewhat bastard piece, but it is better than a lopsided one.

- The best way to provide a missing decoration if you can't find one is to have one made by an expert cabinetmaker. If you have the expertise, try tracing a pattern from the part you have, and cut another one out from a piece of similar hardwood. You'll probably need some special woodcarving tools for this, and a lot of patience.

STICKY DRAWERS

Try to determine the cause before proceeding with the problem of a sticky drawer. Usually you'll find missing or broken drawer runners (bottom edges). You can replace these easily with a piece of scrap hardwood and some brads (Fig. 5-18). Often, the cause is unevenness of the chest itself, which pinches the drawers and causes sticking. Check with a level and put something under the

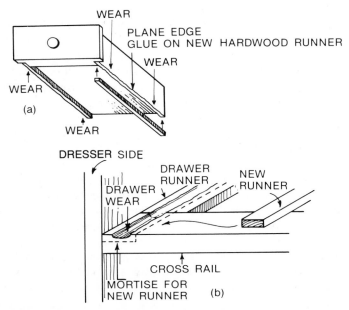

FIG. 5-18 • Replacing worn drawer runners.

short legs. A little soap or paraffin on the runners may be enough to cure minor problems.

If the piece is pretty old, you may find that the runners or guides (the boards that the runners ride on) are worn and uneven. Add thin strips of wood to worn runners. To fix worn drawer guides, rabbet out the old one until smooth, then shim up to their former height with rail strips. An easier method is to install plastic bumpers or tape in the worn areas.

If the drawer itself is wobbly, check the joints. Hopefully, they're dovetailed. If so, gently tap the joint apart, being careful not to break any of the tenons. Remove old adhesive, reglue, and clamp as described above. Here, corner clamps may be helpful to keep corners square. Other joints can be fixed in the same way, of course, but nondovetailed joints will probably fall apart again under hard use. If possible, and the piece is otherwise valuable to you, replace the old joints with a dovetail.

SPLITS IN LARGE FLAT PARTS

Usually caused by poor drying of the wood before assembly. Even a piece that has been around a good many years may crack and split if placed in a house with excessive humidity. Whether the problem is in a dresser top, bureau side, or table leaf, the solution is approximately the same.

Remove the part from its neighbors by unscrewing, removing glue blocks, knocking apart, or whatever. If a piece is only partially split, you are better off cracking it all the way, odd though that may sound. A partial split is the very devil to glue properly. If you complete the job that nature will probably finish anyway, you'll have some nice surfaces to slap glue onto. Properly glued and clamped, the split will be just as good as new—maybe better.

For a heavy piece, bar clamps are very useful, and so are the homemade wedges discussed on p. 94. Be sure to allow plenty of time for drying. The thin panels found in the sides of chests or cupboard doors cannot be fixed in this way but are easily replaced by a piece of the same thickness. Note that these panels "float" in their slots and are not glued. These panels are made floating so that they will have room to expand (and contract) with the moisture in the air. Still, they do occasionally split, particularly if the inside is not finished. To prevent such splits, give the inside a coat of linseed oil, sealer, varnish, or shellac. This will help keep the moisture content the same on both sides.

Sometimes you can close up hairline cracks by removing the panel and soaking the inside with wet rags for a day or two, then nailing a thin strip of wood over the inside length of the split.

WARPS

Warped boards are usually long ones such as tabletops, doors, and similar large areas. The cause of warping is the same as that for splits and cracks—that old enemy, moisture. It is good to remember when doing your own refinishing that most warps could have been avoided by the simple expedient of applying a coat of some kind of sealer to the interior surface of the part. These finishing materials keep moisture out of the wood—at least, to roughly the same extent that the "finish" finish on the other side does. You should know that sealing the underside of a truly valuable antique may lessen its value. Antique experts like to be able to examine the bare wood.

In any case, it is uneven moisture absorption that causes warping. The most effective cure is a fairly drastic balancing of the moisture, by wetting the unfinished side while drying out the other, if possible. There are as many ways to accomplish this as there are ways to skin a cat—steam it, put it over a radiator with wet rags on top, etc. The best way seems to be to lay the unfinished side over wet grass in the bright sun. Remember that the dry side is the one that curves in and should receive the damp treatment.

You must, of course, remove the top in the manner described above under "Splits." If the warp is a "simple" one, in which the boards are curved in the same general direction, use the grass method (or some other wetting gimmick). Sometimes the warp is more complex, however, with a "twist" longitudinally as well as a warp. If such is the case, put a big rock or other heavy weight over the part that is more out of shape than the others.

You should be able to see the effects of your labors in a few hours, by the end of the day anyway. When the board is just about as straight as you can hope for, put it back where it came from as tightly as possible. Clamp any loose edges, as you would have for a table leaf, to a couple of straight, dry boards to help keep the piece from warping back again. Some experts feel that it is acceptable to attach permanent cleats to the underside of table leaves that are prone to warpage, while others feel that this destroys the value of the piece, since cleats will be visible when the leaves are in place. Our preference is to try all else first, and use cleats only if the case is hopeless. Apply cleats if you use them immediately after "de-warping."

The wet method will work in most cases, but there are times when it won't. According to the experts, the warp in such cases is caused not by moisture absorption but by internal stresses in the wood. This has to do with the way it is cut—radially, tangentially, etc. (see Chapter 2). Regardless of what it means, there is a cure for it, rather difficult but the only way (Fig. 5-19). Preferably with a power saw, cut a series of kerfs in the underside of the piece about 3 inches apart and to a depth about **two-thirds** of the thickness of the

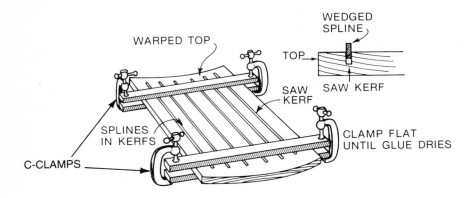

FIG. 5-19   •   Using wedged splines to eliminate warping.

board. Make wooden splines to fit the grooves, preferably in a slightly wedged shape. If the part is curved so that the kerfs are in the concave (edges curled upward) side, then tap the splines in slowly, forcing them into the glued grooves with a mallet. If kerfs are on the convex (edges curled downward), cut the splines thinner and do not force them at all. Glue loosely and liberally into the saw kerfs. Clamp flat against some straight boards. Another, really more effective way to cure warpage is to cut the part into several small boards, alternating them as they are put together. This is delicate work, and usually ruins the looks of the top.

As soon as your de-warped part has dried out, screw or glue it immediately back where it came from. You may find, however, that in the wet process, some boards have fallen apart. These will have to be glued back together in the same way as described above under "Splits." This may be a good time to insert a couple of dowels in badly warped areas. Since this is a little tricky, however, with a chance of drilling crookedly through the top, you shouldn't attempt it without a drill press or drill-press attachment for a radial-arm saw (see p. 105 on working with dowels). Remember that minor warpage is not always a bad thing. As a matter of fact, it is often prized in truly old antiques.

LOOSE SCREWS

Loose screws (Fig. 5-20) are mainly a problem at hinges, where the weight of a door, leaf, etc., exerts constant pressure and sometimes pulls the screws out of their original tracks. In many cases, the screws point into tabletops, veneer, etc., so that the time-honored trick of replacing the loose screws with longer ones runs the risk of popping through the finished surfaces. This will work sometimes, but it is dangerous—and you can't do it more than once. The use of larger screws

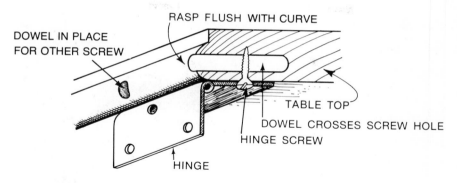

FIG. 5-20 • Using dowels to fill screw holes.

is also limited by the diameter of the hinge holes. The best and easiest way to cure loose screws is to fill the screw hole with wood chips, splinters, toothpicks, etc., and glue. When the mix dries, the screw should go back in tightly again. When wood is too dry or splintery, or into the end grain, you may have to crossbore from a relatively invisible spot and insert a dowel into the screw area. The dowel should be tight and well glued, and afford an excellent surface for the screw to bite into.

Alternative methods of tightening up screw holes are:

- Fill hole with wood dough, such as Plastic Wood (Fig. 5-21).
- Fill with epoxy putty.
- Fill with wood expander.

All these methods have validity. Which one you should use is a matter of opinion and the needs of the job at hand.

WORKING WITH DOWELS

There are many cases where a joint, split, or other defect can be strengthened by the use of dowels. Some of these have been indicated, and other uses will come to you as you proceed. There are times when dowel work does not require a high degree of accuracy, as in many end-to-side joints. The beginner is urged to try his luck there and not attempt to use dowels to put together side-by-side boards in a tabletop as a first job.

When putting two boards together edge to edge, dowels are often of excellent value in adding strength and reducing warpage. To use dowels in this way, accuracy is vitally important. Any slight displacement of the dowel will result in unevenness, which is difficult to correct.

FIG. 5-21 • One way to tighten up loose screws is to fill the old screw holes with wood dough or a similar substance; then drill new holes for the old screws. Always use a drill bit slightly smaller in diameter than the screws or use a special screw-hole bit available at most hardware stores.

Make sure to use grooved birch dowels for edge-to-edge work (Fig. 5-22). You should also have a drill press—an electric drill at any rate—plus dowel pins and, unless you're a real pro, a doweling jig. The jig is set to certain dimensions and ensures that each dowel hole is straight and accurately bored.

After all the holes have been drilled in one side, insert dowel pins into each hole and very carefully line up the other side. Press the undrilled piece onto the pins and the point will indicate exactly where to drill into that side to ensure correct alignment. Holes on both sides should be countersunk to collect excess glue and provide greater strength (Fig. 5-23). Use clamps, as always.

PATCHES

Chapter 6 covers patches of a cosmetic nature, such as those in veneers and those made to repair gouges and burns. Some experts can patch almost any part of a

FIG. 5-22 • Dowels always hold better if they are grooved to collect more glue. You can groove your own dowels with a tool like this. (*Courtesy of Dremel*)

piece of furniture and make it look good. They can cut a part of a chair leg, bureau top, desk surface, or anywhere else, fit it, plane it, sand it, stain it, and make it look like new. There may come a time when you can try this, too, but there are a lot easier things to learn first. If a structural part needs patching, our advice is to take it to a cabinetmaker—or don't bother with it. There are two exceptions, as noted below.

Mortise-and-tenon joints • Sometimes even the excellent mortise-and-tenon joint can be damaged through hard wear. Since the tenon is unseen to the eye, you can usually do a decent job of patching. To do so, cut off the broken tenon, and make the second mortise where the old tenon was, pretty much matching the mortise on the other side. Then make a new double tenon to bridge the gap and fit into the two mortises. You don't necessarily have to cut a blind tenon, even if the other one is. It's easier to cut all the way up to the top of the new tenon if you find the blind mortise too difficult. Fill the joint with plenty of glue (casein or hide) no matter how you cut it. If the joint is subjected to severe stresses, it may be wise to add small dowels across the sides into each end of the double tenon.

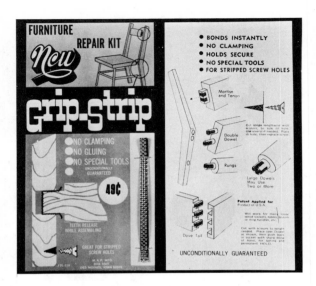

FIG. 5-23 • Another gadget for holding dowels (and other things) tightly in place is "Grip-Strip". (*Courtesy of M.A.P. Mfg. Co.*)

Butterfly patches on the undersides of chairs • Butterfly patches will often be the only cure for such things as split seats. First cut the patches in the shape of a butterfly, then lay over the underside of the two pieces as they will be when put back together. Trace the outline of the patch on the seat bottom and chisel out. Place the pieces together, glue all around, and insert the butterflies. Clamp the patches down and the pieces against each other. The seat should hold for a very long time.

Cosmetic Repairs — Restoring and Reviving

This chapter is concerned with the *appearance* of a piece of furniture—how to improve its looks rather than its structure. With people, improving the structure also does wonders for the appearance, but that's not necessarily true for furniture. Matter of fact, a piece often looks worse after major surgery. (But so do people, don't they?)

Anyway, it is assumed here that either the piece has had its major structural alterations, or that it never needed any. It just looks bad. The veneer is broken or unsightly, there are gouges or bruises, or maybe it's just plain dirty.

The last brings up an important caveat. Many beginning restorers automatically assume that they'll have to strip the old finish off to make the wood look decent. This is not necessarily true. Very often, years of neglect and abuse have simply built up a solid layer of dirt and grime. Before you commit yourself to the time-consuming job of stripping and refinishing, take a few minutes to try out a cleaner–conditioner on one section to see what happens. This can do no harm and may save a lot of unnecessary labor.

━━━━━━━ CLEANERS AND CONDITIONERS ━━━━━━━

There are a lot of **cleaners** sold in supermarkets and hardware stores for reviving old finishes, but you can't do any better than a mixture of 3/4 boiled linseed oil and 1/4 turpentine. Properly applied, this conditioner will not only remove the dirt, it will also disguise scratches, clean up haziness, and restore the natural grain and color. It should be applied hot for badly soiled areas. There are a number of commercial products sold for the same purpose as this mix, and they are all pretty good, but try them out in a small, innocuous area before applying them to the whole surface.

If the cleanser-conditioner worked as magically as you hoped, you won't have to go any further. Just apply a coat of wax or two or some furniture polish to bring back the color.

Particularly bad areas, such as grease spots, can often be removed with simple green soap, available at most drugstores. On the other hand, if the piece isn't in too bad condition and just looks a little bit dirty, you can use good old white soap and water. Be careful with water, though, since it can cause a whitish haze in shellac and lacquer (and the odds are heavy that one of these will be the finish on store-bought furniture). Even so, this condition, too, can be cured (see p. 117).

FIG. 6-1 • With any luck, your old furniture can be reconditioned as good as new with an instant furniture refinisher. The tung oil is used as a final finish. (*Courtesy of The Hope Co.*)

——————— TYPES OF FINISHES YOU'LL FIND ———————

Might as well get into this now as anytime. At first, it looks impossible to determine what kind of finish was used on a particular specimen. It isn't as difficult or mysterious as it may seem, however.

One myth that should be dispelled quickly is the furniture-store pitch about the superduper varnish on whatever it is they're trying to sell you. True varnish finishes simply cannot be applied in a mass-production factory environment. Any piece bought in a furniture store will undoubtedly have a lacquer finish—not a bad finish, at that, but not varnish.

Furthermore, both varnish and lacquer are relatively recent inventions (around the turn of the century), so any piece that has been around awhile is almost certainly finished with shellac. We have to hedge with "almost" because there is a good chance that the piece has been refinished already, perhaps more than once.

After awhile you'll be able to tell if a piece has been refinished or not just by looking at it. There are always telltale signs of scraping and sanding on a piece that has been refinished. Look at the carvings and around the edges. Any traces of steel wool? Or look where there are chips or nicks in the finish. What's underneath? Another finish? Finally, look underneath to see if there are signs of two types of finishing materials. It may take awhile to recognize these signs, but after you've gone through the process yourself a few times, the signposts will be unmistakably clear.

But even if you've found that the piece has been refinished a couple of times, does that help you determine what finish was used? No, it doesn't (although a *lack* of a second finish on an old piece will tell you that the finish has to be shellac).

——————— TESTING FOR FINISHES ———————

The only sure-fire way of determining which finish was used on the piece at hand is through the wonders of chemistry. Don't get scared. It isn't all that complicated. The following tests will do the trick.

SHELLAC

To test for **shellac**, wrap a piece of cloth around the end of your finger and dip into some wood alcohol. Rubbing alcohol won't do, as it is more than three-fourths water. Since undenatured alcohol has been known to tempt people's palates, the manufacturers refrain from calling it "alcohol." Instead, you'll find it called by such names as "shellac thinner" or some combination of syllables with "sol" in it (Solox, Quakersol). Also, if you have a fondue pot that uses an alcohol lamp, "thinner" for use in that can be used.

Anyway, while you're waiting with your alcohol-dipped finger for this essay to conclude, it has probably dried off. So dip it again and rub it across the surface of the piece. If the surface dissolves, you can be sure that it is shellac.

LACQUER

Use the finger-in-the-rag trick to test for **lacquer**, too, but dip into lacquer thinner. Lacquer will respond in a rather unique way to lacquer thinner. It will start to look funny, like it was suddenly worn or scuffed up at that particular spot. But soon this look will disappear, as the highly volatile thinner evaporates, and the finger-dipped area will look glossy and smooth again (more so than before, usually). Now you know that you've got the right stuff.

VARNISH

Put away that piece of cloth and rest your finger a bit. The only thing that can touch **varnish** is paint and varnish remover. Put a little bit of that in a spot where it doesn't matter much, then let it work. But paint remover will affect lacquer and shellac, too, so try their solvents first. Then there are those nasty little exceptions that screw up the scientific certitude we all yearn for. *Sometimes*, lacquer thinner will react with *some* varnishes. But there is a difference. Lacquer thinner causes varnish to crinkle up, and it doesn't get smooth again after the thinner evaporates. Furthermore, varnish leaves the hardest surface, so try to dent any questionable surface with your fingernail. If it doesn't yield, you can be pretty sure it's varnish.

OTHER FINISHES

There are other finishes, of course, **paint** being the most obvious. But there are also more exotic finishes like a **combination** of shellac and some primitive forms of lacquer. You may find this in pieces dating from around the time of the Civil War until after World War I. As far as cleaning is concerned, just treat these finishes as you would shellac. Special treatment is required, however, if you're trying to remove this finish (see p. 130, "Removing Shellac").

There are, of course, many other time-honored finishes applied by professional and amateur refinishers. Very rarely are these applied at the factory. Some of these are **boiled linseed oil, clear sealer**, and **French polish**. None of these presents any special problem in cleaning. They either wash off or have worn off spontaneously by the time you start fooling around with them. The only exception is wax, and wax may be used either alone (even though it shouldn't be) or over some other finish. If the piece has been around awhile, you can bet it got a couple of coats of wax at some time in its career.

HOW TO REPAIR DAMAGE TO THE FINISH

If you can see or suspect that a finish has a coat or more of wax, this must be removed before you can clean off the gook and grime. A can of turpentine or mineral spirits and a little rubbing should remove most of the wax and leave the piece ready to he cleaned.

WHITE SPOTS AND RINGS

You usually find these on shellac-finished tables, although they can occur with lacquer and less often with varnish. The culprit is usually a wet glass set down on the surface. Almost any fluid can damage the surface of unprotected shellac, however, which is a good reason for keeping such finishes well waxed.

But lectures on what should have been done aren't exactly helpful when you have a problem. The cure for the condition depends on how deep the scar is (here we go again into the hedging department).

The best way is to start off easy and work up to the most traumatic method. If the white discoloration is more of a hazy look than a true ring or spot, you may be able to get it away with the old refinisher's trick of rubbing a little cigar ash in with some good old-fashioned spit.

If that doesn't work, and it won't for anything other than the mildest cases, the next best bet is to polish the white area with a piece of fine (3/0) steel wool and a little oil. Any kind of light oil will do, really—lemon oil, mineral oil, corn oil, olive oil, sewing machine oil, linseed oil. As a matter of fact, almost any kind of nonwater or nonalcoholic fluid will do, such as turpentine or mineral spirits. Rub lightly but for quite awhile.

This treatment should get off the majority of white spots, but if it doesn't, mix some common table salt into the oil. If *that* doesn't work, you'll have to resort to pumice, but be very careful not to rub too hard or long. Mix the pumice into a paste, using water until it reaches a creamy consistency. Apply with oil as before. Use a padded sanding block, if you have one, to rub the spot with the pumice and oil mix and don't bear down too hard. The pumice may scratch the rest of the surface badly if you aren't careful.

If nothing else works, try a commercial product designed for this work. Whatever you use, wipe if off with a damp rag, let the surface dry, then follow with a healthy coat of furniture polish.

Somewhere along the line, before or after the polish coat, it may be apparent that the area you removed the spot from is going to stand out like a sore thumb. In that case, you may have to apply the same treatment to the entire surface so that it all looks the same.

SCRATCHES, GOUGES, AND OTHER WOUNDS—WAX STICKS

Many shallow scratches can be removed from the finish by using a cleaner-conditioner as mentioned earlier. If that doesn't do it, a piece of the nutmeat from the same source (a walnut for walnut wood, etc.) rubbed diagonally across the crack a number of times should darken the scratch enough to make it fade away.

If the wood has been stained, you can try to match the stain with something similar. You can also try plain oil colors mixed to match the existing finish.

For deep scratches, gouges, etc., some filling is necessary, and there are several products used for this. Each has its own champions, so we'll give you the lowdown on each and urge that you try them and decide which is best for you.

The easiest materials to use are plain old wax crayons (Crayola, or one of those), which are melted over a sootless alcohol lamp and dripped into the wound. Most finish colors can be matched to one of those big crayon assortments that contains a lot of browns and reds. Mix these with some black, white, and/or yellow and you can arrive at a conglomeration that will duplicate anything.

Mixing itself is a little tricky. Shave off some wax chips, heat them, and keep adding other colors until you get the shade you want. You have to heat up the mix every time and let it cool, because you can't tell whether it's orange or purple when it's hot. The stuff cools rapidly, though, and shouldn't take too much time altogether.

When you get the mixture to just the shade you want, heat it up again and start dribbling it into the scratch. Scrape off the excess with a dull knife and level the scratch fill. Give the top a little stroke with a finger to make it nice and smooth.

If the job looks good, it is wise to coat the entire surface with a coat of two parts alcohol and one part shellac. This prevents the wax from bleeding into varnish or lacquer. Then varnish the whole surface where you'll be applying a new finish.

The new finish may contrast with the other surfaces, so either varnish the entire piece or rub the varnish coat with steel wool to give it the desired degree of dullness.

It should be noted here that you don't *have* to use Junior's crayon box.

There are special wax sticks, found in furniture shops and some hardware stores, which are made expressly for this purpose. Buy them if you prefer.

DEEP WOUNDS—STICK SHELLAC

A second approved method is use of a shellac stick. This treatment is preferred by professionals and does render a more invisible, professional look. Shellac is not easy to use, however, and cannot be removed easily if you foul up the job (wax can be pulled right out again). Our recommendations would be to use the wax for smaller, less conspicuous repairs, and to use stick shellac for bad or obvious places. Shellac is available in many different shades, and you heat and combine if necessary. Use an opaque stick for deep wounds and a transparent one for shallow marks.

To apply stick shellac, use your alcohol lamp to heat the blade of a knife. Also heat the end of the shellac stick, scrape off a little of the molten mass, apply it into the hole. If the hole is deep, you should use several coats rather than filling it all at once.

After the hole is filled with hot shellac, smooth it out with your hot knife, or—better—a flat spatula. Leave it slightly higher and rounded in the center of the patch if it is large.

When the material has cooled, cut it level with the surface using a razor blade, sharp knife, or the flat side of a chisel. Then finish the surface with some very fine "wet or dry" paper and light oil.

Remember that nothing is going to stick—shellac, glue, or whatever—if the area to be filled is dirty or soiled. Clean thoroughly, and stain (if you're going to) before applying the patch. Also, you can patch edges and corners with stick shellac if you made forms out of tongue depressors and masking tape, filling the area so formed.

Stick lacquer is also available and is used in the same manner as stick shellac. Another material you can use is wood dough, but this doesn't give a very good finish. The best usage for this is for inconspicuous places, or as a filler in deep wounds over which stick wax or shellac is applied.

CIGARETTE BURNS

For a burn that is not too deep or extensive, treat like any other wound in the surface—with wax or shellac sticks. Here, though, you should dig out the burned materials and leave a nice, clean hole. Use a razor blade to dress the wound.

When the burn is quite deep, the entire surface may need refinishing. With solid wood, first sand down the surface to bare, unburned material, then stain and finish as outlined in Chapters 7 and 8. If a burn goes through a veneer top, patch the veneer as described later in this chapter, then refinish as in Chapter 8.

There is a possibility that the burn is covered by your fire or homeowner's insurance policy. If the burn is slight, most companies will not pay, on the grounds that there was no actual fire. Deep burns are also questionable because of the lack of a real fire, but you can make a case that a deep burn goes beyond a mere "scorch."

The best line of attack here depends on how expensive the burned piece was and how badly it was burned. If the burn is slight and easily fixed, don't bother to make a claim for a number of reasons (including the $50 deductible). When the piece will cost considerably more than $50 for a refinishing job by a professional, is ruined beyond repair, or is drastically diminished in value—a possibility with valuable antiques—it may pay you to make a claim. Whether you'll collect or not depends on the policy of the company and the whim of the agent. The law is not settled in the matter (at least not at the time of publication).

DENTS AND BRUISES

A little dent in the surface of an antique can be passed off as making it more authentic, but it can be an eyesore in most pieces (it's all in the mind, really). With any luck, dents and bruises can be removed from all but the hardest woods (hard-rock maple, for example).

Wood fibers act in much the same way as the pores of sponges. If you fill them with moisture they will swell. Look at your doors and windows in humid weather, or our old friend warp (p. 103). This difficulty is an advantage when it comes to dents, however, for it is the moisture absorption of the fibers that eradicates the dent.

There are several ways to utilize the moisture absorption principle, like merely laying some water in the depression and watching it swell. But this doesn't work very well on most hardwoods. The best general solution for any dent is to steam the dent up to level with a regular household iron and a wet cloth. Lay the cloth over the dent with the iron on top. Turn the iron onto a low or "synthetic" setting and let it work for a half-hour or more. Keep half an eye on it while you go about other chores, so that it doesn't swell up too high, but chances are that the cure will fail in the other direction rather than going too high.

If regular steaming doesn't work, you can try sticking a needle into the depression, making some tiny holes for better absorption, then proceeding as above. The swelling will either close up the holes or render them too small to notice. Give the needle a little whack with the hammer to make it penetrate the the surface; 1/4 inch or so will be plenty deep enough.

All that water won't help the finish any, so you may as well remove it from the area before you begin. This will help the absorption process. When you're done, refinish as described in Chapter 8. You might get away with just redoing the area you worked on, but chances are you'll wind up refinishing the whole surface.

Be careful, by the way, with old pieces and dents near glue lines. All that heat and steam may loosen up the joints. For such cases, put a piece of wet blotter into the depression, press a marble or similar rounded object over it, and hold the iron on top of that. Turn the iron on a little hotter (medium range or higher) since it is so far from the wood. No matter how you do it, try to keep the water and steam away from the glued areas.

Very hard woods, as mentioned above, will not succumb to the seductions of steam; but, then again, they are very hard to bruise. If it does happen, the fibers are probably broken rather than compressed. You will either have to sand the surrounding surfaces to minimize the abruptness of the dent, or fill the area with a shellac or wax stick as described earlier in this chapter.

CLOUDINESS, HAZINESS, BLUSHING

Cloudiness, **haziness**, and **blushing** refer to the same phenomenon, which is nothing more than a gigantic white ring or spot and should be treated accordingly. (See p. 113 for details.)

What causes the condition is that some sort of moisture gets into the finish either through excess humidity in the air, a lack of heat in the room, or something similar. The water that collects on the surface causes the same problem over the entire surface as that wet glass did to the top of the cocktail table.

If the finish is cracked or "alligatored" in addition to being cloudy, proceed to the cure for the condition, which follows immediately. "Reamalgamation," as the corrective process is called, will fix up clouding in addition to alligatoring.

CRACKING, CRAZING, ALLIGATORING

Furniture that is directly in the path of hot sun or left for long periods in a hot attic will often develop a condition known by such various names as **cracking**, **crazing**, **crawling**, or **alligatoring**. Technically, the terms have somewhat different meanings. A crawl is a large craze, for example. The condition is often accompanied by clouding or hazing. Regardless of the size or pattern of the cracks, the cure is happily much simpler than the explanation of the terms.

As mentioned above, the finishing material is usually either shellac or lacquer, both of which can be dissolved and spread around again without removal. The technique is known as **reamalgamation** and is accomplished by applying a solvent to the finish with a rag or brush. The solvent "melts" the finish enough so that it can be redistributed or reworked over the entire surface.

The first step is to find out what the finish is (see p. 111). When that is settled, use denatured alcohol to reamalgamate shellac and lacquer thinner for lacquer. If you run into one of those intermediate early twentieth-century finishes, use three parts alcohol to one part lacquer thinner. That should cover all the bases except for varnish. (See "Cracked, Chipped Varnish," p. 119, for this problem.)

REAMALGAMATION TECHNIQUE

The process of reamalgamation is the same regardless of the solvent used. First, remove all traces of the wax finish carefully. Next, apply the solvent with a *clean* brush. Buy a new brush if you have any doubt whether a brush is clean—a lacquer brush for lacquer, a shellac brush for shellac. About 2 or 2-1/2 inches is the best size. It's a good idea to experiment in an inconspicuous spot before attempting to treat a large surface.

You should make sure to have a level surface when applying the solvent, at least over large areas. It is also best to apply the solvent in long, wide, even strokes across the grain and then rebrush with the grain. This will often be enough for minor cracking, but if it isn't, just keep repeating the process until the cracks are gone.

The one thing you'll have to watch for if you keep adding more and more solvent (it's very volatile and evaporates rapidly) is that you don't cut too deep with it. The key point is when the surface is free of all cracks but still has a few brush marks or mild blemishes. Try stopping there and waiting until the surface dries. In a way, what you're doing is applying a new coat of the finish and you don't expect a perfect look until it dries, so don't expect it here. Afterward, if it still looks lousy, give it another go. But it should dry up looking pretty nice.

Once you're satisfied with the general look, it may be well to give the surface another coat. This is more desirable with shellac than lacquer, but it won't hurt a lacquer finish either. After that's applied, give the surface a rubdown with fine 3/0 steel wool and a coat of wax or polish. Then step back and admire your handiwork.

It may be well to read the respective descriptions on how to apply lacquer or shellac in Chapter 8, since reamalgamation requires similar techniques. One thing about shellac, in particular, should be considered—not to apply it in damp weather.

CRACKED, CHIPPED VARNISH

Varnish will sometimes crack, although not half as easily as lacquer and shellac. Often it becomes chipped, too, and the cures for both are essentially the same. Unfortunately, varnish revamping is a much more difficult and chancy proposition than reamalgamation. Here, you'll have to buy special chemicals called **amalgamators**, which are sold at larger paint and hardware stores. They are sold under various trade names but mainly contain acetone and/or other harsh ingredients. Watch out for these chemicals and try them out in a very out-of-the-way place to see if they will work for you.

You can always try another method, which is also used for chipped varnish surfaces. Buy one of the modern synthetic varnishes (see p. 152) and work it into the cracks or chipped areas, applying a second, third, or more coats until the depressions are completely filled. Then paint over the entire area with a final coat.

As you have probably determined for yourself, you may very well be better off removing the entire finish and starting over.

BLACK RINGS OR SPOTS

Logically, it would seem that this problem would belong with or near our discussion of white spots. But there is a rather profound difference. White spots are nearly always superficial and easy to eradicate. Black spots are quite another matter. They are almost always caused by water that has penetrated the finish and gotten right into the wood itself. Flower lovers, attention, because this condition is frequently caused by water condensing on a vase. The fact that the vase just sits there for days at a time is the reason that moisture penetrates so deeply. This can happen to shellac in a day, and may take a couple of weeks for varnish.

No matter what the cause, the cure lies in first removing the finish from the entire surface. This is really the only way to get at the bare wood. Once the piece is stripped, the rest is easy. The black spot is then bleached out rather easily with oxalic acid. You buy the acid crystals, then dissolve them in water. You have to know from the name of the product that it isn't very bright to drink the solution or get it in your eyes. But it isn't all that awful a product. It won't even hurt your hands unless you have a cut or scratch, in which case you should wear rubber gloves. If oxalic acid scares you, regular household ammonia works almost as well.

All you have to do is to rub the oxalic acid over the spot and it should disappear, but there is a problem if the wood has been given a coat of stain (which it probably has). The stain, too, will come out, so you may well treat the entire surface with the acid so that it will look the same all over. The oxalic acid will leave tiny crystals on the surface, so wash it with vinegar before refinishing. Restain, too, if desired, before refinishing.

SCUFFED FINISHES

If your furniture looks like Junior's shoes after a hard day on the sandlot, it may respond to similar treatment as the shoes. "Similar," not "exactly," since you would probably use a special "scuffy" polish for the shoes, and you use plain wax shoe polish for the furniture. The reason for this is that shoe polish is like a big wax stick anyway and is easier to use if you find a respectable color match.

The shoe polish will not only bring some color back to the wood but will also fill the gouges and imperfections. To do the best job, precede the wax treatment with a coat or two of colored polish (dyes in mineral oil). Follow afterward by a coat of plain paste wax over the entire surface.

GREASE SPOTS

Surface grease is no problem and is easily removed with soap, detergent, or cleaner–conditioner, as described in the beginning of this chapter. Occasionally, however, the grease penetrates to the bare wood, mainly because of a thin or crumbling finish.

Deep grease spots that have penetrated into the wood can be eliminated by using a dry cleaning fluid like those used for clothes. Benzine, Energine, or similar products should get rid of most animal stains. Acetone is better for vegetable oils. Use a small brush and try not to let the cleaner get onto areas other than the stain proper. Apply liberally until the grease spot is gone, wiping dry with a Kleenex after each application.

CHIPPED OR PEELING PAINT

Painted furniture has either an opaque lacquer or an enamel finish. If this has peeled, there really isn't anything to do except strip it and repaint (or use another finish if the wood looks okay). One expert suggests trying to glue down a large "peel" as long as it is flexible and smooth, but this isn't a very satisfactory cure. Whatever caused the peeling (moisture probably) is still there underneath, and there seems little doubt that you'll wind up stripping the whole thing anyway.

Chipping is a condition that usually can be masked, if not exactly cured. You can try, anyway.

The first thing is to find out whether the finish is enamel or lacquer. Lacquer thinner will cause lacquer to react in the usual way, won't affect enamel at all. If you have a lacquer surface, reamalgamation (see p. 118) should do the trick. Enamel is a little more difficult. You have to find a matching color and apply several thin layers until the chipped area is brought up level with the surrounding area. Feather the chipped edges before starting, and sand with 6/0 sandpaper between coats. Allow 24 hours between layers.

If a lacquer chip is extra-large in size, reamalgamation won't work and you'll have to apply new lacquer using the same method as with enamel. No doubt your new surface is going to look a lot shinier than the old one, so try to dull the spot by buffing with 3/0 steel wool.

MILK PAINT

In case you have an old-fashioned milk-paint finish, you should consider yourself lucky. Weird finishes like this are considered valuable by antique freaks. If ordinary cleaning won't make the finish look any better, leave it alone. These finishes have a certain charm, even when sort of ugly.

You can even fix up milk paints, but it's a tricky job at best. The oldtimers used sour milk mixed up with whatever happened to be around. Black, for instance, was made of the soot from kerosene lamps; brown and other earth colors were literally that—various forms of clay, sand, etc. Red was made from blood, blue from blueberry juice, etc.

REPAIRING VENEER, INLAYS, ETC.

Wood veneers are usually the most beautiful part of furniture. When something happens to veneer, the piece takes on a seedy look and is often tossed away. Here lies one of the great subjects for worthwhile restoration, because veneer is not difficult to fix and the piece will look amazingly better once the job is done.

Loose or blistered veneer can often be reglued as is, warming up and melting the old glue (probably fish or hide) with an iron. Cover the area with waxed paper and thin padding. Slit any large blisters along the grain with a razor blade if you can't get under them. When the blisters do go down, there will probably be an overlap at the slit, because the wood has undoubtedly been swollen. Use a new razor blade and pare off that part of the veneer that overlapped. It's tricky, yes, but it can be done with a steady eye and hand.

If the veneer came loose at the edges and allowed dirt to get inside, the best thing to do is break that piece off and scrape off the old dirt and glue. Hopefully, the break will occur at a natural point and not be noticeable when it is reglued. You can always fill any larger cracks with stick wax or shellac, but it shouldn't be necessary.

Inlays are nothing more than strips or bits of veneer and should be treated accordingly. Since these are smaller, you can often lift them out completely, scrape off all the old glue and grime, then lay on a dab of Elmer's.

Missing veneer or inlay material is bad news but maybe not as hopeless as it appears. It should be possible to match the old veneer somewhere (after all, there aren't that many types of woods). Maybe you won't find an exact match, color for color or grain for grain, but you should be able to find a piece that will do. If it's a small inlay, perhaps you can take out all the pieces that match and put in a whole new series or section that is completely different but looks okay because it isn't an obvious mismatch. We much prefer replacing entire sections of veneer to patching (see below).

Where do you find all this wonderful stuff? Well, if you've been doing this awhile and listening to the oldtimers' advice about saving good veneer, you may find a piece right in that little old workshop. Failing that, a local cabinetmaker may have a matching piece, or you may be able to find a similar piece and steal from that (tedious finding it, though). If you can't buy a piece, try a specialist such as Constantine, who was recommended before but whose address is worth repeating: Albert Constantine and Son, Inc., 2050 Eastchester Rd., Bronx, N.Y. 10461.

PATCHES

Many authorities on furniture repair tell you how to make patches for badly damaged surfaces. We feel the same way about this type of patch as we did about patches for broken arms, legs, and spindles. Either make a new part or fix the old, but patching a piece in the middle strikes us as futile. If the piece isn't worth the trouble, it isn't worth the trouble. If the piece *is* worth the trouble, take it to a pro. Patching is a delicate art that you can fool around with on a relatively worthless piece if you enjoy the work. But if the piece is any good, don't mess with it at all. Take it to a guy who know what he's doing.

For the record, though, here's how it's done for a solid surface:

1.   Find a piece of seasoned wood that will approximate the piece in color and grain. Wood from an old piece is best, but be sure to thoroughly remove all finishing materials, dirt, etc. Lay it over the area to be matched to find the best grain match.

2.   Cut the piece in the shape of a diamond, arrow, parallelogram or anything but a square or rectangle. For some reason, 90-degree angles show up too easily. Sand thoroughly.

3. Lay the new piece over the surface to be patched and delicately scribe around the perimeter. If the patch is so deep it distorts the shape, make a template of the top and transcribe.

4. Dig a **grave** using the scribed perimeter. The grave should have vertical edges and a level bottom to match the cut piece as exactly as possible.

5. Try the patch in the grave and trim, cut, or sand away any cutting errors.

6. When the patch fits perfectly, lay it in with casein glue to fill the cavities. The patch may extend slightly above the surface and be sanded or cut down to level.

Veneer can be patched in the same way if desired, except that the grave is only as deep as the veneer. If you must patch inlays or veneer, find a place where the old veneer was matched or the grain ends naturally, and replace the entire section. You've got to be a pretty good cabinetmaker to put a patch in veneer and make it look halfway decent.

HARDWARE RESTORATION

They don't make hardware the way they used to, so if you have original brass drawer pulls, keyhole plates, hinges, escutcheons, etc., don't discard them just because they don't look too good. Solid brass can be cleaned up with ammonia or a commercial brass cleaner. Stubborn areas can be scrubbed with lemon rind or hot vinegar and table salt. Remove the hardware if it's easier and dip into a cleaning agent. Rub the cleaned surfaces with 3/0 steel wool, then clean with warm, soapy water, rinse, and dry to give the hardware just the right look.

Brass-plated hardware is best cleaned with commercial brass cleaner or rottenstone and boiled linseed oil in a thin paste. Wipe off the paste with more linseed oil, then polish. Wash with warm, soapy water as above.

If the hardware is ruined beyond repair or missing, you're probably better off replacing everything than by trying to match what you have, especially if it comes in pairs like hinges (Fig. 6-2). The place for this is again Constantine's, 2050 Eastchester Rd., Bronx, N.Y. 10461. They may even be able to match what you have, but don't bank on it.

PLASTIC REPAIR

A lot of new furniture is made out of plastic, both hard and soft. The hard laminates, often referred to by one of the brand names, such as Formica, are best protected by a silicone-base wax. The wax helps prevent wear and makes cleaning easier. Soft plastic, usually vinyl, can be protected by one of the vinyl preservatives sold commercially. Those used for car tops are as good as any.

FIG. 6-2 • If you can't restore the old hardware, there are lots of fine replacements like these almost invisible hinges and matching knob/rings. (*Courtesy of Gries Reproducer Co.*)

When a hard plastic surface becomes worn or dull, we again turn to the auto industry for a single-step cleaner–polish. Pour a little on the worn area and rub with a soft cloth pad in the long direction. Rub until the gloss reappears, then wipe dry. Apply a coat of wax to the entire surface. Never use abrasive cleaners on laminated plastic.

When laminated plastic comes loose from its wood backing, it can be replaced by scraping off the old adhesive and gluing back into place again with a countertop adhesive. Clamp down until the adhesive dries.

LEATHER REPAIR

Leather has been around almost as long as wood, although it usually doesn't last as long. It can be revived, however, if it hasn't cracked or otherwise deteriorated.

To bring back the old glow and also to preserve it, give it an occasional rubdown with saddle or castile soap. Don't use regular furniture polish or anything similar, since these materials contain harmful solvents.

To clean dirty leather, mix up some mild soap flakes (not detergent) with warm water and a teaspoon of vinegar. Apply to the leather with a soft, clean rag and wash off with clear, lukewarm water. Finish, when dry, with a little leather dressing. All these materials can be obtained from a saddle or leather shop in your community. Sometimes shoe repair stores carry the same or similar materials.

REPAIR OF MARBLE TOPS

Marble is basically limestone and quite porous. Because of this, it is rather easily scratched and stained below the surface. If ordinary cleaning won't remove dirty marks, then you can bet that the mark is a deep stain—which takes some doing.

The only sure-fire way to restore a damaged marble surface is by literally grinding it down. This is done in stages, using various-grit abrasive papers and some sort of powder such as rottenstone or tin oxide (available at most drugstores). Start with a very fine grit such as 10/0 to see how deep the scratch or stain is. Some may come off with just one. treatment. If this does nothing, skip to a 3/0 or even 1/0 grit for severely damaged surfaces, then keep rubbing evenly across the surface, using finer and finer grits until the finish is like new.

If there are professional marble finishers in your area (try the Yellow Pages—you'll be surprised), it's best to take advantage of their professional skills. Marble-topped pieces can be quite valuable, so whatever you spend is probably worth it. (See p. 235 for tips on maintenance and care, plus removal of common stains.)

FRENCH POLISH

Sometimes French polish is used as a reviving or reamalgamation technique. See p. 162 for a complete discussion of this unusual finish.

7

Preparing Wood Surfaces for Finishing

If you're looking into finish removers for the first time, it all looks a little scary. All the cautions about wearing gloves, not getting things in your eyes, working in a well-ventilated room, and *lye!* Who wants to fool around with *that* stuff?

Well, you aren't going to hear any soothing words from us. We're just as scared as you are. It isn't perfume and rosewater you're fooling with here. Lye, in particular, is mighty treacherous stuff. If you consider, for example, that the most highly recommended remover for thick layers of paint and varnish is a paste of water, cornstarch, and Drano, then you realize that this ain't no game for sissies.

But don't go away yet. We've just given you the bad part of the news. The good news is that you don't *have* to use Drano (which *is* lye, by the way). There are a lot of ways to skin this cat, many of them quite innocuous and all of them a lot safer than lye.

THE BAD NEWS DISPOSED OF

Let's get right into the question of using lye. A lot of furniture-refinishing pros will tell you that it's really not as bad as it sounds. "With proper precautions . . ." and all that—but our view is that yes, it's fine for the pro, who *knows* all the precautions and no-no's and is skillful and experienced enough to obey them. If you play your cards right, someday you may be a pro, too, but until you are, we say that anybody who uses lye ought to have a hole in the head (which they will if it's spilled there).

Lye is a caustic alkali, which is the opposite of acid but has similar effects, such as eating holes in things. If you insist on fooling around with this stuff, buy a can of powdered Drano or other brand-name drain cleaner. Pour about three quarts of water into a pail (not aluminum, since this will cause poisonous gases) and then dump the lye slowly into it. Never pour water into the lye since it will boil up like a volcanic sea. Use a 10-quart pail so that the water goes less than halfway to the top. Use *cold* water. Even when pouring the right way (lye *into* water, don't forget), you get a strong reaction, so be careful. It's hot as well as mean.

That done, stir in some cornstarch or wallpaper paste to make the mixture sort of pasty. Don't stir it with your fingers or Grandma's silver spoon. Use a long-handled cotton dish mop, which will also be your tool for applying the glop to the furniture.

Be sure to work outside or in a warm basement with adequate drainage. The only effective way to remove lye is by washing the piece down with a garden hose or by applying huge buckets of water. Don't work on your lawn or other garden spot. The excess lye will eat all the vegetation away so hungrily that it will be probably never come back.

If you're still game after reading this far, spread the mixture lightly over the entire surface of the furniture and let it stand until it looks like its work is done. Check a corner with a scraper to see how much of the finish comes off. When it looks like the lye is down to the finish (1 to 10 minutes or so, depending on the thickness of the coatings), quickly take the garden hose (if you're outdoors) and wash the powder off as completely as possible. Scrub or scrape what is left until there is no remover remaining on the surface.

Yet another caution here—for the furniture this time. If you let the lye work too long, you will "burn" the wood, turning it black. Be especially careful to scrub the lye out of cracks and crevices before it gets a chance to do damage to the surrounding wood. It can also raise the grain of many woods, so be very sure you remove it all.

After you're sure you've removed all traces of your brew, neutralize the caustic effect by applying an acid. The best and cheapest acid is plain household vinegar, preferably white. Wash the surface thoroughly with the vinegar and some clean rags. Then let the piece stand for about a day to catch its breath.

WHY BOTHER?

If you've followed us faithfully so far, the logical, legitimate question is: Why should anyone bother? The answer is that lye is cheap, and it cuts stubborn finishes like mad. It's something you should know about, particularly if you run across something that can't be touched by other methods. It can remove thick layers of paint and varnish in one fell swoop. The same result might take four or five applications of paint and varnish remover.

So, if you must use it, use it. But be careful. Wear gloves and goggles, at least the first time. And don't worry too much about darkening the wood. You can always bleach it back into shape again (see p. 134).

AND NOW THE GOOD NEWS

Actually, you can remove practically any finish from any piece of furniture without resorting to lye. If you don't want to bother at all with messy chemicals, you can remove the upholstery and take the piece to one of various types of dip-and-strip shops present in most urban areas. Some of the bigger ones use lye vats, but many smaller ones dip the piece in the same kind of removers you'd probably use yourself.

The price is nominal, from $5 to $15 for a small chair to $50 and way up for a big job. If you're really lazy, you can have the shop strip off the upholstery for you, but you pay for the labor. Matter of fact, many of these places will do the whole refinishing and repair job. So who needs a book?

Before broaching the subject of what chemical to use, we should discuss whether you should use chemicals at all. There are other ways to remove finishes, the two most well known being sanding and heat. But neither of these is really worth discussing because chemicals are so far superior. If you use sandpaper, the job is unbelievably difficult, and you can hardly help gouging the wood or ruining the patina, even if you're a pro. As far as heat is concerned, it's a great way to remove paint from your house siding, but don't mess with a blowtorch on furniture. Other sources of heat, like those new warming irons or heating tools that keep being invented, are simply a waste of money. That leaves the chemicals.

WHICH CHEMICAL REMOVER?

Having established that the best way to remove an old finish is with the chemicals, the next question is which chemical to use. "Chemical" is used here in the general sense that includes things like alcohol. Alcohol is, in fact, as effective a remover for shellac as lacquer thinner is for lacquer. If you know what type of finish a piece has, you can use either one of these solvents in a similar way to reamalgamation. (To determine what type of finish you have, see the tests described on p. 111.)

After you have determined what the finish is, read on to see what the best remover is. But you should know one thing before you even bother with this. If you're the impatient type and want to get to the job as soon as possible without fooling around, get yourself a gallon or two of the paste-type paint and varnish remover. It will remove not only paint and varnish, but shellac and lacquer, too. Don't even bother to read the special methods below but skip directly to "Selecting a Varnish Remover."

REMOVING SHELLAC

The remover or solvent to use with shellac is, of course, denatured **alcohol**. Since some shellac finishes are of the tough variety mentioned earlier, it is a good idea to mix one part lacquer thinner in four parts alcohol before you even start the job, just to play it safe. This mixture will kill the toughest shellac.

Pour alcohol onto the surface to be removed, wipe with No. 0 steel wool, and remove with a clean cloth. Keep adding alcohol and wiping until the surface is down to bare wood (or whatever else is underneath). It is best to do this in small sections. Dip the legs into the jar of alcohol as you work on them to help conserve the alcohol. When it looks like the job is done, give the entire surface the once-over with a clean cloth dampened in more alcohol.

When you're done with this job, you may never wish to see alcohol again, but it isn't really an unpleasant job. You should, by the way, be sure to work in a well-ventilated room. Alcohol fumes can be very toxic, especially in such large amounts.

REMOVING LACQUER

If your tests show that lacquer is the finishing material, **lacquer thinner** will make mincemeat of it. To make the job go a little smoother and faster, add one part alcohol to four parts lacquer thinner (the opposite of the mix above for shellac). Remove in a way similar to shellac.

Remember, again, that you can remove both shellac and lacquer with paint and varnish remover if you prefer.

SELECTING A VARNISH REMOVER

Varnish is one of the most durable finishes and consequently is one of the most difficult to remove. For many years, lye was the only thing that would touch it, but modern science has come up with some very effective removers during the past few decades. It is now possible to purchase a **varnish remover** that not only does a fast and effective job, but which is harmless, odorless, and nonflammable. There is quite a debate among experts as to which of the dozens of types and brands is best, but it doesn't matter a great deal to the average person. The best advice is to browse around a store that sells the stuff and read the labels on a couple of cans. Buy the one that appeals to you most and follow the directions on the can. To really find out what suits you best, try a little of this and a little of that. Sooner or later, you'll decide for yourself what suits you best.

The biggest divisions among paint and varnish removers are these: liquid or paste, wax or nonwax. The more you get into refinishing, the more you'll find that there are times when you'll prefer each of them. For a large, level surface, you'll probably want to use the liquid. Paste (really a jellylike substance) is better for vertical surfaces. And whether you want wax in the mixture depends on how much you want to do at a time. Wax simply retards evaporation, but it also leaves a residue that is hard to get off.

For once we're going to be bold and brave and give you an opinion. Unless you're going into this whole business in a pretty big way, you're better off with the pasty, nonflammable, waxless stuff. It's the easiest to use, although it's also the most expensive. The savings in using the other stuff, though, is miniscule considering the time and effort you save by using the best.

HOW TO USE
PAINT AND VARNISH REMOVERS

Start small. Don't tackle a house until you've learned how to work on a chair or table. Once you learn the method, it's really not hard, but you have to learn. So practice on something little, or something of the neighbor's.

The first thing to do is to find a decent place to work. Outside is best, weather permitting, which is not too often. Even if your family is used to your idiocies, don't try to take off paint or varnish in the living areas. Use your work area and spread a lot of old newspapers around. Handy though they may be, removers are messy. If you've followed the previous advice (p. 59) about building a work platform, this is a good place to work on the smaller pieces. It's helpful to keep the work surface as near eye level as possible. Try to situate yourself in a well-lighted area, and work on horizontal areas as often as you can, turning the piece as necessary and doing one surface at a time.

Read the directions on the can. Most removers come in big cans and you'll have to pour it into an old jar or coffee can. Most say to shake the can thoroughly. Use the old brush you've been saving and apply the remover evenly and thickly in one direction over the surface. Don't brush it around, but let it kind of lay there. Try to do one surface at a time, but work exceptionally large surfaces in 4-square-foot sections.

FIG. 7-1 • The first step in the refinishing process is to remove all the hardware. (*Courtesy of Benjamin Moore and Co.*)

Let the remover stand for quite awhile, at least 10 to 15 minutes, until the varnish is all crinkled up. If you know there are many deep layers to come off, put on several thick coats of remover, cover with burlap, and let soak overnight. As soon as the crinkling begins in earnest, but not before, take out your old putty knife with the rounded corners and start scraping. A wider bladed knife is good for larger surfaces, but be sure that none of them has sharp corners, as they will gouge the wood.

Many experts recommend water-rinse removers, but we're not sure why. For one thing, this almost mandates outside use, unless you have one of those old basements with drains built into the floor. Even then, we don't care much for basements with paint remover all over. Maybe these people all live out West, where the sun shines all day, all year, all century. We Easterners work mostly in our workroom, and the thought of turning the hose onto something down there makes us a little nervous.

Another thing that bothers us about water-rinse removers is the realization that many glues don't take too kindly to water, and it does raise wood fibers. This is no doubt an idle worry, since people use the stuff all the time. But would they use it on veneers? We wouldn't; water can be very harmful to veneers and lots of other joints.

Our preference is for the slower but safer method of scraping the big peels first with a putty knife, followed by wiping off the glob with burlap, rags, newspaper, or fine steel wool. Steel wool used from the start like that can be expensive, but it does do the job nicely.

It should be apparent by now that although we are cowardly about lye, paint and varnish removers don't scare us much unless we have a cut or other open wound. Not that we like it in our eyeballs, but it doesn't really bother your skin unless you leave it on too long. If you're nervous or have sensitive skin, by all means use rubber gloves. They do slow up the work, though. Goggles aren't a bad idea, but they get sweaty and then you can't see. If you get any in your eyes, or it starts to sting in any area, wash it quickly with water and you shouldn't suffer any ill effects. It's a lot safer than lye, under any circumstances.

CARVINGS, MOLDINGS, AND ALL THAT

You've got to know that the methods outlined above are of little use when it comes to the cracks and crevices of carvings and deep moldings. Chemicals can get into the corners all right, but a putty knife or steel wool isn't going to get it out.

There are a number of ways to get around this problem (Fig. 7-2). A wire brush will get into the more shallow crevices, and, if you're careful, you can even use the type that fits into your electric drill. The safest and most effective method is to use an old toothbrush. (A general rule for this business is not to throw *any* brush away.) In addition to the toothbrush, which, incidentally, can be used for cleaning teeth before you use it on furniture, you can work on carvings with toothpicks, orange sticks, turkey skewers, pieces of broken glass, or almost anything with a sharp point that fits into the cracks. Bamboo skewers used for shish-kebabs are ideal. Don't worry too much about harming the finish because probably nobody will be able to see in there anyway. You do have to get rid of the old paint or whatever, since it will be very noticeable if you don't.

To clean rungs or other turned surfaces, skip the scraper and start with steel wool, using a relatively rough grade such as No. 1 or No. 0 to begin with, followed by a finer one.

WHEN IT'S ALL OFF

After you've taken all the varnish off it is a good idea to give the whole area an alcohol bath. This will remove the remover and lots of other dirt, grime, and bits of softened paint and varnish. If you used a wax-type remover, substitute turpentine or mineral spirits.

You may find that certain areas simply will not respond to anything you do. This is particularly true of large pores such as those in oak or in end grain. Here, you can try simply digging out the varnish with a pointed instrument dipped in alcohol. Meat skewers or bamboo sticks may help. Sometimes a sharp knife will have to be used with brute force. Hopefully, you will encounter little or no end grain, and that the remover will take care of it. Unfortunately, end grain soaks up any kind of liquid like crazy and it's a job getting anything out. Sanding may be the only recourse here, and even that might not work. You can just let it go and disguise it somehow to match the final finish (bleaching, staining, oil paints, pigment, etc.)

OTHER REMOVERS

It's apparent by now that lye isn't our favorite substance. It is a court of last resort, however, if nothing else works. Before you resort to it, however, there are several other removers that can be considered in addition to those given:

Arf'n'Arf • Arf'n'Arf is a variation of the alcohol–lacquer thinner stuff mentioned above. Mix half of each this time, which should work on various shellac or lacquer mixes and even some varnishes. It's less work and mess than paint remover.

Trisodium phosphate • Trisodium phosphate (TSP) is a sort of mild lye which is a lot safer to use and doesn't have all the scary warnings on the label and stuff. It's very good to have around for a lot of things, like tough cleaning jobs, taking the shine out of painted floors before tiling, and removing old paint and varnish from hardwood floors (much quicker and a lot cleaner than those sanding machines). Use it on furniture as a sort of compromise before you resort to lye. But it isn't a first choice for this usage, since it can also turn wood dark or black. Treat it the same as lye, except that it doesn't need a vinegar rinse. Mix 1 pound with about 6 quarts of water. It's cheap, too.

Ammonia • Ammonia is the court of last resort, one step beyond lye, because the fumes are decidedly dangerous. If you've used the very mild versions in household cleaners (they won't work here) you know what we mean. This is the pure version, now, and should be used only outdoors if at all. Or, if you are really desperate on a winter day, open every window in the area and make sure there is cross-ventilation. To use, pour the ammonia on the area and rub with a piece of medium-grade steel wool. Do the whole piece at once, then go back and wet it all over again. The finish should come off this time in big satisfying globs. We hate to say it, but this is the best stuff to use on milk (refractory) paints. Even lye doesn't work as well on these stubborn finishes. But better yet, take our earlier advice and leave on the milk paint to keep that antique look.

TO BLEACH OR NOT TO BLEACH

Now that all the finish has been removed from your incipient work of art, take another look with a critical eye. This is what the wood looks like in its native

(a)

(b)

FIG. 7-2 • Old finish is removed (a) from difficult cracks and carvings (b) by using an old toothbrush or a long, thin strip of emery cloth. (*Courtesy of Benjamin Moore and Co.*)

state (somewhat dowdy perhaps, but as native as it's ever going to look). Personally, we like the unbleached natural look with a coat or two of satin varnish (Fig. 7-3).

There are two reasons for bleaching: one, the natural wood color doesn't suit your fancy; two, the wood has been unnaturally darkened or stained for any one (or more) of a variety of reasons. This may happen over the whole surface or just in certain areas. If you aren't that familiar with woods and the wood has been stained or darkened overall, maybe you won't even realize that it isn't the natural color.

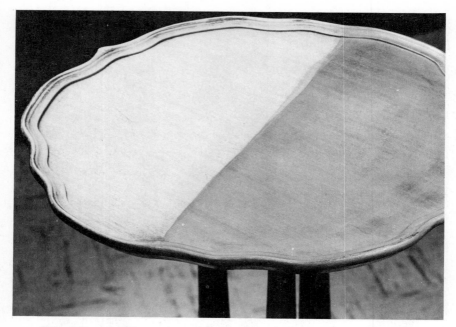

FIG. 7-3 • This newly stripped table top illustrates the difference between bleached (left) and unbleached (right) wood. (*Courtesy of Sherwin-Williams*)

When there are intermittent dark areas caused by water rings, lye, mismated patches, or other factors, you can either stain the whole thing to match the dark part or bleach the dark areas to match the light. For staining, see the latter sections of this chapter. To bleach the dark areas lighter, there are several methods, but the easiest way is to pour some full-strength laundry bleach (Clorox or whatever) over the spot and rub it over the dark areas. Keep doing it until the area is as light as you want it.

Sure, there are other erudite and complicated ways of doing this, but why fool around with all that stuff when laundry bleach can do the job in a jiffy? When the color is light enough to match the rest of the piece, rinse thoroughly with water and the job is done.

You may note a grayish or whitish cast to the wood after you've bleached it. Don't worry too much about it, as it is a temporary condition, caused by loosening of the surface fibers, which will go away once the finish is applied. The only time you might want to fool with it is on softwoods. With softwoods, the phenomenon may still be noticeable after finishing. To prevent this, rub softwood with some 2/0 steel wool before proceeding.

BLEACHING TO CHANGE COLOR

If your motive in bleaching is to alter the color of the wood, the ground rules change considerably. Household bleach is a little slow-working for a major job like this. Two ways to do this are in favor with most refinishers. The first method, and the old standby, is oxalic acid. Unlike lye, this product is not nearly as awful as it sounds. As a matter of fact, the problem with oxalic acid is that it isn't really strong enough. It does a fine job on open-grained woods such as oak, ash, and chestnut, but is not too effective on most other woods.

Oxalic acid can be picked up at most paint and drug stores in crystal or powder form. The only way to use it is in "saturated" solution or in a liquid that has absorbed all the powder or crystal that it can. The way to determine this is to add the acid to a container of hot water until the water can no longer absorb the acid. A rough guide is approximately 1 ounce of powder or 2 ounces of crystal per pint of hot water. With some woods, maple in particular, it helps to throw in a pinch of tartaric acid powder to the mix (also available in drugstores).

Apply the stuff to the entire surface of the piece and let it stand for 10 to 20 minutes. Wear gloves, at least the first time. Then wipe it off with a damp cloth. If the color isn't quite light enough, repeat the same application until it reaches the degree of lightness that pleases your eyeballs.

This method can be used to spot-lighten dark areas, but you might as well resign yourself to bleaching the entire surface. You can try it on a spot, but you're almost sure to do the whole thing to make it look uniform.

TWO-STEP BLEACH

This is a fairly recent development and one that the light-finish lover should welcome with open arms. The "two-step" name comes from the fact that, oddly enough, there are two parts to the operation. You can buy this type of bleach, called by various names (one is Blanchit), in most paint and hardware stores. Keep trying, someone will have it.

To use, apply number 1 (A) first with a large nylon brush. Let it stand for about 20 minutes, then apply number 2 (B) in the same way. If you use the same brush, wash it out before applying the second stage. Let number 2 just keep working until it feels like quitting. When it dries, the surface should be considerably lighter.

These bleaches vary quite a bit in actual application, so be sure to read the manufacturer's instructions carefully. His product may not work in exactly the same way. Some, for example, require mixing of both numbers before application. As you can probably guess by the potency of the solution, rubber gloves are a necessity.

STAINS

LIGHTENER STAINS

You don't have to bleach wood to make it lighter. The **lightener stains** are just what the name implies, true staining compounds that make the wood lighter instead of darker.

Lightener stains are "wiping" stains (see below), which are rubbed into the soft part of the wood. The stain is wiped on, allowed to sink in, then wiped off, leaving the more absorbent parts full of pigment. Since the pigment is light, the wood takes on a lighter tone, just as the more widely used dark stains give the wood a darker look.

WIPING STAINS

Wiping stains are the most familiar to the amateur woodworker and should not be sneezed at by the professional, either. Virtually all stains you buy at the paint or hardware store are wiping stains. That is, you wipe them on, let them work awhile, then wipe them off. Wiping stains contain pigments that are absorbed by the softer fibers of the wood and bring out the grain more dramatically.

Wiping stains are very easy to use and are great for softwoods. Pine, for example, soaks up a lot of the stain and looks beautiful afterward. Poplar and basswood also respond well. Fir is not so good, because of the wildness of the grain. These stains come in a wide range of colors, but not wide enough if you're trying to do something fancy such as matching another piece. And they are no good for close-grained hardwoods, because there isn't enough absorbency to have much effect.

You should always try out any stain on a scrap of matching wood or in an inconspicuous area of the piece you're working on. If the color is exactly what you want, you can use a *sealer* stain, which locks in the color and acts as a finish coat as well. This is fine and may save you some work, but don't use it unless you're quite sure you'll like the result. The penetrating sealers are usually synthetic resins that penetrate the wood fibers and harden them against further changes. You may wind up having to bleach the piece back to what it was before—or worse. So check the label carefully and avoid sealer stains except as stated.

If you prefer a wiping stain to the others below, don't be put off by the fact that the store doesn't stock exactly the shade you want. These stains can be mixed, and you can get practically any shade you want by the judicious intermingling of just three of them—maple, mahogany, and walnut (Fig. 7-4).

FIG. 7-4 • You can create almost any color shade you want by mixing tinting colors into standard stains. (*Courtesy of Benjamin Moore and Co.*)

Although most furniture should be properly sanded before application of the finish (see Chapter 8), wiping stains have a linseed oil vehicle, which does not raise the grain, so this cuts down the sanding job a little. The color of any of these stains, however, is not as attractive or bright as the dye-type stains below.

WATER STAINS

You won't find **water stains** at the local hardware store, but it doesn't really matter, because it is doubtful that you'll be using them anyway. They are very popular with furniture factories because they are fast and cheap. And they do a nice job.

The nice effect that water stains impart to woods is due to the fact that they contain aniline or synthetic dyes, and these dyes give the wood a sharp, brilliant color that is much admired. Aniline dyes come in little packages of powder that cost less than half a dollar a quart at Constantine's, 2050 Eastchester Rd., Bronx, N.Y. 10461. They are mixed one packet to a quart of boiling water and applied with a spray gun. At least that's the best way, and it's a little tricky. You can apply them with a brush but that's even trickier. And worst of all, water stains will raise the grain of the wood, necessitating a more difficult sanding job. Further sanding may even remove the color from high spots.

One nice thing about water stain is that you can mix up a batch of a color and save what's left indefinitely. If you put labels on the bottles, you can stock up quite a collection of colors, and reproduce any you want to use more of by following the same mix as on your label.

On the whole, though, we don't find water stains worthwhile for the nonprofessional furniture refinisher. For the less showy jobs, we recommend wiping stains and, for any real *pièce de résistance*, our personal preferences are the alcohol or non-grain-raising stains discussed below. Matter of fact, if we had our way, we wouldn't stain at all except for some white softwoods, such as pine (see the discussion below on this).

Generally speaking, no wood surface need be sanded or smoothed before applying a stain. In most cases, make sure that the surface is dry and dust-free, but moisten the surface for water stain. The stain is mixed according to your preference and tested on a scrap of the same wood or an out-of-the-way place.

When the color is just right, apply the stain in long, straight strokes using a regular 2-inch paintbrush. Tap the brush on the edge of the container after each stroke and go back over the part you just did, picking up surplus stain again, repeating the process until the surface has a nice even look without streaks. Keep the surface as flat as possible the whole time to avoid running. Work quickly so that drips or large blobs won't have time to sink into the wood.

ALCOHOL AND NON-GRAIN-RAISING STAINS

Basically, the **non-grain-raising (NGR) stains** you can buy at some stores are the same thing as **alcohol stains**. And alcohol stains are the same as water stains except that they don't raise the grain of the wood. You make an alcohol stain the same way you make a water stain, with aniline dyes. But this time you mix the powder with denatured alcohol instead of water. Ordinarily, mix one packet of powder to a quart of alcohol. You may find, however, that the darker colors such as walnut and red mahogany are too intense and should be diluted with twice as much alcohol, maybe more. Add or subtract as much as you want, mix them, match them, etc., in the same way as with water stains. This time, though, you'll find that it's difficult to save the leftover stain because the alcohol evaporates so quickly. If you cover the jar extra tightly, it may last for awhile at least.

As we all know by now, alcohol evaporates very quickly, which creates another good–bad situation. The good part is that you can put another coat of stain almost immediately after the last one, because it dries so quickly. The bad end of it is that you've got to work superquickly and evenly and not go over the last brushstroke, because it'll be half dried up by the time you return to it. So lay it on quickly and evenly, and it should work out fine. If it's too light, you can add another coat in a few minutes. You can also apply one color on top of another to add a little more brown, red, or whatever shade you want intensified.

Always err on the light side when working with these stains. If you put the stuff on too dark, you'll have to get the bleach bottle out again to lighten it. On the other hand, it's very easy to add more color.

Alcohol stain should always be covered with a coat of half-shellac, half-alcohol after the job has been completed to your satisfaction. Alcohol stains do tend to bleed, so give it a coat right away and follow with at least one coat of varnish as soon as possible. The final finish for this type of stain should be a hard varnish to prevent the stain from bleeding through.

TO STAIN AT ALL?

This question of whether to stain at all is not as frivolous as it may sound. The best woods—hopefully, those used in the furniture you're refinishing—don't need any stain and, at least in our opinion, look much better in the natural state. Included in this group are

butternut	chestnut	oak
cedar	mahogany	rosewood
cherry	maple	teak

Woods that must be stained—if they are to look like anything—are

ash	beech	pine
basswood	gumwood	poplar

These lists do not, of course, cover all the woods available. Any woods not named are optional. Stain or not to suit yourself.

Further, there are a lot of "woods" that aren't really used much in furniture making. If the furniture salesman tells you that his dining-room set is made of apple, or something similar, he either doesn't know what it is and is telling you what the stain looks like, or he's an out-and-out crook.

Woods used for inlays may be one of the exotic wood varieties because there is not much wood used to make inlays and the maker can afford to splurge a little. These woods include holly, myrtle, tulipwood, satinwood, violet, and zebra wood. Almost without exception, wood this expensive is not stained.

Nobody says that you *can't* stain rosewood if you want to. Matter of fact, it is still done very often by furniture manufacturers because people think rosewood should look red instead of the usual natural brown.

You should also remember that your finishing material, as well as a filler, if used (see below) will darken the wood somewhat. Before you plunge in and apply a hard-to-get-rid-of stain, why not try out a little varnish, or whatever you plan to finish with, on an inconspicuous corner and see how it's going to look. You may decide to forgo the stain after all. Actually, wetting a spot with pure water will give you a pretty good idea what the wood will look like after finishing. In general, if you're not sure whether a piece should be stained, don't do it.

SEALER COAT

At the outset, it should be emphasized that the sealer under discussion here is *not* a sealer *finish*.

Sealer finishes are penetrating sealers used mostly on floors, although their use on furniture is increasing (see p. 158). The **sealer coat** referred to here does one specific job only: it locks in the stain so that it doesn't react with the finish coat of varnish or other final finish.

A thin coat of shellac is, we think, the best sealer for *any* finish, although others feel that the sealer coat should be a thinned-down version of whatever you're using for a top finish. Experiment with both if you have the time and energy, but remember that a mixture of half shellac and half denatured alcohol will work under anything. If you're lazy and don't like to think a lot, use it for everything and relax.

If you insist on fooling around, here are the sealer coats recommended for the various finishes:

- Shellac: the half-shellac, half-alcohol mix recommended above.
- Lacquer: half lacquer, half lacquer thinner. Use two coats.
- Varnish: half varnish (*not* synthetic) and half turpentine.

You can also buy, at the drug or paint store, **sanding sealers**, which are shellac and varnish and some other stuff all mixed together. It's pretty effective and dries very quickly.

No matter what you use, wait for it to dry and then give it a general sanding. If you're going to use a wood filler, a light rubdown with 3/0 steel wool is all you need at this point. When the finish coat is going on directly over the sealer, the surface should get a thorough going-over. You can either use 4/0 steel wool or a 7/0 garnet paper, but make sure that the surface is completely smoothed before proceeding. A *complete* sanding doesn't mean a *hard* sanding. On the contrary, the touch should be very light, although even and thorough. Be especially careful on corners and edges not to cut through the entire sealer and into the stain.

WOOD FILLERS AND WHEN TO USE THEM

Wood fillers are another of those things that you're going to hear all kinds of arguments about. Some people use them all the time, others very rarely. It's primarily a matter of taste. Fillers give the surface of the wood a very smooth, hypersatiny, mirror-flat surface. Many people like the look, others prefer a more natural look, which a filler does diminish. As should be evident by now, we are generally in favor of the natural, so we are not particularly wild about using fillers unless absolutely necessary. Even the pro-filler folks have to agree that a filler makes for rather poor adhesion of the finish.

Certain woods, however, are so open-grained and porous that it is difficult to give them any finish at all unless they are filled. We're not adverse to having you try a finish without a filler even on these, but you're taking a chance. Most people prefer the use of a filler with the following coarse-grained woods:

ash	elm	oak
beech	hickory	rosewood
butternut	locust	walnut
chestnut	mahogany	teak

As far as we are concerned, these are the *only* woods that should be treated with wood filler, and we're not even dogmatic about that (Fig. 7-5). We will be fairly dogmatic about the next list. It names those woods that should *never* be filled. There is really no point to it, since they are fine-grained and don't even accept a filler unless it's so watered down as to be invisible anyway:

basswood	ebony	pine
cedar	fir	poplar
cypress	hemlock	redwood
	maple	

HOW TO USE WOOD FILLERS

There are two kinds of filler, paste and liquid. Liquid fillers are best for fine-grained woods, but there isn't much point in filling fine-grained woods, as we've mentioned.

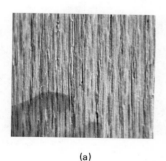

(a)

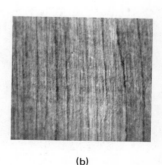

(b)

FIG. 7-5 • Open-grained wood (a) should be filled. Close-grained wood (b) neither needs nor is helped by wood filler. (*Courtesy of Benjamin Moore and Co.*)

Just for the record, though, in case you want to fool around with different colors or effects, liquid fillers are brushed onto the wood surface like any other coating. If there are still some pores unfilled, another coat may sometimes be necessary. When completely dry, sand off the top first with 5/0, then 7/0, abrasive paper.

Paste fillers are the ones most often used, and they now come in almost any color in a premixed state. You may prefer a transparent filler with no pigment, or a white, blue, or green pigment for special effects, but ordinarily the filler is the same shade as, or slightly darker than, the stained or natural wood. You can buy neutral filling material and mix up your own shades with your own pigments if you prefer, but it's easier and just as good to buy the premixed fillers to start with.

Filler comes in paste form with directions for thinning on the label. If the directions are confusing (and they probably are), just add turpentine until it reaches the consistency of heavy cream. Wet the area to be filled beforehand, then apply filler to the surface with a brush or squeegee (Fig. 7-6). Work the stuff around and back and forth until it penetrates every pore.

Let the mixture stand for about half an hour, then wipe it off with a piece of cardboard, cloth, or squeegee. Follow this with a clean cloth or piece of burlap, working this across the grain until all traces of filler have disappeared (Fig. 7-7). Then take a clean cloth and wipe slowly and carefully one last time with the grain. Let dry for 24 to 48 hours. Touch up lightly with worn 7/0 abrasive paper and dust thoroughly. When dry, apply a coat of sealer as

FIG. 7-6 • Filler can be applied with a number of tools including a brush. It should be applied heavily and worked around both with and against the grain until it penetrates every pore. (*Courtesy of Sherwin-Williams*)

described above. When the final finish is to be enamel, a varnish sealer must be used or there will be no adhesion between the enamel and the filler.

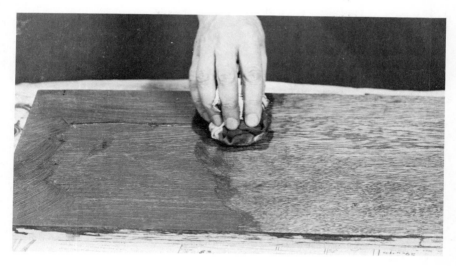

FIG. 7-7 • After filler has set for about half an hour, it should be wiped off, primarily against the grain, with a piece of cloth. (*Courtesy of Sherwin-Williams*)

The
New
Finish

Lots of fact-obfuscating nonsense has been written on the subject of furniture finishes. The fact of the matter is that, once the surface has been properly prepared, it's easy to apply one of the many really excellent products and obtain a good, hard and beautiful finish.

Proper preparation for a *re*finished surface consists of following the advice that has been given in the previous chapters. If you've followed the steps for removal of the old finish, plus whatever intermediate steps such as staining, filling, etc., you prefer, all you have to do now is select your finish and apply it.

If your furniture is new, however, and the finish is going onto raw wood, you'll have to sand carefully and thoroughly. Start with a medium-grit sandpaper and work down to a superfine one, with several grades in between for best results. (Much of the better unfinished commercial furniture is well sanded already and just one very fine sanding is all it needs.) Use garnet or silicon carbide paper rather than the cheaper grades, and wrap strips around a sanding block for faster, better work on level surfaces (Fig. 8-1).

Whether your piece is new or old, and no matter which finish you'll ultimately use, remember to present a perfectly smooth, dry, and dust-free surface to the finishing material (Fig. 8-2). You'll be rewarded in kind by a corresponding extra beauty and smoothness when you're done.

FIG. 8-1 • As a final refinishing preparation, sand the entire surface lightly with a very fine grade of abrasive paper. (*Courtesy of Benjamin Moore and Co.*)

WHICH FINISH?

Hang onto your hats for some more direct, uncompromising nonhedging. We don't see any cogent reason for anyone to use any final finish other than quick-drying varnish. Why should you? Varnish, particularly a modern synthetic, offers ease of application, relatively fast drying time, a fine-looking warm glow, and—best of all—a hard surface that is impervious to water, alcohol, dirt, grit, and most of the blows of children.

Sure, there'll be loud dissenters to this advice but they can't punch any holes in the reasoning. For all-around use, and this is what you'll be dealing with mostly, varnish is unbeatable.

Now for the other side, and we'll try not to set up any straw men. We also like the looks of shellac, but shellac simply will not hold up under the onslaught of most liquids. Shellac is even easier to apply than varnish, it builds up a beautiful finish—but it doesn't last. We would recommend shellac as an alternative choice for pieces that won't get much wear—mirrors and picture frames, hatracks, underpinnings of chairs. Shellac also gives a nicer look to pine and other light woods. But why fool around with pieces that might get liquids spilled on them?

Lacquer is wonderfully fast-drying and imparts a lovely clear finish, but it is best used with expensive spray equipment for best results. Why get involved in that if you don't have to?

FIG. 8-2 • Make sure the surface is completely dry and free of all surface dust, dirt, etc. A shop vacuum comes in very handy here. (*Courtesy of Benjamin Moore and Co.*)

Forget linseed oil unless you have a real mania for that sort of finish. It's difficult to apply, takes up to a year (no kidding), and you can easily botch it and have nothing but a gummy surface to weep onto. You can also put varnish stains into the forget-it category. These are a combination of the worst qualities of both stain and varnish and shouldn't be bothered with unless you have something you want to spruce up quickly for a garage sale. The same holds true, although not quite as vehemently, for sealer–stains.

One other finish worth considering is penetrating resin sealer. This type of finish is perhaps the easiest to use and gives a very nice finish that wears quite well. We don't happen to like the looks of it as well as varnish, but we have no objection to your trying it out and liking it as well or better. For the natural look, it can't be beat.

Another finish that perhaps tops all the others for looks on certain older pieces is French polish. This is a specific use of shellac that is probably the ultimate in brilliance. But it's tough to apply and its looks are not for everybody.

Two more comments and we'll go on to the how-to.

Wax is not a true finish but a dressing over other finishes. It should *never* be used on bare wood. Wax over bare wood gets gummy and grimy. The "wax" finish consists of several coats of thin built-up layers over a sealer. You don't notice the sealer, because it is transparent and nonglossy, but it's there (or should be). Actually, though, this type of wax can and usually should be applied to *any* finish.

Shellac is very often used as a first coat under the other finishes such as varnish. This is ordinarily over a stain to seal the color in, but it is a good way to build up a good base quickly, stain or not. One coat of varnish over a coat or two of shellac is excellent. Or, you can try what many of the pros do—give the piece a couple coats of shellac, then finish off with varnish only in vulnerable places such as table tops.

A LITTLE ABOUT SHELLAC

We'll start with shellac because of the previous paragraph. In other words, although you may want a varnish top coat, you may want to save some time and get a thicker finish by first applying a coat or two of shellac. Or, you may want to use shellac exclusively. But you wouldn't go the other way; that is, use varnish or any of the other finishes *under* shellac.

PREPARING SHELLAC

Shellac is made from the secretion of the lac, an insect, found mostly in India, that inhabits banyan and fig trees. These secretions are powdered and immersed in alcohol. How much of the secretion is in solution is indicated by the "cut" of the mix. (A 3-pound cut, for example, means 3 pounds of lac per gallon.) It is recommended that the beginner use a very light cut, usually by adding alcohol.

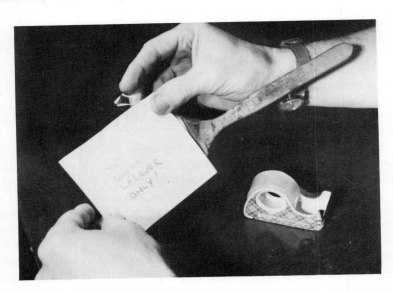

FIG. 8-3 • No matter what finishing materials you use, it is best to keep a separate brush for use with each one of them.

How much alcohol depends on the cut purchased and the degree of cut that you want to use. It's not all as complex and scientific as some deliberately obscure experts like to say it is.

The novice "shellacker" would use about a one-pound cut. It's much easier to apply when very thin. If you love formulas and pinpoint accuracy, check Table 8-1 at the end of the chapter, but if you're inexact like the rest of us, just cut the usual 3- or 4-pound cut with half again as much alcohol (1 pint to each quart) or close to that. As you progress, you can cut progressively less, but you should always add *some* alcohol to make it flow more smoothly.

Make sure not to buy more shellac than you need. It evaporates quickly and will be unusable within a year at most. If the mix you buy is dated, as some are, buy the freshest mix available. Buy white shellac, too, unless you like the dark look of orange. Orange is preferred by some refinishers for very dark woods.

HOW TO USE SHELLAC

As mentioned, cut the shellac about half or maybe a little more with alcohol. Get yourself a clean 2-inch bristle brush and stir the two together in a coffee can or soup bowl (those low peanut cans are ideal, but that means you have to eat all those fattening peanuts first). Don't shake the shellac. It causes bubbles. Use a new shellac brush each time if you can, or wash the old one out thoroughly with alcohol, then soap and water.

Just before you're ready to lay on the shellac, go over the surface once more with a dry cloth, then a tack cloth (see p. 153 for making these). Put the largest surface up on your work platform or work bench and start with that.

Dip the brush back into the mix, give it an extra stir or two, then apply the fully loaded brush to the surface. Brush the shellac onto the wood in long, even strokes, lapping slightly each time. It doesn't matter too much whether you go with or against the grain, but brushing with the grain is a good rule of thumb for everything. Once you've covered the surface evenly and completely, stop. Don't worry about a few brush strokes showing. They'll fade as the shellac dries.

After you've done one surface, turn the piece around so that the part you've just done isn't on the bottom. Work on that in that way until all parts are covered. Since you won't be finishing the bottom, the piece can stand until dry, which won't be long, maybe 1 hour or less for the first coat.

When the first coat has dried completely, rub with 3/0 steel wool. Wipe with a dry cloth to remove all traces of steel fragments, etc., then apply a second coat. A third coat of shellac is usually recommended, although two will do in many cases. The real aficionados go for four, five, or more coats, but that's a bit much for the average refinisher.

FIG. 8-4 • When preparing for the final coat, a "liquid sandpaper" will dull the sheen and give "tooth" for the finish to come. (*Courtesy of Sherwin-Williams*)

If the shellac coat is the final one, you will probably want to rub off the high gloss a little. The best way to do this is with steel wool. The grade of steel wool is dependent on how much gloss you want to rub off. To take off just a wee bit of the shine, use the finest grade you can find, 6/0, 5/0, or whatever. To produce the more popular "satin" (dull) finish, 3/0 is best.

After the steel wooling is complete, rub thoroughly with a clean cloth and put on an application of wax (see p. 231). Don't, by the way, pay much attention to the oft-repeated but silly advice about using water or oil when sanding. The effect is only psychological.

If you're following the shellac with a coat of varnish or anything else, two coats of shellac will be plenty, followed by a good rubdown with 3/0 steel wool. Be sure to dust thoroughly before applying varnish.

VARNISH

Varnish is made of resins (gums) or synthetic resins plus linseed oil, drying agents, and enough turpentine to make it flow easily. It is the best all-purpose finish for the do-it-yourselfer, mainly because of its toughness and relative ease of application.

Which of the many bewildering types of varnish you should use is really a moot question. They all really give the same look, regardless of names and minor variations. There are some guidelines, though. Look for one that is quick drying. This type is just as good as the long-drying variety and much more convenient. If you're looking for superhardness and a clear finish that doesn't darken the wood, the newer polyurethanes are tops (most varnishes darken the wood slightly). If you do buy a polyurethane varnish, make sure that it is the oil-modified type. If the label says to use mineral spirits for cleaning, you have the right kind. But you should also know that polyurethane is one of the few varnishes that shouldn't be used over shellac, lacquer, or a filler (unless these other finishes specifically state that they can be used under polyurethane).

The one type of varnish you must avoid like the plague is spar varnish. This type is made with very little drier so as not to dry out in the sun. It remains, more or less, constantly tacky, which is fine for boats and other outside uses, but sort of nasty when you sit on it.

PREPARATION FOR VARNISHING

The one problem with all varnish is its tendency to pick up specks from the air and show them prominently on the surface. For this reason, it is imperative that you work in as dust-free an environment as possible. The room should also be warm, around 70°F being ideal. This seems to shoot down basements for workrooms, because they are neither warm nor dust-free. You can, however, remedy this if you're serious about doing much refinishing work there.

Most of the omnipresent basement dust comes either from the concrete itself or from the floor above. The way to get around this is to put in a ceiling (the suspended type is the easiest as it goes around pipes and all that). Wall yourself in on all sides, and put tile on the floor to cover the concrete. If you have enough head room, the floor should be raised slightly by using 2- by 4-foot "sleepers" underneath a plywood or hardboard subfloor. If you don't want to bother with all this, move temporarily to a dry room in the main part of the house and put down lots of newspaper.

You should also give the surfaces to be varnished another once-over with a **tack rag** just before you start. You can either buy prepared tack rags at the paint store (if not, write Bond Chemical Products Co., 2100 W. Fulton St., Chicago, Ill. 60612) or make them, which is much cheaper but a pain in the neck. To make them, take a worn piece of cotton—handkerchiefs are ideal—and soak it in warm water. Wring it out lightly, then sprinkle with turpentine. After that, pour on a couple of teaspoonfuls of varnish. Fold the cloth and twist it a few times, repeating until all the liquid is wrung out of the now-dry rag. Let it dry a day or so and it's ready for use. Obviously, it is wise to make a few at a time if you're going to bother, but be warned that they may dry out. The best way to prevent this is by storing them in an airtight container like an old tobacco can. As a matter of fact, it can be dangerous to leave them lying around because of the possibility of spontaneous combustion. Rags can be used over and over again if necessary. Simply sprinkle them lightly with water and turpentine, then fold them after use, storing as described.

Another gadget you'll need for varnishing is a **pick stick**. The best ones are the homemade kind of burnt varnish on a cotton swab (Q-Tips, for example) or little stick. To make burnt varnish, place a small pan in a pan of water, add some crushed rosin (available at music supply stores if not at your paint store), and heat until it melts. Then add a small quantity of varnish to the melted rosin (about one part varnish to six parts rosin). You can also use a toothpick or a small sable artists' brush for the same purpose.

If you want to make another gadget that will simplify things greatly, make yourself a varnish pan out of an old small pot or frying pan. Bend up the handle somehow to make it fit under your thumb, and attach a wire across it to run your brush across. Pour your varnish into this and you won't have to bother with tapping the bristles or guarding against dipping the brush too far into the can.

HOW TO APPLY VARNISH

We recommend shellac as the first coat or two and varnish as a final finish only, but there is nothing wrong with using varnish all the way if you prefer—with one exception. If you used stain, you *must* use at least one shellac coat under the varnish as a sealer. If varnish is the first coat, then it should be thinned slightly, about one part turpentine to six parts varnish. (The other coats will be put on full strength.)

Varnish is best applied with a good-quality, 2-inch natural bristle brush. The most important thing about the brush is that it should be clean. If you don't have many brushes around, keep buying new ones each time you varnish until you're overwhelmed by them. That way, you're sure of a clean brush and the old ones can be used for painting. You can also apply varnish with a pad, if you want.

Don't stir varnish, ever, because it causes tiny bubbles in the liquid which make a smooth finish impossible. Never dip the brush into the varnish more than one-third of the way (hence the usefulness of the varnish pan). And don't drag the brush across the rim of the can to remove excess varnish. This also causes bubbles. Instead, tap the bristle tips lightly against the inside of the container above the surface of the liquid (or use your varnish pan wire as described).

When brushing varnish, apply only a moderate amount of pressure on the handle (Fig. 8-5). Do not bend the bristles. Flow on with parallel strokes, then cross immediately by brushing at right angles to the original direction. Finish by

FIG 8-5 • Apply varnish with a really clean brush and flow on very gently. The best method is to apply one coat with the grain, then one against. (*Courtesy of Benjamin Moore and Co.*)

stroking lightly (**tipping off**) with just the bristle tips of an almost dry brush (Fig. 8-6). Work parallel to the grain only when tipping off. This last step eliminates brush strokes and assures a coating of uniform appearance (if you do it right).

To wipe varnish on with a cloth pad, dip the folded pad into the varnish, getting a generous quantity into the cloth. Spread the varnish on with long strokes applied parallel to the grain. Don't rub hard, and make no attempt to work the varnish into the surface. Wipe up runs or sags as soon as they are noticed, since varnish seldom levels out completely if allowed to set.

As you work, no matter which method is used, lift off any dust that has settled with your pick stick. If allowed to stay too long, the varnish will harden and you will have to dig the speck out, spoiling the finish.

When more than one finish coat of varnish is applied (and you don't really need any more if you've applied a couple of coats of shellac underneath), each coat should be dried thoroughly and then sanded or steel-wooled with a very fine grade of either material. We prefer steel wool, but, again, it's a matter of personal preference. You don't really need wet-or-dry paper, by the way. Wetting with water or oil is for the factories to keep their automatic machines from getting too hot. If you use paper, again we recommend the best—silicon carbide, aluminum oxide, or garnet paper.

When sanding, always work with the grain to avoid scratching. And use light pressure, even with steel wool. All you're out to do is dull the sheen a little,

FIG. 8-6 • The last step in applying varnish is to "tip off" using just the ends of the bristles—and always with the grain. (*Courtesy of Benjamin Moore and Co.*)

so don't attack it like you would if you were trying to really "sand" it. Sometimes it's hard to see how the surface looks with all the dust on it, so brush off an area to see if you've achieved the desired satiny-smooth look. When it looks good enough, dust thoroughly and finish with a tack rag before applying another coat.

THE FINAL STEP

The final coat (and the only one if you've used shellac first) goes on like any other, except that the last coat is "rubbed" to give the furniture the highly desirable satin look.

Let the final coat dry for about a week, even with quick-drying finishes. This allows it to harden as well as dry. When ready, rub with 3/0 to 5/0 steel wool or make a paste of powdered pumice and a light oil such as motor or machine oil. (Don't use drying or linseed oils here.) Rub the paste over the surface with a folded pad of heavy, lint-free cloth.

Rub over the surface with straight strokes, parallel to the grain, and using only moderate pressure. Continue until the surface feels perfectly smooth, then use a clean, dry cloth to wipe off all remaining powder and oil. This rubbing operation will leave the surface smooth to the touch but slightly cloudy or dull in appearance.

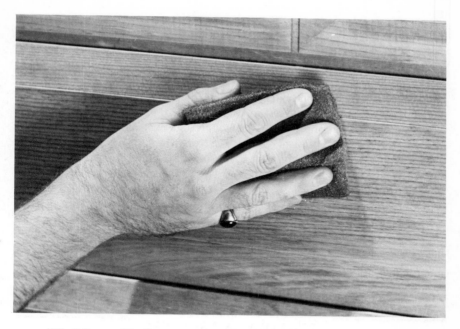

FIG. 8-7 • The final step may be a rubdown with very fine steel wool.
(*Courtesy of Sherwin-Williams*)

To restore the high luster that is preferred by some people, a second rubbing or polishing is required with a still finer powdered abrasive (Fig. 8-8). Mix a second paste of powdered rottenstone and oil and again rub in parallel strokes following the grain. After the surface has been polished to the luster desired, wipe off all paste and oil by rubbing repeatedly with clean cloths until the surface is so dry that it "squeaks" when rubbed.

USING (OR NOT USING) LACQUER

You really shouldn't have any occasion to use **lacquer**. It is nice when it's sprayed on by pros at the furniture factory, but you have to be a real fanatic to buy all that gear and suffer with spray particles all over the house. Brushing lacquers are okay, but not as good as varnish. There seems to be little point in discussing it, but for the record, here's how you do it.

Lacquer is similar to shellac in composition except that acetone is the thinner instead of alcohol. It was intended originally for the usage it still mainly enjoys, spraying on the production line. Lacquer dries extremely quickly (1½ to 2 hours), but is difficult to brush. As you are applying it, it is drying. Going back and forth over the work to smooth it becomes a problem, because it is setting as you work. Lacquer, by the way, is very often mixed with pigment for use on cars and other fast-spraying jobs, just as varnish is mixed with pigment and sold as enamel.

A good brush is a necessity here, and it must be natural bristle, because nylon may dissolve in the acetone. When you buy the lacquer, buy twice as much lacquer thinner. You will want to thin the lacquer with an equal amount of thinner and you'll need the rest for wiping up.

Mix the lacquer and thinner, then apply one coat quickly, letting it soak into the wood. Allow it to dry for an hour or two, then rub briskly with 3/0 steel wool and dust thoroughly. Give it a turn with the tack rag.

Now brush on the next coat with long, full, and bold strokes, working from the unfinished area into the finished, lapping the prior strokes lightly. Watch out for accumulations in carvings, turnings, and other such areas. Tip off the excess in these areas with the point of your brush.

This should be enough, since additional coats only gum up the first two. But you'll probably want to get rid of some of the shine by rubbing the finish as you would with varnish (see p. 156).

THE MAGIC OF PENETRATING SEALERS

Most furniture refinishers underutilize the really excellent **penetrating sealers** that have become available during the last decade. Once you're hooked on varnish, it's hard to kick—something like that. But we *have* tried penetrating sealers and liked them very much. They don't look good on everything, and maybe that's why we forget about them. (Our favorite varnishes can be used on anything, so we just automatically use them most of the time.)

Anyway, penetrating sealers are just fine for the beginner. They are extremely easy to use, requiring less time, skill, and equipment than varnish. They dry quickly, thus reducing the problem of dust collecting on the surface during drying. They are resistant to moisture, alcohol, acids, alkalis, heat, cold, burns, scratches, grease, and abrasion. The elastic quality of the tung oil or synthetic resins used as a base allows the sealer to sink into pores, fill cavities, and saturate the surface, actually becoming part of the wood. Sealers are also easy to repair, and a quick extra coat renews the finish instantly. It doesn't run or leave little "curtains" of sealer that have to be shaved or sanded down afterward.

So why not use them all the time? Because its "natural" look doesn't work with many types of furniture. The piece must have a soft, mellow sheen to begin with. The surface must be very smooth and well sanded, with all holes and defects filled. And you must like the wood the way it is. Penetrating sealers are completely invisible. They just lock into the wood fibers and stay there, keeping

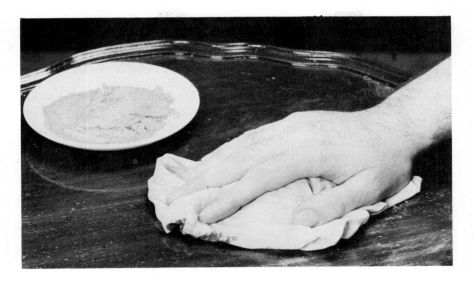

FIG. 8-8 • If all the rubbing down has made the surface too dull for you, a final going-over will restore some of the luster. Oil and rottenstone (in the bowl) is the treatment chosen here. (*Courtesy of Sherwin-Williams*)

out foreign objects but imparting no sheen whatever unless you use a dozen coats, which defeats the purpose. The furniture will look, in other words, like it doesn't really have a finish on it. For the better-looking woods, this is great, but it's not so good for the poor relations.

If you have a piece that you think will look nice with a sealer, go to your paint or hardware store and look through his probably meager stock. Read all labels carefully. You'll want a *thin* sealer, one that contains *varnish* instead of wax. This type will give the piece just a little bit of desirable gloss and is best for the typical antique or modern furniture. Exceptions are Colonial, Early American, etc., which may look best with a wax type. More open-pored woods, such as unfilled oak or chestnut, also look better with a *thick* sealer.

APPLYING SEALER

One peculiarity of sealer is that it should be strained before use. The best way to do this is by stretching a piece of nylon stocking over the top of the open can. Some of the sealer will well up through the stocking. Take a clean, lintless cloth and dip it into the sealer that came up through the stocking. Apply this to one section of the piece at a time. (Wait 12 hours after sanding the wood, 24 hours after applying stain.)

Apply the sealer with a circular motion of the cloth, working across the wood grain. Let the sealer sit for about 10 minutes and wipe off any excess with a clean, lintless cloth.

Now here we have some fun. If you like to dip into things with your bare hands, as we do, sealers are the thing, because the next step is hand rubbing. This should be done as soon as the excess is wiped off. Simply rub your hands over the just-finished surface, warming the mix and helping absorption into the pores (of the wood, that is). This also removes air bubbles and ensures even lapping of the finish.

Continue that process over other areas of the piece. Be sure to wipe off any excess that is not absorbed. Allow the piece to dry for 24 hours before proceeding to the next step, which is, of course, smoothing. With a piece of 3/0 steel wool, smooth gently. Wipe with a clean cloth and then a tack rag. This process removes bubbles and provides "tooth" for the next coat.

AFTER THE FIRST COAT

There are those who, after the first sealer coat, would go to wax or varnish. Try them out, to see what effect you like best. Penetrating-sealer addicts, on the other hand, prefer to apply several more coats of sealer in the manner described previously.

If you're going the sealer route all the way, and the wood you're working with is dark, you'll want to try a little **crocus cloth** on the second coat. Available at some hardware and paint stores, crocus cloth is impregnated with jeweler's rouge (iron oxide), a powder that turns light wood fibers reddish. This coloring agent, if you decide to use it, cannot be removed once it's applied.

Crocus cloth is used instead of the clean, lintless cloths used on the first coat. It gives the wood an extra smoothness, as well as the reddish tint, that enhances the beauty of dark woods (dark woods are the only ones to be treated with crocus cloth). Wrap crocus cloth around a smoothing block for best effect.

Allow succeeding coats of penetrating sealer to dry for 24 hours in good weather, at least 36 if the humidity is high. Apply a third coat after abrading the surface as previously described. Since penetrating sealers don't alter the color of the surface, you may not be able to tell the job has been done after the second coat. A third coat may be desirable, or even a fourth or more. One expert recommends up to 21 coats, but we don't see any sense in that. The old Long Island rule of thumb is: keep adding until it looks good to you. Sort of unpoetic, but useful.

Anyway, whenever you have this feeling that you've put on as many coats of sealer as you're going to, you'll probably want to give it a rubdown, just for fun. The easiest way is to go at it with some 4/0 or 5/0 steel wool. Or, after the final coat has dried for about a week, use powdered pumice and some lightweight mineral or machine oil. A blackboard eraser, by the way, makes a good applicator for the pumice–oil mix. Pumice and oil should be mixed to a light cream consistency. Although it isn't necessary, a wax or varnish coating over the penetrating-sealer finish will make it last longer.

───────── LINSEED OIL FINISH ─────────

It should be emphasized here, although it's been mentioned briefly before, that when **linseed oil** is discussed in conjunction with furniture, it is always *boiled* linseed oil. That doesn't mean that you throw some raw oil into a pot and start brewing. It means that you buy the boiled variety in the first place. And it's not really "boiled" at all; it has had drying agents added during its manufacture. Just be careful that the label says "boiled" instead of "raw," because raw linseed oil is sold side by side for use in paints. The raw stuff hardly ever dries, like spar varnish, which makes it great for exterior use, but useless for furniture.

Linseed oil makes a lovely finish in most people's eyes. We aren't particularly enamored of it, although it does look terrific on some antiques. Even so, it is the very devil to work with because you're never finished. If you like that feeling of satisfaction when the job is finally finished, stay away from linseed oil. After we describe the process, you'll see why.

Linseed oil is mixed two to one with mineral spirits or turpentine. Make sure the surface to be finished is perfectly smooth, wipe with a dry cloth, then a tack rag.

Heat the mixture in a double boiler (never directly over heat because of the fire hazard) and apply with a lintless cloth. Do the flat surfaces first, then go to the carved or grooved parts after the mix has cooled. (If a piece has too many of these areas, the finish shouldn't be used at all.) Keep rubbing it into each area for 5 to 20 minutes or until the wood can absorb no more.

After each section has absorbed all the oil it can, wipe away the excess, changing cloths as soon as they become saturated. Remove all traces of oil from crevices; otherwise, the oil will either harden or become sticky. (That's why it shouldn't be used when there are too many crevices.)

Next, rub each part of the piece with polishing cloth for 10 to 20 minutes. A firmly woven, hard cloth is excellent for developing a nice luster, although flannel can be used, too. Keep rubbing until you can set your hand on the part and it won't pick up oil.

At least four coats of this are required, with at least a week's drying time in between. But four coats are not going to satisfy the oil cultists, so you'll probably be going at it like this every week or two for 4 to 6 months, maybe a year. Really, about 8 coats are best and 12 or more are not beyond the pale.

As if that isn't enough to discourage all but the true believers, you are hereby warned that another coat or two is necessary every 6 months to a year to keep up that satiny sheen. Furthermore, the underside of tabletops, etc., must be kept oiled, too, or the wood may warp.

If you're at all impatient, don't go anywhere near this technique. Impatience will ruin the best-intentioned attempts. By rushing between coats, you may find that the surface becomes gummy or sticky. Each coat must be completely, *thoroughly* dry before applying the next one. Use the hand test described above scrupulously, and don't skimp with the elbow grease when rubbing.

One other thing. Either rinse out or get rid of those oily rags as soon as possible. There is a real threat of spontaneous combustion from oily rags. And watch out for fire when boiling the mixture. Even in a double boiler, the possibility exists.

SEALER-STAINS AND VARNISH-STAINS

Sealer-stains and varnish-stains are mentioned here only for the sake of completeness. We don't recommend either. The **varnish-stain** is a cheapy type that belongs only on cheapy furniture or somewhere where you can't see it. The only time we might recommend it is to cover up some really ugly grain or something, but there are better ways to do that (heavy stain, colors in oil, dyes, paint).

We really have nothing against **sealer-stains** except that, as explained in Chapter 7, you're pretty much stuck with the color of the stain once you start to apply it. If you put a stain on first, you can fool around with it a bit to make it live up to your expectations. Once you have the color you like, then you apply a sealer as described above, to achieve the same purpose as a sealer–stain.

WAX FINISH

Wax is also mentioned here for the sake of completeness, although it isn't really a finish. Wax should never be applied to bare wood, What you're doing with a wax "finish" is putting on an extra-heavy-duty wax coating over a thin finish of something else. That something else can be varnish, shellac, or whatever, but usually it's a penetrating sealer. (See p. 231 for a discussion of proper waxing.)

FRENCH POLISH

French polish is an old finishing *technique* rather than a finish in the pure sense. It uses some old favorite materials, shellac and linseed oil, but the application is different. You can use it, incidentally, when simply restoring furniture as well as in refinishing. It can be applied over old finishes as well as new.

To start with, if working with an old finish, remove any old wax. Use turpentine or mineral spirits for this job. Let the surface dry completely, then dust and wipe with your tack rag. Make a pad about the size of a baseball out of old shirts or other lint-free cloths, dip the pad into boiled linseed oil until it is saturated, then squeeze out most of the oil. Now dip the pad into a thin cut of shellac (1 pound or less) and rub it onto the surface. But keep reading before you start, because the way you rub it on is vitally important. The secret of French polish is that you cannot start or stop the wiping process while the rag is on the surface.

Don't lay the pad on the surface and then start wiping, but begin your stroke outside and continue it onto the surface. *Don't stop*—ever. Just keep wiping and wiping in a circular or figure 8 pattern until the cloth gets dry or your arm gets tired. Then keep wiping toward the edge and off without stopping until the rag is completely clear of the surface.

When you have the rag onto the surface, wipe fairly hard, hard enough to force the shellac deep into the pores but not so hard the pad sticks or stops. When the pad starts getting dry, work over to the edge, stop, apply a few drops of linseed oil and a teaspoon of shellac. Keep doing this until the entire surface is covered. Let dry for about 24 hours, then do it over again. Keep going until the surface has just the right glow. The more your work, the better it looks.

You may find that the glow you've produced is a little too glossy. High gloss is a definite feature of French polish and the reason it was a lot more popular in the days of the Louis's than it is now. If the finish does wind up too shiny for you, you can dull it by application of a pumice–oil mix as described above or by rubbing it down with very fine steel wool.

Although French polish doesn't sound too hard—and it isn't, really—it does take practice. The novice should definitely try it out on a less-beloved piece before attempting it on the baby grand. (It looks great, incidentally, on pianos.) One thing about it, though, is that you can easily repair mistakes. If you leave the rag in a spot too long (in spite of our earnest remonstrations), a little alcohol will wipe off the spot. Of course, you'll have to start over.

Don't be put off by the people that think French polish is old-fashioned (it is). Try it once. You might like it.

PAINT

Enamel, in spite of the fact that it is nothing more than varnish containing pigment, gives a completely different effect than the finishes discussed so far. Most furniture is not suitable for the opaque finish that enamel gives. Paint hides the grain and the color stands out so distinctively that the effect can be unpleasant unless judiciously used. Semigloss enamel is sometimes used on furniture, but it is not as long-wearing as pure enamel.

In general, there are three reasons for painting furniture:

- Some furniture styles were painted originally and may be in need of re-painting. Such styles includes variations of Louis XV, Louis XVI, seventeenth- and eighteenth-century Italian, Sheraton fancy chairs, Windsor and Hitchcock chairs and rockers, and early Pennsylvanian and Southern furniture.

- Many new (and some old) pieces, primarily unfinished types, lack natural beauty of color and grain. Most of these are made of pine, poplar, and beech, and come either knocked down or assembled. Any piece that has a grain that is unpleasant to your eye is a candidate for painting.

- The appearance of some furniture may be improved by painting. Such furniture may include Mission style and late Victorian pieces, and furniture that has been damaged by stain, wear, etc. Heavy Mediterranean, Moorish, or similar pieces may look better painted than stained.

HOW TO APPLY PAINT

There are three important steps to be followed in obtaining a successful paint job. First, you must choose a quality paint. Enamel is best, but semigloss may be used if you want a duller look. Never use latex or other water-soluble paints. Second, you must prepare the surface properly. Third, you must apply the enamel properly.

Proper surface preparation involves the condition of the furniture. Wooden furniture in good condition simply requires a good cleaning with odorless paint thinner to remove oil, wax, or polish. Afterward, sand lightly. This will dull the gloss and will provide a surface to which the new finish can adhere. Be sure the furniture is clean and dry before applying the enamel. If the wood furniture is in poor condition, it should be completely stripped of its old finish (see Chapter 7). Fill any holes or cracks with plastic wood or water putty and let dry thoroughly. Finally, sand as smooth as possible and apply an enamel undercoat. When this has dried, you are ready to apply the enamel topcoat.

Unfinished furniture is usually sanded in the factory. But it's a good idea to sand it lightly before you apply the undercoat. If you apply a second undercoat, sand lightly between coats.

METAL FURNITURE

To renew wrought iron and other metal furniture, clean thoroughly first. Next, sand away any traces of rust. Prime the spots of bare metal with a quality metal primer such as zinc chromate. Let the primed areas dry, then apply the enamel. Follow the same procedure for aluminum furniture.

The final step to a bright new finish is the proper application. Load your brush generously; flow the enamel onto the surface in long, smooth strokes with the grain. Don't reload or cross-stroke. Then with your nearly dry brush, go over the surface with the grain, once again using long, smooth strokes. This method provides even coverage and eliminates any excess that might cause runs.

Here are a few additional hints. Remove hardware, drawer pulls, and metal fittings beforehand. Those that can't be removed should be covered with masking tape. If the pulls and handles are to be enameled, it's easier and more efficient to take them off and paint each separately. Place chairs and small tables upside down on your work platform or on a bench; it's a more convenient height. Do the underneath surfaces first, then put the pieces right side up and finish.

AEROSOL CANS

Paint for every purpose now comes in aerosol cans. You can buy either enamel or lacquer in this state. These cans are great for outdoor furniture or cheaper indoor types. They are best for small jobs rather than large, as there is ordinarily a great waste of paint. Always spray outdoors if possible. To use any kind of spray paint properly, hold the sprayer (the can, in this case) about 6 inches from the surface to be sprayed, then move it back and forth in a direction parallel to the surface. Holding your arm steady and just moving the wrist is the cause of most spray-paint failure. Instead, keep your wrist steady and move your entire arm. It takes a while to get the hang of this technique, but try it on an inconspicuous surface and you'll soon catch on. Be careful about letting the paint build up in one spot. It runs terribly.

EPOXIES

If you're painting something that will have to stand a lot of punishing wear, the new **epoxy paints** may be just the thing. The finish is not as attractive as enamels but it dries faster and is not subject to dust specks. It's great stuff for outdoor use, kids' or kitchen furniture.

These extremely durable paints should be mixed with a hardener and applied per manufacturer's instructions.

TABLE 8-1 • Shellac-Cutting Chart

Store-bought	to	Desired cut[a]	Parts alcohol	to	Parts shellac
5 lb		3 lb	1		2
5 lb		2 lb	1		1
5 lb		1 lb	2		1
4 lb		3 lb	2		1
4 lb		2 lb	3		4
4 lb		1 lb	2		1
3 lb		2 lb	2		5
3 lb		1 lb	4		3

[a]A 1-pound cut is thin, 2-pound medium, 3-pound heavy.

Elementary Upholstery

You have probably heard some highly conflicting stories about the art of upholstery. Some tell you that it's as simple as pie; others throw up their hands in despair because it's so difficult.

It's again time to hedge. Both sides are right, but they're talking about different things. There is furniture that's easy to reupholster, and there's a lot that's very difficult (Fig. 9-1). Whole books, classroom courses, and home-study guides have been written on the art of upholstery, so it can't be all that easy.

On the other hand, a child can reupholster a dining-room chair seat. A teenager can put a new cover on a kitchen chair, and most adults can repair seats and backs in stuffed furniture with some guidance. Now, take an involved piece with upholstered cushions, complicated welting, and fabric that's attached with no visible means of support—now we are beyond the average do-it-yourselfer and this book.

What this book *will* tell you is how to make some of the more elementary repairs that won't take too much time and drive you up the wall. If you want to do more than that, fine, get yourself another book. The rest of you refinish the thing and take it to the upholstery man. He'll do it faster and better and leave you more time for the art you're expert in (by now)—refinishing.

FIG. 9-1 • Overstuffed Early American furniture can be very difficult to reupholster. Take it to someone who knows what he's doing. (*Courtesy of H. T. Cushman Mfg. Co.*)

SOME PRELIMINARY PRECAUTIONS

So far, a fairly orderly sequence has been followed, from acquisition of a restorable piece to the final finish coat. Now backtrack a little to the time when you first started to look for your restoration victim. Obviously, if the piece is all wood or metal, there is no place for reupholstering at all. But if it does have upholstery, where does the process fit in?

The first time you should think of upholstering is when you're buying. Most areas have laws relating to upholstery. There must be a tag saying that the upholstery on a used piece of furniture has been thoroughly cleaned. If the tag isn't there, forget it. You're only borrowing somebody else's trouble.

So now your lovely clean piece is home and you're looking it over. If you now decide that the poor innocent victim needs a complete overhaul, you can forget about the upholstery for awhile. To completely refinish an upholstered piece, you're going to have to remove all the fabric, whether you put it back on yourself or not. You can decide later how and when the new upholstery job should be done. (You'd be foolish to put the old fabric back on. As long as you've removed it, install something new unless it's true gold thread or something—an unlikely prospect.)

But suppose that you decide only on reamalgamation or a similar process? Will the fabric have to be removed? Probably, unless you're very neat. Even if you could work with it on, maybe you want to take it off anyway. What kind of shape are the springs in? Is the padding in place? Unless the springs are sagging, the only way to look is to remove the fabric. Chances are great that you'll want your newly restored piece reupholstered as well, but if you don't *have* to, you at least have the option of thinking about it.

The next question is whether you can do all or part of it yourself. If it's just a chair seat and back, it may be one of those easy jobs you can do yourself. If not, then better line up somebody who'll do it for you. These people are tremendously busy in most localities and you may have to wait weeks or months. So call one, if you can find one, and tell him what you want done. Find out if he's interested in the job and let him know around when you'll bring the piece in. This is a lot less frustrating than scurrying around looking for somebody when the finish is all bright and satiny and you can't wait to have the upholstery back on to see how it looks.

REMOVING THE OLD FABRIC

An important step is often overlooked in our haste to get at it with our paint removers. You have to take off the old fabric, and it's not simply a matter of tearing it off to get at that bare wood. The old pieces of fabric, no matter what shape they're in, will serve as the pattern for both pro and amateur reupholsterer. But a pro can play a new pattern by ear. For him, difficult; for you, impossible. So take it off (all off) gently. You should use a tack puller or the claw of a hammer to remove the old tacks. If you can't find the tacks, remove the welting that may cover them. Or pry off a corner of the fabric with a screwdriver and see how the fabric was applied. If it was blind-tacked, you can pretty much plan on sending the thing to the upholsterer, because this is a pretty tough thing to do. But you don't necessarily have to redo it the same way.

You can attach everything from the outside (maybe) using one of the easier methods described below. But take a good hard look and try to envision what the piece would look like that way. It may look fine, but chances are it won't; otherwise, the manufacturer (or the last guy who did the reupholstering) would have done it that way himself.

Okay, so finish with the fabric removal, working at all the visible edges until the more hidden ones show themselves. Mark where each piece came from and store it somewhere where you can find it when you're ready for it.

LOOKING AT THE SKELETON

With the fabric gone, you'll see what you really have. You'll see what the wood looks like without a stain, and how awful the old thing looks underneath. Unless you're very fortunate, you're going to find sagging springs, worn webbing, loose padding, and a peck of dirt. You may be somewhat disillusioned to find that that lovely piece of furniture is basically just a couple of pieces of wood, some ugly springs, pieces of burlap, and moldy cotton batting.

Take a look at the padding. It may be made of many things: cotton batting, animal hair, excelsior, Saran, Tampico, or other fibers. Remove and examine it. If it isn't too awful, maybe you can use it again. But you'll probably prefer to replace it with foam rubber or one of the other materials. Foam is certainly more comfortable, but doesn't always retain the original shape unless expertly installed.

You don't have to worry about the padding now; just set it aside, even if it's in shreds. You can use it to guide you in cutting the new stuff. By now you should have exposed the springs. Check all the springs to see if they are broken. In a good chair or sofa, the springs themselves are probably in good shape, but they may well have slipped their moorings.

Most springs in better furniture are tied to the webbing and each other in a semi-intricate pattern. Each spring is tied to the frame adjacent to it, then to the other springs on all sides, plus diagonally. They are also attached to the webbing below, to metal strips, or to wood cleats, depending on the construction.

Underneath the springs is the webbing, which is tacked to the bottom of the frame. Sometimes, in nonstuffed construction, the webbing is the only thing under the upholstery. Webbing is 2- to 4-inch strips of jute which hold up the springs and other seating or back material.

TACKS, STAPLES, AND ALL THAT

For years upholsterers were famous for working with a mouthful of tacks, spitting one onto a tack hammer and deftly setting it exactly where it was supposed to go. That image has mostly disappeared, unless you happen to know one of the true oldtimers who "always did it that way and ain't going to change at this stage of the game." More than likely, your friendly neighborhood upholsterer has a couple of high-powered staple guns and a more antiseptic mouth.

You should have a good supply of tacks around, anyway, because there are times when you can't get at something with a stapler, and materials that don't take too well to staples. But for most things that were formerly tacked, staples can and should be used instead.

You should know how to use a tack hammer. There are people who've had tack hammers around for years without even knowing that one end was magnetic, much less knowing how to use it.

Upholstery tacks, you see, are pretty short with big heads. They're devilishly hard to hold when starting. Sometimes you can push them into soft wood a little, but not so with the very hard woods. So some bright fellow invented the tack hammer, which has one conventional head (although longer and skinnier than a claw hammer) and one magnetic head. The regular head is for whacking tacks that have already been started. The magnetic end is for sticking tacks to (head first). With the tack intact (you might say) the hammer is aimed carefully at the spot where the tack is supposed to go and whacked down onto it. With any luck you'll miss. But keep practicing and you'll get the knack. Matter of fact, it's kind of fun practicing with an old board. Mark some targets on it and see how close you can get to the bull's-eye. While you're still nervous about it, you'll find that you'll need the other end to finish hitting the tacks in, but as your confidence grows, you should be able to drive them home with a single blow—the smaller ones, anyway.

Speaking of sizes, you'll need large (No. 8) upholsterer's tacks for webbing and thick fabrics, smaller (No. 4) tacks for most materials. Tying springs requires the biggest tacks (No. 12). Staples should be ¼ inch for thin materials, with ½ inch or the biggest available for webbing. We prefer to use tacks for webbing, but you can use staples if they're long enough and you have a powerful staple gun.

Which brings us to staple guns. We bought a dual-action one many years ago which we still use. It has two settings, one for low power and one for high. It works fine, although it's a little difficult to change settings back and forth. Use low power for softer woods and thinner materials, high power for webbing, harder woods, etc. (Why not use high power all the time? Because it's slower.)

If you like upholstering and think you'll be doing a lot of it, two staple guns are really a good idea. Load the low-power job with ¼-inch staples and the high-power one with the longer staples. It saves lots of time and fooling around.

If the webbing is intact and doesn't look rotted, don't worry any more about it. But if it has deteriorated in one spot, it probably should be replaced all over. You can buy webbing (good jute, 3½ to 4 inches wide), a webbing stretcher, and all the other materials you'll need at a good fabric, upholstery, or furniture-repair shop.

Remove the webbing that has deteriorated with a tack puller or a claw hammer and replace as outlined below. Or, if needed, remove all the webbing and start from scratch.

To replace webbing, start with the center row and work from back to front. Set the chair upside down on your workbench or platform and lay the roll of webbing over the back of the frame. Let the edge hang over about 1½ inches and stagger four No. 8 tacks into the frame. Fold the end piece over twice, then place five more tacks in staggered fashion. Run the roll over to the other side and pull taut with the webbing stretcher (butt against the side of the frame, teeth into the material). Put four more tacks into the webbing at the front of the frame, cut off the roll about 1½ inches from the edge. Double the excess back over twice and insert five more tacks.

Install webbing strips from the center to each edge, leaving approximately 1 inch between strips. Then start the same process from side to side. Start at the center again, and weave the strips in and out of the crossing strips. (You'll either have to precut these strips or weave from the roll over to the other side.) Stretch each strip and take in the same way as the other strips.

You will note that webbing is applied here in an unorthodox construction manner. The weight of the springs and everything else above it is in a direction that tends to pull out the tacks! This violates all the principles of sound construction, but there hasn't been any way devised yet to avoid it. It is mentioned here to stress the urgency of making the job as strong as possible. If you are using staples, try to get the coated kind for better holding power.

If not replacing all the webbing, check every strip carefully and tighten up any loose strips. Insert extra tacks where the old ones have pulled out or loosened (use new tacks in new holes). If the space between strips is more than 2 inches, install extra strips, even if they cross over old ones. Better to err on the strong side than the weak.

Webbing is usually applied to chair backs that are upholstered. Here, you don't have the problem of the tacks being pulled in the wrong direction. The webbing is attached to the front side of the chair back in the same general method as the seat.

SPRINGS

REPAIRING SPRINGS

Old springs need not be replaced unless they have deteriorated or are bent out of shape. Clean rusty spots with steel wool, dust, and apply paint or a sealer. There should be one coil spring at each intersection of the webbing. Each spring should be twice the height of the seat frame (5-inch spring for a 2½-inch frame). Buy new springs to replace those badly rusted or deformed.

If any of the twine holding the springs has deteriorated, the rest is sure to follow, so you might as well bite the bullet and replace it all. Buy flax mattress twine from the same sources as the webbing. Sew the springs to the webbing first using a 6-inch mattress needle. If you are tying all the springs, start in one corner with a long strand of twine and make three stitches each at four equally spaced points around the spring. Stitch continuously from spring to spring to avoid cutting twine (see Fig 9-2).

If springs are tied to metal or wood instead of webbing, check the attaching devices to make sure they are sound and replace missing parts, nails, etc. Most of these devices are available from the same sources as the above.

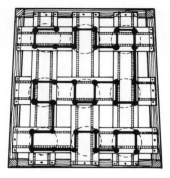

FIG. 9-2 • The underside of a chair showing the pattern for tying springs to webbing.

TYING SPRINGS

As shown in Fig. 9-3, each spring is tied eight times, either to the frame or its neighbors. If most of the twine is in good condition, simply replace the missing strands, if any, with special manila or hemp spring-tying twine. The twine should be attached to the frame with large tacks. If any are missing, replace with No. 12 upholsterer's tacks. Tie twine to the tacks using the method described below.

Single tacks can be used at each juncture of string and frame if the weight isn't too great, but where there is any chance of great strain, double tacks about 3/8 inch apart are much better. To tie string to single tacks, use a square knot. Use a double half-hitch (Fig. 9-4) for double tacks. Don't worry too much if you aren't too big on knots. Tie square knots everywhere if you want, because you're going to drive the tacks in tightly when you're done. You should really learn the half-hitch, though. It's a strong and versatile knot (see "Macramé," p. 208).

FIG. 9-3 • Each spring is attached in eight places, with the twine attached either to the frame or to an adjacent spring.

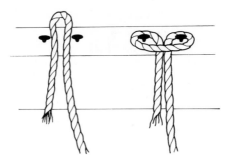

FIG. 9-4 • Tie to the frame with two tacks and double half-hitch.

When retying, proceed in this fashion:

- Back to front
- Side to side
- Diagonally each way

Tie the twine to tacks on top of the back frame, then run the ball to the front, add half a row for knotting and cut. Start with the center row, tie to the nearest edge of the nearest spring with a figure-8 knot, then to the opposite side of the same spring, to the next spring, etc., until you reach the other side (Fig. 9-5). Pull tightly as you proceed, then drive in tacks on the opposite edge and tie tightly. Drive in the tacks all the way.

FIG. 9-5 • Springs are tied with a figure-8 knot.

Next, proceed to the rows on either side of the center and continue until that direction is finished. Start at the center of the side-to-side rows, and finish that way. Then go to the left-hand corner of the back and put some tacks in there. Measure a row diagonally to the front right and add *two-thirds* for knotting. Tie to edge of first spring, loop around the other crossing cords in the center of the spring, then to the opposite edge of that spring. Continue in the same manner until finished, then tie diagonal springs in the same direction. In the corners, this will be only one spring, but it must be done for proper support. Now tie all the diagonal rows in the opposite direction.

This sounds a lot more difficult than it is, and you can get a better idea by studying the accompanying diagrams and the way the old strings were tied. Be sure to realize, though, that the diagram is one-dimensional and does not show that the springs are compressed (if you're doing your job right) so that the center of the seat is the highest point and the edge springs are almost down to the level of the frame. A section through the seat would look rounded from side to side.

REPLACING PADDING

Unless the padding has been badly stained, smells musty, or has deteriorated, it doesn't necessarily have to be replaced. But before you put the padding back on, stretch a layer of new burlap over the springs so that they won't poke through, tacking it all around to the frame. Sew burlap to springs with a No. 4 curved needle and a single long thread of mattress twine. Spread the old padding over the burlap, or replace with foam, cotton batting, or whatever, to a depth of about 1½ inches. Use a pattern if complex. Rubber-cement foam padding to the edge of the frame and to the burlap if on a vertical surface. When using foam rubber, apply 3- or 4-inch strips of muslin to edges where foam hits the frame for greater smoothness. Glue the muslin to the foam and tack down the other edge to the frame. Snip the strips around corners so that they will lay flat.

STEEL WEBBING, NO-SAG SPRINGS, AND OTHER CONSTRUCTION

You may encounter steel webbing if your chair or sofa is fairly modern or has been recently reupholstered. To repair this, use rosin-coated nails. This webbing is stretched in the same manner as burlap webbing and snapped off at each end. Springs are used with this type of webbing, and the number of strands of webbing depends on the number of springs. There should be one row of webbing on each side for each row of springs. Steel webbing is criss-crossed in the same manner as jute. Springs are attached through loops in links. In all other respects, steel webbing is applied in the same way as jute is applied.

"No-sag" springs are a different proposition. These are self-supporting, curved, long steel wires that do the job of both springs and webbing. They are attached from front to back by holders especially made for this purpose, and from side to side by small springs. Burlap is sewn directly to the no-sag spring base (Fig. 9-6).

Other chairs, particularly dining-room chairs, have either a plywood base under the padding, or webbing stretched on the *top* of the frame. It is easy enough to replace the plywood by cutting a similar piece, and webbing is replaced in the same way as it is on the underside.

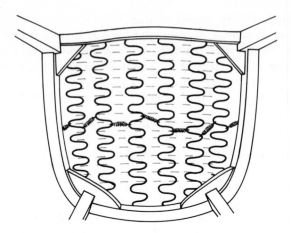

FIG. 9-6 • The underside of a no-sag spring seat.

FABRICS AND
HOW TO PICK THEM

If your town is typical, the best fabric stores are the little hole-in-the-wall places where nobody seems to know where anything is. They have a vast collection inside—if anyone can find anything—and it's a trial of nerves to find what's available, what the *real* price is, and whether it's what you want. But these crazy places traditionally have the most interesting and least expensive fabrics. No matter where you go (and we don't necessarily recommend these places except to the stout-hearted), always be sure to get the best fabric you can afford. That doesn't mean the gaudiest or the newest, but the sturdiest and the best made. Even though there is little perceptible difference (to us amateurs), the better-grade fabric always outwears the cheap stuff by years. Don't ask us why. We don't know either. Something to do with the weave or something.

It is extremely difficult for the novice to pick out a satisfactory fabric, but it is one of those things *you* have to do. God knows what would happen if you left that choice in the hands of the upholsterer. One is tempted to state simply that you should go by price alone, and that really isn't a bad criterion. But you leave yourself wide open to an unscrupulous merchant this way. Keeping in mind the old maxim that you get what you pay for, following are some of the things you should look for when you buy upholstery material.

APPEARANCE

Color • Analyze **colors** you have in the room and those you might add. If you want the room to look spacious and restful and the chair inconspicuous, choose a fabric related in color to that of the wall. Or if you wish to feature the chair, give it an inviting look, or add interest to the room, choose a pleasingly contrasting color. Weigh also the overall room effect; use proportionately more of one hue than of others, more of bright or of soft colors; add accents of other hues, values, or intensities.

The most practical colors do not soil readily, do not rub off, are easy to work on, and are fast to light laundering and/or drycleaning.

Pattern • **Plain fabrics** look well in most rooms and on most chairs and are less expensive than **patterned fabrics**, which require matching. Several plain fabrics give an impression of pattern.

Patterned fabrics usually show wrinkles and soil less quickly than do plain ones. If used, decide where and how they will be most effective; avoid a "busy" room. If combined, one might be a large distinct motif, another a blending stripe, and another a small all-over pattern.

Be sure to see the fabric on the chair; the effect is quite different than that of fabric in folds or on a bolt.

Texture • Blend **textures** as carefully as you do colors. Shiny, smooth, sleek textures usually look well with modern and new furnishings; dull, soft textures often complement fine old woods and furnishings that have begun to show wear.

LABELING

Proper **labeling** of all fabrics, which helps identify fibers, became mandatory when the Textile Fiber Products Identification Act was passed on March 1, 1960. The label must give:

- The generic (family) name. Fibers with similar characteristics are grouped together in 20 different categories. For example, natural fibers include cotton and linen; man-made fibers not sensitive to heat include rayon and metallics; man-made fibers sensitive to heat include acetates and acrylics.
- The percentage of all fibers (using the generic name) 5 percent or over in order of predominance by weight: for example, cotton 75 percent, rayon 25 percent.
- The country of origin, if made outside the United States.
- The registered identification number, house mark, or name under which business is conducted.

Read and interpret labels accurately; for example, a small percentage of a certain fiber may add glamour but little quality and may increase the cost. Some fiber characteristics important in the selection of chair-cover fabrics are as follows:

Cotton, the fiber from which many chair-cover fabrics are made, is strong, durable, and easily laundered, but should be treated to make it resistant to shrinkage. Special chemical finishes, resins mainly, can impart added properties not inherent in the fiber. They can make the fabric crease or wrinkle resistant; soil, spot and stain retardant, or water repellent. Chemical additions may make the fabric easy to care for and mildew and flame resistant. Good-quality finishes should last as long as the fabric, and in most instances are best applied by the manufacturer; a few can be sprayed on at home. Some add considerably to the cost; also they make the fabric less pliable and more resistant to handling and to shears, pins, and needles.

Man-made fibers in chair-cover fabrics are usually used in blends (two or more fibers blended together to make the yarn), in combinations (different fibers for lengthwise and for crosswise yarns), or in blend combinations (a blended fiber yard for one direction and a single fiber yarn for the other). These man-made fibers add characteristics such as crease resistance, stability, and easy care. However, special treatment is needed for rayon and acetates to prevent shrinkage.

The American Standards Association has set criteria for a **voluntary labeling program.** An AS-L22 label would indicate minimum performance of a fabric for its end use and directions for its care. A fabric so labeled meets specifications regarding breaking strength, dimensional change (shrinking, stretching), colorfastness, permanence of finish, and seam slippage. Recommended laundering and/or drycleaning procedures should also appear on the label.

The National Retail Merchants Association has designed a set of "Sure Care Symbols" which give explicit instructions for care of fabrics. These symbols, if used, are permanently affixed, usually printed on the border of a fabric.

COLORFASTNESS AND WEAVE

Labels should indicate **colorfastness** and specify whether fast to light, laundering, drycleaning and/or gas fumes. Labels usually indicate "resistance" rather than "proof." The term "vat" in the label indicates good colorfastness.

How the fabric will wear depends on the fiber or fibers used, the yarns from which the cloth is woven, and how the cloth is woven.

Tightly twisted **yarns** usually wear better than those loosely twisted; a two-ply strand usually is stronger than a one-ply strand. Pull out and untwist both a lengthwise and a crosswise thread to see how it is made.

A firm, compact **weave** holds its shape better than a loosely woven fabric of similar texture and weight, and dust does not sift through easily. However, the fabric should be pliable enough to shape to the chair, and to handle. Smooth fibers, bulky heavy yarns, and loose weaves often fray with wear and cleaning.

Balanced weaves, with about the same number of pieces of yarn both ways and with all yarns of about the same size and strength, wear better than those with thick filling yarns and thin warp yarns, for example. A twill weave (diagonal ridges) may resist wear and soil better than a plain weave of comparable quality. A satin weave may have long surface yarn to catch and be pulled by buttons, sharp edges, and claws.

TIPS

If the **design** is printed on the surface only instead of woven the same on both sides of the material, draw a yarn or follow the weave partway across the width at the cut end. If not printed true, you usually have to cut with the design rather than with the grain. Fabrics off-grain neither wear nor clean well, unless given special finishes to help them keep their original shape. These finishes should be guaranteed to last the life of the fabric. Some fabrics that are set off-grain in finishing can be improved by steam pressing.

Estimate yardages for different **widths** of material. Wide fabrics are economical if back and arm pieces can be cut from half the width; if not, a narrower fabric might be a better buy.

MEASURING

From 4 to 8 yards of fabric are required for the average stuffed chair, and a couch can be almost anything, depending on the length. If you want to get a good estimate the easiest way, line up all the pieces you previously removed in a more-or-less tight pattern about 3 feet wide. Find out how long a line you have, and that's about how much you'll need of the new fabric. You can always be scientific and measure each little piece and add it up. But by the time you're done measuring, you could have had the job finished.

APPLYING THE FABRIC

You should have a hand in choosing the new fabric, but you don't have to put it on yourself. Unless it's just a chair seat and back or something similar, our advice is to take the chair and the new fabric and give it to a pro. Whether you or the pro does it, here is where saving all those pieces comes in handy. If the pro is doing it, give him all the little pieces (or leave the old fabric on and let him do the whole job). If you're doing it yourself, lay all the pieces together on the fabric and horse them around until you get the most economical use of the material without wasting any.

Using the old pieces as patterns, cut out all the pieces at once, marking them as you go along. Attach the pieces to the frame in approximately the same sequence as you removed them and you shouldn't get into too much difficulty. The big problems come when you try to hide the tacks or attach two pieces together. The pros have lots of ways to solve these problems, but they're much too complex to describe here. To simply hide the tacks, use fancy upholstery tacks, or glue some welting on over the area where you used the tacks. Some fabric shops will make custom welting for you out of your fabric.

SIMPLE CHAIR SEATS

Here is a simple job that almost anyone can do to get the feel of working with fabric. Most dining room or kitchen chair seats are pieces of plywood covered with fabric and a little padding (Fig. 9-7). There aren't any springs; sometimes there is webbing, but located at the top of the frame.

Chair seats are ordinarily screwed to the frame through braces at each leg. Remove the screws from underneath and the chair seat is free. Pull off the old fabric and save it for a pattern. Cut out a new piece of fabric and stretch it over the padding, tacking on the underside (here, a staple gun is best, especially for leather and plastic). If the edge is rounded or curved, snip the inside edges of the fabric to make it cover better without bunching.

The best way to replace the padding is to make a new pad out of foam rubber. Use a 1½- to 2-inch slab of firm foam rubber for most seats, and drill ¼-inch holes every 3 inches in the plywood bottom to let the rubber "breathe." The foam should be attached to the plywood with rubber cement around the edges and with a big cement "×" in the center.

Lay the seat back on the frame and put the screws back in. Job's done.

ONLY FOR THOSE WHO SEW

Someone who already knows and enjoys the art of sewing and has a machine and related equipment will no doubt find upholstering an easier and more rewarding experience than those who are inexperienced. A lot of the problems associated with upholstery are easy to solve for people who already know how to make clothes, slipcovers, and draperies. If you have this type of skill, you are urged to delve more deeply into the mysteries of upholstery.

FIG. 9-7 • Replacement of a dining room chair seat, like the one shown above, is relatively simple. (*Courtesy of Armstrong Cork Co.*)

Creative New-Old Techniques

It's pretty safe to say that there is nothing new under the sun when it comes to furniture decoration. On the other hand, like the furniture styles described in Chapter 4, decorative finishes come and go with the fashions. Decoupage is one example. An ancient art, it was in a state of popular limbo until the last decade. Limed or pickled furniture finishes were very "in" 20 years ago but are not too much in vogue now (except for floors). Some sort of painted decoration was used on the oldest furniture found in Egyptian excavations. For a long while, good furniture wouldn't be caught dead with an opaque finish. Now, antiquing kits with their opaque enamels are all the rage, and the advent of plastic furniture has brought a revival of vividly colored furniture.

FANCY PAINTING TECHNIQUES

The art of painting furniture a plain color was discussed in Chapter 9. For many people, the color alone gives the piece the desired finish. Others like to further embellish their work. This is a rather dangerous area, and it is suggested that anyone more than mildly interested in the art purchase the book previously

FIG. 10-1 • Painted furniture can be highly artistic, as exemplified here. (*Courtesy of Western Wood Moulding and Millwork Producers*)

recommended, *The Art of the Painted Finish for Furniture and Decoration* by Isabel O'Neil (William Morrow & Company, Inc.). A quick survey of just some of these techniques is given here (the necessary materials are summarized on p. 48).

STRIPING

For **striping** a contrasting color is painted onto a section of the piece at hand. Some areas suggested are along the edges of a chair seat, in the moldings along the edge of the top of a coffee table. Sometimes a square or diamond pattern can be imposed with striking effect on a large, dull surface. The ways to use these are myriad, too myriad. Used in poor taste, you can ruin the effect totally. The best advice is to use striping sparingly, if at all, and to try out the color with erasable chalk in a trial run to see how it will look.

Stripes are painted onto the desired area with a long-haired sable brush— No. 6 for most lines, No. 3 for lines under 1/16 inch in diameter. The brush is carefully tapped on the side of the container to avoid runs and then pulled along the desired area with the arm fully extended and the shoulder muscle doing most of the work. The brush is held high up on the handle with the bristles as far away as possible. Keep the strokes free, steady, and at an even pace. Once started, you can't stop and worry about what you're doing.

Obviously, this is no job for the faint-hearted. You have to plunge right in and do it without hestitation. It is essential to practice the technique on scrap wood or a piece of hardboard until you get the feel of it. Confidence will come with practice. It helps to start with moldings, because you have a natural line to follow. Also, no one will tell if you use masking tape, even though it isn't the best way to learn the technique.

DISTRESSING

There are two kinds of **distressing**, physical and painted. Physical distressing is done to newer furniture to make it look older. The piece is beaten with a hammer, chains, keys, bricks, ice picks, and/or any number of other instruments to give an antique look. To make "wormholes," distressers have been known to shoot several rounds of BBs or buckshot at a tabletop. This scarring, believe it or not, can materially increase the value of the furniture.

Distressing can also be done with paints. To do this, paint the most ex- posed areas of a newly enameled piece with little dabs of paste-type remover. As soon as the paint starts to wrinkle, give the areas a sharp dab with a towel or other absorbent cloth (wiping smears the remover around.) Let the piece dry for 24 hours, then apply a coat of satin varnish with high wax content. You can, if you prefer, use sandpaper instead of remover. This is safer but doesn't look quite as authentic.

This technique works best with a coat of brown under the top coat. The remover is allowed to work down to the undercoat and then stops. It is also important to apply the most remover to the areas that would receive the most natural wear. There are also much more complicated variations of this and various combinations that are too involved for this brief discussion. A little imagination and further reading will help if you wish to pursue the subject further.

MARBLEIZING

Marbleizing or **faux marbre** (fake marble) was practiced at least as early as 2200 B.C., when it was sometimes used on Mycenean pottery. There are a lot of really artful and beautiful ways to achieve this look, but a short cut that works pretty well is by applying a glaze or toner (see "Antiquing" below) to an enameled surface, then spreading a large piece of clear plastic lightly over it. Pat the plastic lightly with a cloth to make sure that wrinkles and air bubbles are gone. Pick up the plastic quickly and carefully, making sure not to drag it. Slightly different but similar effects can be achieved with different colors and/or by use of a sponge, burlap, a feather, newspaper, or a combination of these.

TORTOISE SHELL

This **tortoise-shell effect** is best created by working on a small area at a time. Apply a heavy amount of glaze, then tap the surface lightly with your fingertips, changing the angle of your hand each time. A similar appearance is achieved by tapping the surface with a short bristle brush, beginning in the center of the area and working toward the edges.

SPLATTERN

Use a stiff bristle brush, such as an old toothbrush, for the **splattern effect**. Dip the ends of the brush into the paint and "spring" the bristles with your finger to throw a fine spray of glaze over the enameled surface. Practice on a piece of paper first to check the effect and remember that too much glaze on the brush will make it splotchy.

WATER-STAINED WOOD

Water staining is a traditional and interesting look created by first coating an enameled surface with a glaze, rubbing with cheesecloth as for standard antiquing (see below), then splattering the surface with mineral spirits. The toner will spread out in the spots where liquid has fallen, creating an authentic water-stained look.

OTHER "IMPERSONATION"

If and when you get really good with an artist's brush, you can make any surface look like anything. And that means *anything*. The humblest wood can look like rosewood, bamboo, inlays, snowflakes—anything, really. Most of these techniques are much too complex and require too much skill and practice to be discussed here. Again, see Ms. O'Neil's book for details.

ANTIQUING

Antiquing is a technique not too much different from some of the ones described above. It, too, is deceit, designed to make a wood look like something it isn't. It has become very popular, with ready-made kits available from almost every paint manufacturer. The effect of an antique finish is very pleasant, and it certainly is an effective way to give a newer piece the patina of age. It is difficult to understand, however, why people use antiquing methods such as this on furniture that is already plenty old enough on its own. One guess is that antiquing does away with some of the messier parts of the refinishing process, such as removing the old finish.

The process widely known as antiquing is nothing more than a glaze finish over an enameled surface (Fig. 10-2). You can buy one of the prepared kits or make your own glaze or "toner" as follows:

3 tablespoons of gum turpentine

1 tablespoon of varnish

1 teaspoon of desired oil color(s)

Oil colors can be almost anything, depending on the base coat, but most common are the earth colors:

raw umber (grayish tone)	burnt umber (brownish tone)
raw sienna (reddish tone)	burnt sienna (reddish-brown tone)

Mix the glazing liquid and the oil colors thoroughly. Remember that very small amounts of oil color go a long way.

Undercoat • Prepare the piece in the same way as any other enameled piece [Fig. 10-2(a)]. Do not rub the enamel with pumice, however. Make a tooth for the glazing liquid on the final coat of enamel by lightly rubbing with 3/0 steel wool or fine sandpaper. Wipe the sandings from the piece with a clean cloth, then a tack rag.

Glaze coat • Use a flat, wide brush for large surfaces, painting one side of the piece at a time [Fig. 10-2(b)]. Long, even strokes with the grain of the wood will produce the most desirable effects. A thin coating is best, but pay special attention to carved surfaces, painting them first to allow more absorption of the toner.

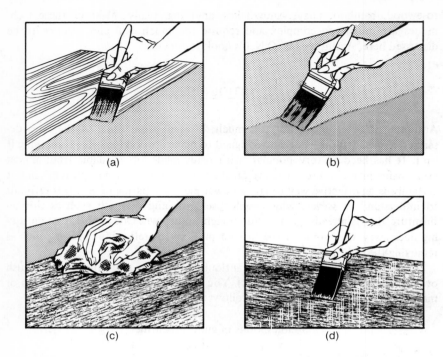

FIG. 10-2 • (a) Apply undercoat with a brush and let dry one to four hours. (b) Apply glaze coat and let sit 15 to 20 minutes before wiping. (c) Wipe the glaze around with a clean cloth, working to create highlights by rubbing off more glaze in natural wear areas. (d) Varnish all areas subject to wear—or the entire job, if you want. (*Courtesy of Sherwin-Williams*)

Do one flat surface at a time, allowing the glaze to sit for 10 to 20 minutes before wiping. Then wipe with a soft clean cloth. Use a circular motion, starting at the center of flat surfaces and working toward the edges. Turn your cloth to a fresh portion after each wiping. Leave the center of each surface lightest with the color gradually darkening toward the edges.

Blend further by patting the surface with clean cheesecloth and finish blending with a dry paint brush. Work the brush from the center toward the edges. Wipe off the brush on a cloth to remove excess glaze. Wiping off and blending is not at all difficult when only a small amount of glaze material remains on the surface. It gives a slightly noticeable but most effective appearance.

For carved surfaces, moldings, and turnings, proceed as for flat surfaces. Remove excess glaze material from depressions with a dry paint brush. Wipe the brush off on a cloth. Highlight by wiping the glaze off the raised areas with a clean cloth, leaving the glaze in the depressions for contrast [Fig. 10-2(c)].

Protective coat • A glazing liquid you have prepared yourself should have a **protective coat** for greater wear and durability.

- When the glaze is completely dry, apply a coat of clear varnish [Fig. 10-2(d)]. (Do not use varnish that has a yellowish color.)
- Allow 1 week for the varnish to dry.
- If the surface is too shiny, rub carefully with pumice powder and mineral oil.
- Make a paste of the powder and mineral oil and apply with your hands. Rub the surface until a satin finish is obtained. Wipe the surface with a clean, dry cloth to remove the pumice and oil.

A commercial glazing liquid may also require a protective coat. The label will state if a protective coat is needed. If one is needed, then purchase the protective coat in the same brand as the glazing liquid.

Wood-grain effects can be created by using the above techniques but using a dry brush just lightly tipped in glaze. Apply in long, even strokes, with the grain of the wood, but in irregular lines.

THE DOPE ON DECOUPAGE

In eighteenth-century Europe, things of beauty were highly prized. In the homes of nobles and wealthy merchants, even the most mundane of day-to-day articles was likely to be richly finished and lavishly decorated. Particularly popular was Oriental hand-painted lacquerware, brought from China and Japan over the long and dangerous sea trade routes.

Because of the relative scarcity of such pieces, European craftsmen evolved a method of simulating the elaborately engraved and gilded products of the eastern masters without the painstaking and time-consuming work involved in the originals. Called **decoupage**, it involves the application of a cutout print or picture to an object, then applying many coats of varnish to make the print recede into the background and actually appear as part of the surface underneath. Some of the work of these craftsmen survives in museums, and on the rare occasions when one can be found for sale, it is almost sure to command a handsome price.

MATERIALS YOU'LL NEED

Line up all the materials before you start. First you'll have to decide what surface you wish to cover. It might be a tray, a tabletop, the lid of a jewel box, a piece of furniture, or just a plain board that you intend to use as a decorative wall hanging.

The print that you select should be clear, clean, not too thick, and printed on one side only. It should be a complete unit, like a flower or bouquet of flowers, that will make up the entire decoupage design. Magazines, greeting cards, and wallpaper are just a few sources of attractive prints.

Quality varnish is essential. You will need clear satin varnish *and* clear high-luster varnish. You will also need a separate receptacle into which to pour the varnish; work out of this receptacle to avoid contamination, and make sure the varnish does not become dirty while you are using it. If it does, strain it through nylon hose.

Other materials needed are a good brush, fixative, turpentine, linseed oil, white glue, superfine abrasive paper (the finest you can find), pumice, and cuticle scissors.

STEP-BY-STEP INSTRUCTIONS

Sand the wood surface of the object to be covered so that it is clean and smooth. Wipe it off, then apply several thin coats of flat wall paint (either latex or alkyd type) as a background color harmonious with the colors of the print you will apply. (A stained surface may be substituted for paint.) Sand between paint coats with 10/0 wet-or-dry sandpaper, keeping both paper and surface slightly moist with water. Always remove sanding residue—after every sanding or rubbing operation—with a tack cloth.

Next, apply a thin sealer coat of clear satin varnish. Allow it to dry thoroughly, then rub down the surface with 4/0 steel wool until the varnish is absolutely smooth. Once again, use the tack cloth.

Protect the print from damage, smudges, or shredding by treating it with three or four very light spray coats of artist's fixative, available in aerosol cans. After the fixative has dried (it only takes a few minutes), use cuticle scissors with curved blades to cut out the print.

Apply a thin, even coat of white glue to the back of the print and carefully flatten it into position on the wood surface. Place a clean, damp cloth entirely over the print and press-roll away all excess glue and air bubbles with a small wooden roller or similar tool. Wipe up all excess glue with the damp rag. Allow the glue to dry thoroughly before proceeding. Remember, patience is the key.

You'll need all the patience you can muster for the next steps, which are also the most rewarding to the decoupeur. These are the repeated varnishings and rubbing downs. Five coats of clear varnish should be applied before sanding smooth with 10/0 wet-or-dry sandpaper, following the moistening procedure used earlier. Then rub down the surface with 4/0 steel wool.

Repeat the sanding and rubbing operations between each five-coat application of varnish. Apply a minimum of 10 or 15 coats in order to have the design recede completely into the varnish. It is not unusual to apply 30 or more coats to achieve truly distinctive decoupage.

(Some decoupeurs alternate coats of clear satin and high-luster varnish to achieve a faster film build. Others prefer clear satin only for its superior rubbing characteristics. Clear flat may be used as a final coat if desired.)

When you are satisfied with the appearance of your product, apply a good paste wax in very small quantities on small areas. Rub to the desired sheen and polish, if a protective coating of wax is desired. Some decoupeurs use beeswax especially imported from England. Others, to obtain a high polish, use a very fine steel wool dipped in a finish compound of linseed oil and fine pumice powder, omitting the wax.

From your first attempt at decoupage you will see endless possibilities, from fine furniture to one-of-a-kind gifts. When you are thinking of gifts, remember that color prints of children or family pets are sure conversation pieces—and highly valued by the recipient.

Decoupage is a very complex technique, and we have touched here only on the highlights. There are several excellent (and lengthy) books written on the subject; and, if you get bitten by the decoupage bug, you will probably want to read all of them. The one thing that nobody can teach you is patience. Decoupage is both craft and art, so remember that Rome wasn't built in a day—nor was the Mona Lisa. Take your time, and take pride in your work. You'll have better results—and more fun.

GILDING

"Gold fever" has long been a killer of men and a lightning rod for adventurers and thieves, to name just a few. The mystique of gold is sometimes puzzling, even when understandable. "Runs" on gold take place when confidence in paper money diminishes (witness the dollar decline in the early 1970s). Why it is such an important standard and such a powerful symbol of wealth and majesty is beyond the ken of most of us. But deny it we can't. There is a magic about gold that prevails everywhere and in all ages.

In the days of the Pharaohs, gold foil came into use as a way to cover more mundane offerings to the gods when gold itself became too scarce or too dear. Throughout the centuries, the art of gilding grew to be an exclusive craft, then a hobby indulged in by the very skillful. Now, it's a luxury indulged in by the very rich.

If you can afford to pay for gilding papers, welcome to an exacting, painstaking, but highly rewarding art. The many variations and derivative arts are beyond the pale of this small discussion, but we can give you a few basics, just in case you have some extra gold leaf you want to play with.

THE CLASSIC WAY (CONDENSED)

Any feeling that **gilding** involves a simple application of gold leaf should be quickly dispelled. Long before a bit of leaf is applied, the surface must be carefully and lovingly prepared. Serious gilt lovers will want to read many of the good books on this subject, but the merely curious, too, must be admonished that complete reading of the minimal instructions is necessary before attempting even the first step. It is also wise to practice the technique using less precious leaf, such as aluminum or Dutch metal.

Burnished gold is the more common of the gilding types and involves the placing of gold leaf over a coat of "bole" or clay size, which has previously been applied over "gesso," thin coatings of plaster of paris or gypsum. For details on these processes, see one of the many books on the subject. A matte finish is accomplished by laying the gold leaf directly onto the surface without bole or gesso, but most people prefer the burnished look. Gold leaf is applied to the delicately prepared surface by an even more delicate operation. The surface is coated with a solution of half water and half denatured alcohol, with a drop or two of rabbit-skin glue added (no kidding).

The gold-leaf paper is applied by means of a special camel's-hair brush, which is first rubbed lightly against your cheek to make it electrostatic. The brush, known as a "gilder's tip," is pressed lightly against a piece of leaf. The gold is picked up as a result of electrostatic friction.

The leaf is delicately laid onto the wet surface of the piece and smoothed quickly with the gilder's tip. One by one, each leaf is laid onto the surface and smoothed.

After the gilded surface has dried, the raised sections of carvings and other highlights are burnished with an agate stone tool. The tool is applied with gentle pressure, polishing only some of the gilt away so that the red bole is visible here and there to impart a soft glow.

SOME EASIER WAYS

The method described above is the best. The effect is magnificent, the effort stupendous. But there are relatively easy ways to give your furniture a gilded look, without going through the entire involved process just partially described above. The easiest way of all is to stir some finely ground bronze powder into a varnish or shellac. Bronze powders come in many colors, including, but not limited to, bronze. Gold, for example, comes in six shades, including the most popular one for gilding, usually called "pale gold."

Purchase the powder of your choice from an art-supply or large paint store, and mix into your favorite shellac or varnish. Because of the powder, the liquid will have to be thinned a little more than usual. Mix in a little extra alcohol for shellac, a little extra turpentine for varnish. The resultant product is applied just like the vehicle without the powders. Use it just in certain areas or over the whole surface if you prefer. Any kind of gold finish, however, is best used in moderation.

A compromise way to obtain the gilded look without going through the tortures of the damned is to paint the furniture a red enamel before applying gold leaf. The red paint won't have the same warmth as a true bole, but it will take a discerning eye to tell the difference. Chinese red is the best color, but almost any red, particularly the red-oranges, will do.

No matter what undercoat you use under gold, a coat of varnish is a good idea to protect the leaf (although not essential). This is one of those instances where spray lacquer is your best bet. It is available in aerosol cans.

GILT IN A JAR

If you are interested only in gilding highlights, moldings, doing some striping, or other small jobs, we particularly like the little jars of metallic colors in wax that you put on with your finger. They come in gold, silver, bronze, copper, and colors. They are handy and easy to use. Most large paint stores carry them as well as other small jars of gold paint and even one with red bole colors mixed in.

PAINTING WITH DYES

You should have *some* artistic talent to attempt any kind of designs dyed into wood. The dyes go in deep, and it's a job to erase them.

Nonetheless, simple patterns are not too difficult for the average person. One example is a checkerboard-design tabletop. For best results, mark off the square in pencil, then score them slightly. Make a simple guard out of cardboard that fits into the scored grooves and extends just beyond one square.

Use **aniline or synthetic dyes** and mix small containers of the dyes as instructed by the manufacturer. Using the cardboard as a shield, apply the colors with a small brush in the same manner as paint. Work from the center out to avoid drips on finished work. Table legs can be dyed with one of the same colors if desired.

After the surface has dried completely, a light sanding will eliminate any raised grain due to water in the dye. Apply a sealer, and finish in the same way as any other piece of furniture.

FREE-HAND PAINTING

A lot of rockers, Early American chairs, and other Colonial types of furniture seem to benefit from free-hand drawings. Trays are a great place to try your luck. This is literally an "art," as opposed to a skill, which can be learned. You can either paint or you can't, and if you're one of those who can't, skip to "Stencils" below. But if you have some talent in this sort of thing, there isn't any harm in trying.

The best way to try to paint something **freehand** is to study some of the designs that have been used on similar furniture (books, museums, etc.). Trace or copy the design and do the best you can to transfer it to the piece at hand.

Artists' oil colors are the medium here. A standard set of modest size will do, with lots of earth colors and some extra white. You'll also need turpentine, linseed oil, and a set of artist's brushes. Square-ended brushes are best for this type of work.

It is highly desirable to practice on a piece of cardboard or hardboard before forging ahead on the poor defenseless piece of furniture. Work the brushes around to see how they work when turned, etc. Perfect the technique of steadying your hand by keeping the ring and little finger on the surface of what you're painting. And hold the brush as far away from the bristles as possible, with the brush "one" with your arm as described under "Striping" (p. 184).

When you've mastered the technique, go right to it and don't stop or hesitate. If you go at it boldly enough, people will think it's a primitive design. If you stop and start and show your lack of confidence, people will just think it's poor art.

When the painting is over, let it dry thoroughly for a couple of days in the hot sun or in a warm room. Some japan drier in the paints (especially the reds) will help speed this process. When everything's properly dried out, a coat of glaze is usually applied (see p. 187). Clear varnish then may be added for those surfaces likely to receive lots of wear.

STENCILS

You wouldn't want to **stencil** a Queen Anne table, but there are quite a few styles of furniture—provincial, in particular—that may benefit from an occasional stencil or two (Fig. 10-3). Our feeling is that they must be used sparingly, if at all, but bronze-powder stencils are pretty classy. Done right, which isn't hard, a bronze-powder stencil looks a lot more artistic than it really is.

All stencils work best when the finish is tacky. That way, the cardboard or whatever it's made of will stick to the surface and won't move around while you work.

FIG. 10-3 • Stencils are particularly effective in decorating rocking chairs. (*Courtesy of Sears Roebuck and Co.*)

To make your own stencils, place tracing paper over the design to be copied, one piece for each color. Trace the outlines for each color onto the paper, then transfer to the stencil. The outlines are then cut with a stencil knife, single-edge razor, or X-Acto knife. Architect's linen makes the best stencils, but it is not transparent enough to trace with directly.

If stenciling with paint, just apply enamel over the open areas of the stencil, letting one color dry before applying the next. The same applies to bronze powders, but these are more difficult to apply. To get the powders in to the right places, make a flannel, velvet, or chamois "glove" for your index finger. You then tap out some of the powder onto the unused part of the stencil. Work it over to the parts that are to be covered with your finger, smudging into the surface. If the effect is somewhat shaded, so much the better. A glaze over the whole surface, when finished, gives the job the proper antique look.

DECALS

It seems almost sacrilegious to mention **decals** in the same chapter with gilding and antiquing. But there is a place for them, nonetheless, if only on children's furniture. Some of those Pennsylvania Dutch symbols, for example, might look nice on a not-too-fancy rocker. A brightly colored design could be just the thing for a modern chest. Decals have no place on fine furniture, but at least consider them for some of your more outlandish pieces. The more garish, the better. **Decalomania**, by the way, does not mean the state of being bananas over decals. It is simply the proper name for the shorter "decal."

PICKLING AND LIMING

A **pickled** or **limed** (as in "limed oak") finish is basically the same, as are similar finishes that have two different "colors." The colors may be stain and filler, stain and paint, filler and paint, or any combination thereof. Limed oak, for example, is flat white paint or filler with white pigment in the bleached wood pores, followed by a coat of clear lacquer or varnish.

To give any furniture (or woodwork) a pickled look, first apply a stain or paint to a new or refinished piece, then follow with a sealer coat. Work some of the contrasting color into the pores after the sealer coat has thoroughly dried. Use either flat paint (interior wall type) or a pigmented filler, Rub the paint or filler deeply into the grain, follow with varnish or lacquer.

As can be seen from the description of the process, such a method works only on woods with a fairly open grain. If you want to try it with a fine-grained wood, you'll have to make artificial pores, which isn't very satisfactory. The combination of colors, stains, or whatever is endless. The results are often very lovely, sometimes awful. Use your imagination and your good taste, and it should work out well. To be on the safe side, try out the combination on a piece of matching wood or in an inconspicuous spot of the piece to be finished.

NOVELTY FINISHES

Some of the finishes already described can be called novelty finishes, if you want to get pedantic about it. But the term is better used to define those really wild and far-out effects that are used in small doses rather than as an overall thing.

You can probably fill a book with such finishes if you really care about them. Their use, though, is limited, and only rarely do people really use these crazy gimmicks on furniture they care about. Picture frames, lampshades, and other small objects are the chief victim of novelty finishes. Most are more suited to metal and glass than wood. Most are best applied with a spray gun.

JACK FROST

Jack Frost is a specific type of lacquer available in almost every color, opaque or transparent. It can be applied as is to bare wood, metal, or glass. Use a special sealing lacquer undercoat if applied over another finish. The lacquer is sprayed onto the object and in 2 to 10 minutes begins to "frost over." This finish is now available in a brush-on liquid found in some larger paint stores.

CRACKLE

Crackle takes advantage of the fact that a quick-drying finish will crack when applied over a slow-drying one. When two contrasting colors are used, the effect can be dramatic and interesting. Regular lacquer can be used if it is rapid-drying, or special "crackle" lacquer can be purchased if available. Use a slower-drying lacquer, enamel, or whatever underneath; then, while the undercoat is still drying, apply the finish coat. The result will be minute cracking or alligatoring of the top finish. A light coat is best, applied quickly, for the top coat. When the top coat is dry, apply clear lacquer or varnish.

BAKED-ON FINISHES

Two finishes to be baked on are **wrinkle** and **crystal**, both of which must be processed in the oven. Both are special lacquers. Both look as their names imply. Wrinkle is a one-coat job which is the exception to the statement about spraying. It is best brushed on, the heavier the better. After half an hour of evaporation, the piece is inserted into an oven at 180°F, then increased to 250°F after 1 hour. The wrinkles will be baked on hard.

Crystal is applied in two special coatings and placed immediately into the oven with no evaporation. As a matter of fact, the oven should be as leak-free as possible (a self-cleaning oven is great for this). The less evaporation, the better the look. Bake on the crystal finish at 200°F for 2 hours. For a metallic effect, blend bronze powders into the top coat of clear crystal.

FLOCK

Flock is the familiar material found on "flocked" wallcoverings. It is simply pulverized or shredded wool, rayon, or other fibers. The fibers are obtainable in a variety of sizes from 1/64 to 1/2 inch, with the smallest best for this purpose.

Give the piece or area to be flocked a coat of base varnish or binder. The flock is then applied immediately to the tacky base coat, where it adheres and forms a coating. The best way to do this is with a flock gun, which is available at specialty paint shops.

Incidentally, the same method—applying shredded materials to a tacky base—can be used with any number of other materials, such as plastic, cellophane, colored sand, mica, dry bronze powders, crushed glass, or small beads. Larger materials can be applied by hand, smaller ones with the flock gun. Since many of these materials are expensive, always work on a clean surface so that unused material can be swept up and used over again.

TISSUE PAPER

The use of **tissue paper** is a fairly recent fad which imparts an unusual finish to furniture and is particularly useful for unfinished pieces. First paint the furniture with a color you like, then lay cut-up squares of colored tissue paper over the surface, imbedding them into the paint with clear spray lacquer or brushed-on clear varnish. Try it on a scrap piece first before subjecting the furniture to this treatment. This is very "chic" with certain decorators.

DECORATING WITH TAPE

The art of **tape decoration** has become one of the cleverest means of deception in Detroit, where stripes are "painted" and decals are applied that look like a real paint job. Colored pressure-sensitive tape is available in a wide variety of colors that can be used with good results on modern children's furniture or on unfinished furniture.

Here, again, imagination is the key. Stripes, patterns, and designs can all be applied with tape in one or more colors. One woman we know used green stripes alternating with the white porcelain finish on her old refrigerator, making it look like a brand new one. Plastic tape is tough and long wearing.

And don't forget good old masking tape. There isn't anything like it for making straight lines, cutting in, covering windows while painting, and making small patterns. When spray painting, attach newspapers with tape over the areas you don't want covered.

New Seats and Tabletops

The two areas most often worn out on furniture are tabletops and chair seats. Most modern chairs use the **slip seat**, one that is attached to the frame with screws, with a fabric cover attached to a piece of plywood or hardboard. Many older chairs, and some modern ones, use cane, rush, splint, or some form of twine to form woven seats of some description. This type of construction is often used for the backs of dining room chairs as well.

If you have a fondness for these materials, you must acquire the proper kind of chair. You can't put cane on a chair that's made for a slip seat. You can apply a slip seat to a chair that was formerly cane or rush, however, although it may not look so hot.

As far as tabletops are concerned, the best practice, generally, is to finish them the same way they were finished to begin with. But there are many times when the top becomes so badly scarred by burns, lost veneer, etc., that the top must be covered over or replaced by something else.

199

━━━━━━━━━━━━━━━━━━━━━━━ **CANING** ━━━━━━━━━━━━━━━━━━━━━━━

Chairs with small holes drilled through the frame around the seat opening should have **cane seats**. A carefully woven cane seat is very strong and wears well.

Cane for chair seating is made from a Far Eastern palm called **rattan**. The stem, which is covered with beautiful green foliage, grows in length from 100 to 300 feet and is seldom more than 1 inch in diameter. For export, these stems are cut in 10- to 20-foot lengths. The outer bark is stripped in widths varying from 1/16 to 3/16 inch and is cut in strips. Then it is tied in hanks of 1000 feet and is ready for the weaver. One such hank is enough for four chairs with medium-sized seats.

You can buy cane at chair-seating and craftman's supply houses, at department stores, and mail-order houses. One of the latter is the *Cane & Basket Supply Co.*, 1283 S. Cochran Ave., Los Angeles, Calif. 90019. Buy long, select cane (from 15- to 18-foot lengths) for medium or large chair seats. You can use shorter lengths but they have to be tied more often. Good cane is smooth, glossy on the right side, tough, and pliable. The "eye," the lump where the stem of the leaf grew out, should be smooth and unbroken. Poor cane has rough and imperfect spots, does not weave easily, and is likely to split.

Plastic cane is also available. It weaves easily, does not require soaking, is strong, and costs slightly less than other cane because little is wasted. Its smooth, shiny texture is suitable for painted chairs; real cane is preferable for fine old furniture.

GETTING THE SEAT READY

Cut away the old seat with a keyhole saw. Clean any pieces of broken cane or dirt from the holes and the seat rails. Pull out old nails and tacks. Be sure you can get cane through all the holes. Drill through any that are plugged up. File down the inside of the frame so no sharp edges will cut the cane. Do any refinishing before starting to cane.

PREPARING THE CANE

Pull one of the strands of cane from the looped end of the hank, near where it is tied. As you pull, shake the hank so that the cane will not tangle or tear. Roll the strand, right side out, to fit into a 6-inch bowl. Fasten the ends with a clamp clothespin.

Fill the bowl with a 10 percent solution of glycerine in warm water. Soak the roll of cane in the solution for about 20 minutes or until it is soft and pliable. Do not soak plastic cane.

THE WEAVING PROCESS

The usual form of weaving is called seven-step weaving. Weave from the upper side of the seat; first, from back to front, then from side to side, again from back to front, and from side to side, and then on the two diagonals. If you begin in the center of the back, you will find it easy to make sure the rows of the cane are straight. Add the binder last.

Step 1 • Count the holes in the back rail. If there are an odd number of holes, put a peg in one of the holes nearest the center. Do the same side of the center on the front as at the back.

Take the roll of cane from the bowl and wipe off excess water with your fingers or a cloth. Put another strand in to soak while you work. Weave with the eye whenever you can so that you do not roughen or break the strand.

Pull out the peg from the back rail. Push about 4 inches of an end of cane down through this hole and refasten the peg. Bring the cane to the front rail, right side up; take out the peg there and push the cane through. Then replace the peg.

Push the cane up through the nearest hole on one side of the center. Pull it across the chair and down through the opposite hole at the back (Fig. 11-1). As you weave, hold the cane so that it sags a little below the level of the wood seat frame.

Continue weaving toward the side as long as you can weave in opposite holes. Do not use corner holes unless you are sure there will be room for the diagonal and binder canes that must also go through these holes. Leave the rest

FIG. 11-1 • *Step 1*: Start weaving from the center row, back to front, pegging the center row and moving another peg forward each time a row is completed. Punch cane up through the nearest hole to start a new strand.

of the strand to use later. Fasten it with a clamp clothespin to keep it out of your way.

For seats wider at the front than at the back, weave separate pieces of cane. Canes must not be carried across on the underside of the frame to block holes that must be used later. Weave the other half of the seat the same way.

Step 2 • Start at the back on the right side rail as you face the chair, in a hole next to the corner.

Pull the cane up through the hole and across the seat over weaving you have already done. Continue weaving back and forth. If the front rail is curved, weave with separate pieces of cane.

Step 3 • Weave as in step 1 (Fig. 11-2). Keep the strands slack as in steps 1 and 2. Weave in line with, and on top of, the first and second weaving and to the right of the cane you wove in step 1.

Fasten the ends of cane on the underside of the frame by tying them to or twisting them around the cane crossing from the next hole. Trim the end, leaving about ¼ inch. Tie the end wherever you can before starting the next step and then tie as you go along, so that the pegs will not be in your way. Moisten the ends of cane if necessary so they can be tied without breaking.

FIG. 11-2 • *Step 3*: After weaving from side to side over the first set of canes, weave another row, as in step 1, over both previous rows.

Step 4 • Real weaving begins here, as you work from side to side (Fig. 11-3). Start at the back on the right as you face the chair and in a hole next to a corner. Weave over the canes on top and under the canes underneath. As you work, straighten the canes you wove previously. When you are a third or half of the way across, pull the length through that far, being careful that it does not

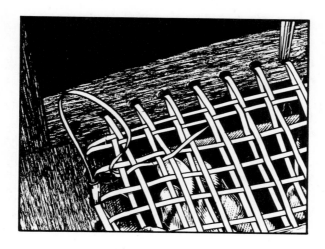

FIG. 11-3 • *Step 4*: True weaving begins here, with the next side-to-side rows. Weave new cane over the rows on top and under the ones underneath.

twist or break. As you pull, keep your hand level with the chair rail. If you lift up, the weaving cane may cut canes already woven, especially if the cane is plastic.

Continue weaving across the row. This draws together in pairs the canes from front to back and from side to side. When you reach the opposite side, put the end of cane down through the hole and peg it until you weave the next row. Pull the cane up through the nearest hole and weave back across the seat, so that the cane passes over the same canes and under the same canes as it did the first time across.

Repeat for the other rows. At the sides, be sure the canes in step 3 are on top and at the right of canes in step 1. Soak the woven cane with a wet sponge or cloth. Using two pegs, straighten rows and force them close together in pairs with hollow squares between.

Step 5 • Start at the back corner hole on the right side as you face the chair, and weave the first diagonal row toward the left corner (Fig. 11-4). You will weave the cane over the pairs from front to back, and under those from side to side, keeping the cane straight from the corner holes. Weave with one hand on top and the other underneath. Pull the cane through when you are third or half of the way across. The cane must lie flat and be so woven that the edges do not bind. Moisten with a damp cloth to help it pull through easily.

Back section ○ Weave the back section of the seat first, using holes on the left and back rails. For the second row, weave from front to back, going over and under the same rows you did before.

FIG. 11-4 • *Step 5*: Weave the first diagonal rows over the pairs of cane from front to back and under those running from side to side. The diagonals in the opposite direction are woven the opposite way—under the front-to-back pairs and over the ones from side to side.

Weave two canes in each corner hole, to make a "fishhead" or a "V." Complete the fishhead on the back corner or finish it when weaving the front corner. Sometimes canes can be kept straight only by weaving a single cane in part of the corner holes.

Weave back and forth until you have reached a place near the center of the left side. If the seat is round or definitely curved, weave only a few diagonals and then begin to skip or double in holes.

Keep the rows straight. If there are more holes on the sides than on the back, skip holes, usually not more than three on the side. If the seat is round, you may double in the holes across the back as well as skip holes on the side.

Make the canes lie straight across the back corner. Check to see that you have skipped enough holes so that the same number are left on the back as on the side. Use a new piece of cane when you need to, or use an end left from previous weaving if you can do so without crossing holes on the lower side of the seat.

Front section ○ Since the first diagonal was woven from back to front, weave the first row on the front section from front to back using holes on the front and right rails.

Canes may curve slightly near the rail. Put them in the holes where they will curve the least. To make the pattern alike on the two sides, weave twice (fishhead) in the hole or holes corresponding to those skipped on the left side of the chair. On the front rail, double in holes on the left and skip holes on the right. Tie ends as you go along, wherever there is a nearby strap to which to tie.

Step 6 • Start at the back corner hole on the left side as you face the chair and weave diagonally toward the front right corner. Weave under the pairs from front to back and over those from side to side.

Weave the front section of the seat first. Complete the pattern started in the first diagonal, so that the corners and the two sides correspond. Each half of the front and back rails also must correspond.

Front section ○ On the left side rail, weave twice in holes skipped by the first diagonal. Do the same on the front rail, right side. On the left side, skip those holes used twice before. Do not carry cane across holes on the underside of the seat. Instead, cut the cane if necessary.

Back section ○ Use a new cane to weave from front to back; double in the back corner hole to match the opposite corner. Weave to the front and double in the corner hole.

On the side rail, skip holes woven in twice by the first diagonal. On the back rail, skip any holes already used twice.

Step 7 • Binder cane is the next size wider than that used for weaving. It is used to cover the holes and to finish the edge of the weaving. If the seat is curved, use one strip long enough to go around. If corners are square or turns are sharp, cut separate lengths, each from 6 to 8 inches longer than the side of the seat where it will be used. Keep both binder and weaving cane wet and pliable. Lay one of the pieces of binder flat over the holes on one side of the seat with the center of the piece at about the center hole. Push one end through the corner hole and hold it there with a peg (Fig. 11-5).

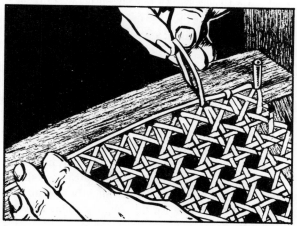

FIG. 11-5 • *Step 7*: Binder cane is pegged at both ends and attached with a long strand of weaving cane at each hole along all sides of the chair.

Fasten the binder at each hole with a long piece of weaving cane or, if the holes are close together, at every other hole. Begin at the end where the binder is pegged. Pull the weaving cane up through the next hole, passing it over the top of the binder and down through the same hole. Bring it up through the next hole on either side of the binder and repeat. Keep both canes right side up, flat and tight. Use an awl or a bone knitting needle if you need to force an opening for the cane.

Repeat around the chair. When the cane is dry, it should be tight enough to ring when you snap it sharply with your fingers. The mesh should be level with the seat frame.

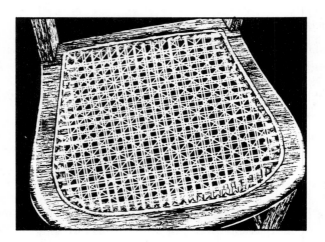

FIG. 11-6 • The completed chair is lovely enough to justify the effort.

USING PREWOVEN CANE

The easy way to weave a chair seat is with prewoven cane. Only trouble here is that the seat must have a groove around the inside edge, with a wooden spline to hold the edges of the cane. There isn't much point in buying prewoven cane for the usual kind of caned seat discussed above that has holes around the edge. You can't tie up the ends of prewoven cane properly without a groove and spline.

If you have the right type of chair, first remove the spline, if it's still in the groove. Save the spline if it's still in good shape. If not, buy a new one from the cane dealer. Set the prewoven cane over the open area, tack it down temporarily in all four corners, and cut it on all sides just slightly beyond the groove. A new razor blade or X-Acto knife is best for this. Dip the spline in water meanwhile to let it get good and wet.

Fit the spline into the groove and cut off the excess (if new) with a sharp knife. Check old spline material to see if it fits all right. Put spline aside for now—but keep it damp.

Apply an even layer of glue inside the groove. Dampen the ends of the prewoven cane placed over the frame. Drive the ends of the cane into the groove with a wooden mallet and a scrap of hardwood wedge, beginning at the back of the seat. Leave the wedge in place at the center back, then drive the sides into the groove, again leaving the wedges in place. Finally, drive the front of the cane into the groove, using additional wedges if necessary. Cut off any excess outside the edge of the groove.

When the glue has dried, remove the wedges. Spread another thin layer of glue in the groove, then place the precut spline over the groove. Drive the spline firmly into the groove with a wooden mallet and an overturned wedge. Move the wedge all around the edge, striking firm but light blows with the mallet. When the spline is in place, let the glue dry and cut off any cane around the outer edge of the spline.

FINISHING

Tie and cut off any loose ends of regular cane on the underside of the seat. Trim off rough places or hairs with a razor blade.

Cane has a hard, glossy surface that does not really need a finish. If you want, however, you may apply a thin penetrating wood sealer to both sides to prevent drying and cracking. To blend the color of a new cane seat with the finish on the chair, apply a chair seat stain. Rub the stain on the underside first, with a soft cloth or brush. Wipe off the surplus, and repeat on the upper side. When the stain is dry, apply a second coat if you want a darker color.

CLEANING

Cane seats can be cleaned with a cloth wrung from a solution made as follows: Place 1 quart of boiling water in the top of a double boiler (or two old basins). Add 3 tablespoons of boiled linseed oil and 1 tablespoon of turpentine. Put boiling water in the bottom of the boiler to help keep the solution hot. Do not place the mixture directly over a flame. Clean both sides of the seat.

SPINDLE-AND-POST CHAIRS

If the chair in question is made up of rounded legs and cross-members, it's known as a **spindle-and-post** chair. The material for seating this type of chair can be made of rush, splint, macramé, or some form of twine, cord, or what-have-you.

To prepare these chairs for their new seats, remove all old material, tacks, nails, etc., and sand down any areas that are sharp or uneven. Most of the finishing materials you'll be using are not designed for hard usage against sharp objects.

MACRAME

Macramé is simply the use of knotted cords in some form of decorative pattern. The cords can be rope, twine, string, or any number of various materials. The important condition is that whatever you use can be knotted. Some of the commoner materials used for chair seating are polished linen or cotton cord, Swedish rug yarn, India twine, Hongkong grass, sisal or hemp rope, manila trawl twine, Venetian blind cord, sash cord, or nylon yacht cord. These materials can be purchased at cordage or marine supply houses, hardware stores, or fabric boutiques. Many mail-order houses have these materials if they are not available locally.

Basic to all macramé work is the understanding of knots. Of all the knots in the Boy Scouts' manual, the half-hitch and its variations are the most versatile (Fig. 11-7).

The infinite variations of the various knotting patterns and materials used in macramé can only be touched on here. The interested reader should refer to the numerous books and specialized magazines on this subject. To knot a chair with macramé, a few simple knots should be learned. The double half-hitch (logically the whole hitch, but not called that) is a good beginning. There are

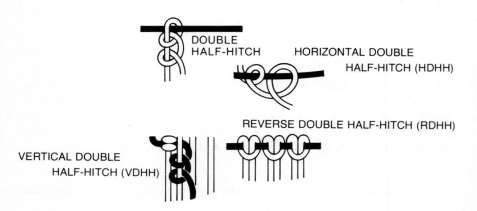

FIG. 11-7 • Basic macramé knots are the double half-hitch and its variations.

three basic variations, depending on what work is to be done. Where the cord is attached to the spindle, the reversed double half-hitch (RDHH) or "nag's head" is used [Fig. 11-8(a)]. Horizontal and vertical double half-hitches are used when the cords cross each other. When the vertical cord is stationary and the horizontal is tied around it, the knot is called a vertical double half-hitch (VDHH). When the opposite occurs, the knot is a horizontal double half-hitch (HDHH) [Fig. 11-8(b)].

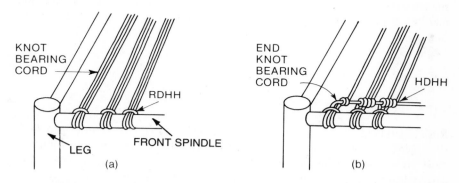

FIG. 11-8 • (a) Macramé cords are attached to the chair spindle with a reverse double half-hitch (RDHH). (b) The knot-bearing coard is then crossed over and tied to the other cords.

"Horizontal" when used in this context means the pattern that runs from side to side. "Vertical" in this sense means those cords that run from front to back. The actual knotting is done with a "knotting" cord, which is a lot longer than the other cords. Usually used horizontal, the knotting cord is worked across the pattern and tied to each vertical cord that it intersects. In some patterns, particularly those where different colors are used, the knotting cord is changed every row or every several rows.

Macramé is not confined to use on spindle-and-post chairs. It can be used instead of cane where the chair has a seat perforated for that purpose. Macramé can also be used in chairs with grooved edges around the seat (the same type of chairs mentioned above that are used with prewoven cane). To use macramé in this instance, remove the spline as described for the prewoven cane and trace a pattern. Transfer the pattern to a "knotting board" (almost anything that you can pin the cords to—insulating board is good). Seats with solid or slip-frame seats can be covered with macramé, too, by using a knotting board.

The macramé process is quite similar to rush work (see below) except that the cords are knotted at the intersections. If you apply the same basic theory to macramé as outlined for cane and rush seating, you may be able to work out your own patterns. One thing you can do with macramé that you can't do with cane, rush, splint, or similar materials is use bright color and pattern variations.

━━━━━━━━━━━━━━ **RUSH SEATING** ━━━━━━━━━━━━━━

Rush can be used on almost any chair with spindle-and-post construction but not much else. Some chairs look better with splint seats than rush (see below), but usually the opposite is the case. Rush is more formal and expensive looking than splint, even though the actual cost difference is minimal; and people in the northern part of the United States, southern Canada, and other localities with similar vegetation can find natural rush, ready for curing, in lowlands and marshes. (Cured rush can also be purchased from most of the same sources as for cane.)

FINDING RUSH IN
ITS NATURAL HABITAT

Rush is gathered from "cattails," whose "flower" is so familiar to most people as the cigarlike "bob" or round brown spike. Two kinds are generally found in most areas—the broad-leaved (about 1 inch wide) and the narrow-leaved. The narrow-leaved cattail is scarcer but much better for this type of work. Look for it in the lowlands. The longer the leaf, the better, with 7 feet or longer being optimum.

Gather the rush when the leaves are full grown, when the stalks are still green and the tips are beginning to turn brown. Late July, August, or early September is the best time. Select perfect leaves and those from the stalks that do not have "bob." Cut the stalks just above the surface of the water or ground. Gather an ample supply. Leaves shrink at least one-third as they cure.

PREPARING RUSH FOR WEAVING

Pull the leaves from the stalks. Sort the leaves, placing together those of about the same width and length, and tie them in loose, flat bundles. Be careful not to bend or break the leaves. Dry thoroughly for at least 2 or 3 weeks in a dark, airy room like an attic or storeroom floor. Do not put the leaves in a damp room, such as a cellar, where mildew might form on the leaves, or in a hot sunny room where leaves become brittle.

Dampen the rush until it is workable enough to twist and weave without cracking or breaking. This may take an hour in warm water in a trough, or 8 to 12 hours if spread on the floor and sprinkled.

Fill the trough about three-fourths full of warm water. Add glycerine until the water feels soft, about 1 cup. Soak the rush, about a handful at a time, in the solution.

Choose long, unbroken leaves of about the same length, width, and thickness. The number of leaves to use in each strand depends not only on the leaves but on the size of strand you want. Usually, two leaves are twisted together; sometimes, if they are narrow or thin, three may be used. A thin strand is best for a graceful, delicate chair but lots of strands are needed to fill the seat and the thicker they are, the faster the job.

Run the leaves through a wringer to take out air from the cells and to make the leaves workable. Set the rollers tight so that the leaves make a sharp crackling noise as they are run through. Draw each leaf quickly over the edge of a letter opener or similar instrument, to take out any air left in the cells.

THE WEAVING PROCESS

Weaving a firm smooth seat takes a lot of skill and practice. How you do it depends on the way you like to do it and how you want it to look. One satisfactory method is described below. You may experiment and find a better one.

With a carpenter's square, mark off a square center opening. Place the short side of the square parallel to either the front or the back rail and the long side against the inner edge of the corner of the back rail. Mark the edge of the square on the front rail. Do the same on the other side of the seat. The two corner measurements may not be the same, but the distance between pencil lines on the front rail must be the same as between posts on the back rail. If the square doesn't fit, make a smaller one out of cardboard.

Weave the corners first until you reach the marks on the front rail. To do this, begin with four leaves, each long enough to reach around three sides of the seat. Make two pairs, each with a butt and tip end together and the flat side of one leaf next to the round side of the other. Use string to tie around each bunch, making a square knot near the fold of rush. Tie the string to post D (as shown in Fig. 11-9) to hold in place.

Choose one pair of leaves, bring them almost to the front rail, and then twist them into a strand (Fig. 11-10). Turn this twist away from the post; keep all other twists in the same direction like a rope. Draw the strand over rail 1, close to post A, up through the opening of the chair, over the side rail 2, again close to post A, up through the opening again, thus holding the beginning of the twist. Lift up the strand from the underside of the seat to shorten its length and thus help to make the seat firm. Lay the strands in position to make a square crossing and straight seam from the corner of the seat.

Pull the strand, without twisting the leaves, across the front of the seat. At post B, twist the leaves, bring the strand over side rail 3, close to post B, up through the opening of the seat, over front rail 1, again close to post B. Arrange the strands as at post A.

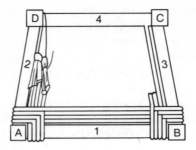

FIG. 11-9 • In order to weave a symmetrical seat, the corners of the seats must be filled in to form a square or rectangular shape.

Pull the strand without twisting to the back and fasten it firmly by winding the ends around the back rail and tying them together or by holding them with a clamp clothespin.

Strands are twisted only over the rails, where they will show, not on the underside of the seat.

Weave the second pair in the same way. Loop the ends tightly around the back rail and fasten them with a clothespin to the first strand.

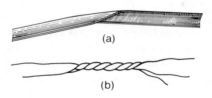

FIG. 11-10 • To weave rush, it must be twisted into strands of two or three leaves.

Tie more leaves one pair at a time in the same loop of string. About five twists fill 1 inch. Use a square every two or three rows to make sure that the corners are square and the rows straight. Use hammer and block of wood to force the strands in place. Keep the seam straight from the corner toward the center of the seat. Add from 4 to 6 inches of another leaf if needed to fill the space.

After the corners are woven as far as the marks on the front rail, fasten the ends on the right-hand side. Tie a piece of string about 18 inches long around all the ends of rush. Loop the ends around the back rail and tie another square knot. Pull the strand taut and keep the rows straight and close together. Remove the clothespins and cut away the rush over the rail that protrudes. If the rush breaks, replace it with another piece.

PADDING

After the front corners are filled in, pad them. The padding is put in the pockets on the underside of the seat at each side of the corner seams. Butt ends and short lengths of rush are folded the length of the opening and forced in flat bundles from the center toward the corner posts. To do this, turn the chair over. Use a wooden ruler as a stuffing tool and poke a bunch of rush into the pocket on the underside of the seat, from the center to the seam. The finished seat should be hard and flat, or slightly rounded, but not overstuffed. Rush shrinks as it dries, so put in enough padding to make the seat firm but not "fat." Both front corners should be of the same thickness.

As you continue to weave around all four corners, add padding about every 3 inches. Back corners take less padding. When you've finished the corners, add the last padding by poking in bunches parallel to the last strands.

SQUARE SEATS

After the corners are filled in, the seat opening should be square. Sometimes seat frames may be square to begin with or have corner blocks that make the opening square. Weave either type according to the pattern in Fig. 11-11, and finish unsquare seats similarly.

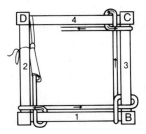

FIG. 11-11 • Weaving the square seat.

First strand • Use the same loop that you had for seats wider at the front or make a similar loop if you are just starting to weave a square seat. Tie in the butt ends of two leaves, one of which is long and the other short. Twist and weave around post A. Loops of string never have to be cut; weaving covers them.

Join the rush • As you leave corner A, add a new leaf. Place this between the weaving the strand, with the butt end hanging down below the underside of the seat for about 6 inches, or the amount of the stiff end of the leaf, and with the curved side toward you. Twist this new leaf with the other two, about twice to hold them together. The butt ends make a seam on the underside of the seat and should hang down rather than be caught in the weaving. Always add a new piece of rush after you finish each corner so that when you are ready to weave the next corner the rush is securely fastened and there will be enough to go around that corner.

Occasionally you may need to use a third piece of rush to fill out the strand, as when crossing twists at the seam.

Corners B, C, and D • Continue to corner B. If the strand is too thick, drop the end of the shortest leaf. This can be cut off or folded in for padding. Twist and weave around corner B. As you leave this corner, again add a new leaf. Continue to corner C and weave as shown. Add a new piece of rush, proceed to weave around corner D, again adding a piece of rush.

Splicing • If rush breaks or you do not have enough to finish weaving the corner, another piece may be spliced in. After you weave the first half of the corner, add a new leaf at the seam with the butt end extending about 6 inches below the seat. Twist the old leaves once around the new to lock it. Then arrange the leaves parallel and twist all three together. If the strand is too thick, pull out the shortest leaf. Continue, weaving the second half of the corner. On the underside of the chair these butt ends will stick down, but at an opposite angle from those used for joining, and will be cut off later.

The rest of the seat • Go on weaving, as for the first strand, around post A to posts B, C, and D, until there is only space for two more rows on the side rails. Continue to make the rush workable by running it through the wringer and zipping it with the letter opener. Smooth the twists. Join a new piece of rush after each corner. Pad the seat as you weave. Keep the strands taut and rows straight by pounding them with the block of wood. Make sure that opposite sides of the chair are alike. Check as you go along to see that the opposite openings measure the same and that you have the same number of twists over each rail. Occasionally force the letter opener quickly between the rows to straighten them and to smooth the strands. Also occasionally, and before the rush dries out, roll and polish the strands with the ruler until the seat is smooth.

If the sides are shorter than the back, fill the sides and then weave them back to front in a figure 8. To help prevent holes near the center, weave around the right side rail twice for the last two strands, proceed to the left rail and weave around it twice. Then weave in a figure 8 over back and front rails until those rails are filled in. Sometimes this process is reversed. Join the rush at the center after weaving the front rail, or after weaving around both rails.

Pull the last few strands through the small opening with a hook made of wire. Weave in as many rows as possible; when you think the seat is filled, add one more strand. Fasten the last strand on the underside of the chair by separating the ends, winding each one around a nearby strand, and tying them firmly with a square knot.

If the unfinished seat is left overnight, fasten the last twist to the seat with a clamp clothespin. Cover the seat with wet cloth to keep the rush from drying out.

EXTRA-WIDE SEATS

Weave until the sides are filled as directed for a square seat. See that the opening measures the same on one side as the other, and the front the same as the back. Complete the filling of the back and front rails by weaving twists in a figure 8, going over and under the front rail, up through the opening, over and under the back rail, and again up through the opening (Fig. 11-12). Do not cross the rush.

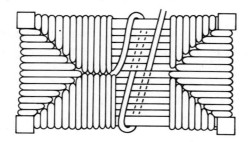

FIG. 11-12   •   Weaving the extra-wide seat.

If you finish weaving the corners on the left-hand side of the seat, weave from there in a figure 8 until the opening is completely filled. You may finish weaving the sides in such a way that you would reverse this, weaving from the right side of the back rail first.

Just before making the figure 8, you may weave twice around the side rail as directed above instead of in single strands.

FINISHING

After you have completed the weaving and padding, trim the butt ends on the lower side of the seat to about 1 inch, so that they do not show as you face the chair. Trim any loose ends with razor blade or shears. Use the rule to pound and even the seat.

On the upper side, trim the loose ends, straighten the rows, and pound with the ruler to mold and polish the twists. You may use a piece of leather also for polishing.

Immediately after you finish weaving, apply a protective coating both to the top and to the lower side of the seat. The suggested treatment is a mixture of ½ turpentine and ½ raw linseed oil (4 tablespoonfuls each). When this is dry (about 24 hours) apply a second coat (3 tablespoonfuls of each). When this is thoroughly dry, apply a coat of stain varnish. Coats of varnish are added until there are no dull spots on the rush.

When first and second coats are still tacky, smooth and even the strands so that when the varnish sets they will be held in place.

A sealer or shellac may be used instead of varnish.

Be sure that no one sits in the chair for at least 2 weeks after the weaving has been completed, so that the finish will have dried thoroughly.

FIBER RUSH

Fiber rush is made from a very tough grade of paper twisted into a strand to resemble rush. It may be purchased in dark brown in widths of 3/32, 1/8, 5/32, and 3/16 inch to resemble antique rush seats, and in multicolored strands in 3/16 inch to resemble new seats.

Prepare the chair as for natural rush. Buy the fiber in 1- or 2-pound lots or in quantity on a large reel. Pound lots cost a few cents more; reels take time and patience to unroll and rewind. Handle that on a reel as you would wire; roll and unroll it rather than pull it. Take off about 25 yards to work with at one time. Tie the end to a nearby strand, and wind it in a roll about 6 inches across. Twenty-five yards of 5/32-inch-wide fiber weighs about ½ pound. Tie string in a slip knot around the roll so that it won't unwind or untwist.

WEAVING FIBER RUSH

Use one strand and weave as you do real rush except that the fiber is already twisted. You may dampen the fiber by dipping the roll in and out of warm water; if too wet, the paper softens and cannot be used. Fasten and join the fiber, and pad the seats as directed below. Cut separate lengths each time you weave around the two front corners.

To begin weaving, fasten the ends of the fiber as for real rush, except alternate hooking and tying ends to a nearby strand to make them less bulky. Each time you weave the corners, tighten the preceding strand.

Join the fiber by one of three methods:

- Fold back the ends of fiber and wire them together.

- Overlap the ends for about 3 inches and tie them together with very fine wire, fishline, or heavy thread.
- Tie the end with a square knot on the underside of the seat.

PADDING

Heavy corrugated cardboard is desirable for padding. Other cardboard or heavy paper can be used but may rattle as the chair is used. Begin padding after 4 or 5 inches are woven on the front rail. If the rails are of even height, cut four pieces of cardboard, one to fit each section of the seat exactly. Force them under the weaving from the upper side of the seat. If rails are of uneven height, two pieces of cardboard may be used in each section. More padding may be added underneath and between. A hole about 2 inches square must be left in the cardboard at the center of the seat to get the fiber through. If brown paper is used, cut it in squares and fold it in triangles.

To fasten the end of fiber, after weaving is completed, pull it to the underside of the seat, untwist the paper, cut it in half, wind each around a nearby strand, and tie. Unfasten joinings that are conspicuous, overlap the ends, and glue or wire them together.

Finish the seat with the oil–turpentine mixture used for real rush and then with a sealer or shellac.

SPLINT, REED, ETC.

Still another type of seat for post-and-spindle chairs is the **splint seat**. Splint is sometimes used as an overall sort of word to include several materials—reed, wide binding cane, and true splint, which is actually ultrathin strips of wood cut into long, narrow lengths. Natural splint comes from native ash and hickory trees and from tropical palm trees. It is interesting to note that rattan, reed, cane, and splint all come from the palm tree (as well as other sources).

Splint is best suited for simple chairs with few turnings, such as Early American ladder-back chairs. It is often used when the side rails are higher than the front and back rails. Although splint looks better, it is a little more difficult to work than flat reed. Flat reed may be used instead by the beginner if he so chooses. Practice with reed will make working with splint the next time a little easier.

Splint and flat reed are used interchangeably indoors. For outside furniture, flat oval reed and wide binding cane are substituted, using the same procedure. All these materials can be purchased from the sources listed at the beginning of the chapter. Paper splint is also available, but you really shouldn't bother with it, since it isn't very durable and isn't worth the small savings in price.

Whether you are using splint or either type of reed, 1 pound should do for the average seat, which is 16 inches across the front. Wide binding cane comes in bunches, with 500 feet ample for the average chair. Most of these materials come in varying widths, with the best size usually somewhere in the middle. It it's too wide, the chair won't look good. If it's too narrow, it'll take you forever to finish.

PREPARATION

The rest of the chair is repaired, refinished, etc., before the seat is woven. If there was splint in the seat before, it may have padding between the layers. The padding can be replaced if desired, but shaped seats without stuffing are actually more comfortable than padded ones. Be sure the wood is dry before you begin weaving.

Pull one of the strands of splint from the looped end of the hank near the spot where it is tied. As you pull, shake the hank so that the splint won't tangle. The "right" side is smooth and beveled; the wrong side splinters when broken. Roll the strand, right side out, into a shape to fit a pan or bowl filled with a solution of warm water and 10 percent glycerine. Clamp the roll with a clothespin.

Let the roll soak in the container until it is soft and pliable—about ½ hour for splint and 20 minutes for reed or binding cane. Each time you remove a roll from the pan, put another one to soak while you work with the one just removed.

THE WEAVING PROCESS

Weaving is done in two directions: the first, **warping**, is the wrapping of the splint around the seat rails. This is done across the long way of the chair so that the second step, **weaving**, can be done across the open rails, the short way of the opening.

Usually, warping is done from back to front and weaving from side to side.

All splints are woven at right angles to the warp. If the front of the seat is wider than the back, weave the center first and fill in the corners later with short lengths.

Warping • Mark a center rectangle or square. Using a carpenter's square, cut a cardboard pattern of a size that will fit within the chair rails. Fit this close against one back post, parallel with the back rail.

Mark the front corner of the square on the front rail. Repeat on the other side of the seat. Check to see that you have enough space for the width of splint.

If the two sides vary, adjust by marking a slightly greater allowance on the shorter side and less on the long side. Mark the center between these two marks on the front and back rail.

Take the roll of splint from the bowl in which it is soaking and remove the excess water with your fingers or sponge or cloth. Put another strand in to soak. Work with the full length of the strand. Temporarily staple one end to the left side rail, with the right side of the splint next to the wood, so that you work with the grain. Pull the strand under, and then up and over the back rail, close to the post, in the exact position and shape you want it to dry. Pull the strand to the front rail, with the outside edge exactly at the pencil mark. Pull the strand over and under the rail and then return it to the back rail.

Continue until you have used all the strand. Force the wet warpers close together so they will not slip on the rail. Hold the end temporarily with a clamp clothespin.

Join strands on the underside. Place a new piece under the old, with the right side down. Staple the strands together in three places, 1 to 2 inches apart, so that at least one of them can be covered when you weave the other way. Pull the strand away from the stick and use pliers to flatten the sharp ends of the staples. Leave enough of the old strand to support the new, but cut off any that would make a double thickness around the rail. Pull the new strand under and around the rail.

Continue wrapping strands. When you reach the center mark, count the warpers to make sure you will have the same number on each half of the seat. When you reach the pencil mark on the right side of the chair, use a clamp clothespin to hold the warper. If work is interrupted, sprinkle the seat and dampen the end to keep the splints pliable.

Design • You can use the old seat as a guide in deciding the pattern of the weave. Or, you can use scraps and ends of splints to try out different designs. You can also work out designs on squared paper, using one square for each warper.

Count the number of warpers on the back rail. This number may be evenly divisible by the number in the design you want to use. For example, 20 strands and a mesh of two under and two over, or 21 strands with a mesh of three over and three under. If the number is not evenly divisible:

• Plan from near the center of the opening and begin weaving accordingly. For example: If there are 23 strands and a mesh of three over three under, weave over one to start the row, continue across until you have used 21 strands and then weave the single strand as on the first side.

• Use a diagonal design. Emphasis then will be away from the side rails where the design may or may not be completed. A diagonal design also is desirable if side rails are uneven.

The second row determines the design. You can move one or more strands to the left for a diagonal design from the right back to the left front of the seat, or you may reverse the direction. For a geometric design, weave alternate rows alike.

The most common design is made by carrying the weave strands over two of the warps and then under two. Other popular designs are two over and three under and three over and three under. For larger seats or narrow widths of splint, the following may prove more satisfactory:

- Over four and under four
- Over four and under two
- Over five and under three

Any designs smaller than two and two are usually too difficult to push together closely enough. Also, any combinations listed above may be reversed. For example, on a larger chair you can go *over* three and under *five*.

How to work the weave • Be sure the strand of splint is long enough to weave across the top of the seat and to join on the underside.

Loosen the last warper thread over the back rail, remove the clothespin, and bring the warper from the front under and over the back rail, then under the preceding warper. Bring the strand diagonally in front of the back post, under the side rail, and turned so that the right side is down.

Pull all strands tight and then weave across, right to left. Pull the weaver thread over the side rail and weave the underside like the top, going over and under the same warpers.

When you join strands, staple from either side. Staples that cannot be hidden can be covered with short lengths of splint tucked under nearby strands.

Flatten the sharp ends of staples with pliers. Continue weaving, cutting the used-up strand where it won't show, even if you waste some of it. Force the joining into position.

The second row in the over-two and under-three pattern starts one warper to the left of the first row, or weave to the right if you want the diagonal in the same direction as on the top of the seat.

Use a stick or a screwdriver to force the strands together. At the same time pull the strands across the rails so the seat will be firm.

On the underside, plan from near the center of the opening, where the design is established, how to begin the row and so continue the design.

When you have woven far enough to see the design, and have space, cut off a length of splint for a warper in the corner of the seat. Hook about 3 inches over the weaver which will continue the design, near the back of the seat. Or just push the strand in rather than hook it over a weaver, if it fits snugly. Bring this warper to the underside of the seat and hook it over a weaver.

Strands may be joined on top of the seat under the warpers to save splint. If the joining is secure, cut off the old strand so that two thicknesses do not show. Also cut the string holding the first strand. Weaving now holds this end in place. Add other short lengths in the corners of the seat, as you have room for them.

Warpers are cut so that ends are concealed under weavers. Use one or two staples and the weaving to hold the joining.

A screwdriver or similar blunt tool will help in aligning the strands correctly as you get near the front of the seat. Continue weaving to the front rail. Finish the underside by weaving as far across as you can and tucking the end under a warper.

If the back of the chair is to be woven, warp strands the long way (up and down). Weave across from the bottom up so that you can push strands in place easily.

Finishing • Trim off "hairs" or rough places with a razor blade or sharp knife. Splint that has a hard glossy surface can be left without a finish. Or you may apply two or three coats of a thin penetrating wood sealer to both sides of the seat. Apply the first coat as soon as you finish weaving. Let each coat dry thoroughly before applying the next. If you want the seat darkened to blend with the color of the chair finish, apply one or more coats of stain before sealing.

—— PLASTIC LAMINATE TABLETOPS ——

Very often a tabletop is warped or scarred so badly that the best course is to either replace it with something else, or cover it. There are plenty of materials around that will cover it adequately.

Of all the available materials, the most versatile is probably laminated plastic (Formica, Textolite, and other brand names). This material comes in many different colors and patterns, but for tabletops the imitation woods are probably most suitable.

Purists will note that this material *is* imitation, and there is no doubt that recovering the table with plastic laminates will doom it forever from status as a valuable antique. On the other hand, when utility is your motivation, there is scarcely another material that will take such punishment. And the newer designs are remarkably realistic looking.

To prepare a tabletop for recovering with plastic laminates, good adhesion is important, as always. So smooth out any badly worn areas, roughen the whole surface just enough to provide tooth for the contact cement and remove all traces of dirt, wax, or any other material that will interfere with good cementing. A washdown with TSP is good insurance.

The adhesive overwhelmingly used here is contact cement, and if you've ever used this adhesive before, you know it means "on contact." Once you lay the materials together they're stuck—but good. Consequently, the prime consideration in this type of work is making sure that the laminate is in exactly the right position before setting it down.

First, the laminate is cut to fit the desired area, leaving about 1/8-inch over for edging (see below). Use a pattern if it's easier for you, cutting the laminate with a sharp utility knife or fine-toothed saw.

After you've trimmed the laminate, apply the contact cement on top of the table and on the underside of the laminate as directed by the manufacturer. It will probably have to set awhile before you can press the surfaces together. If you're a pro at this, you can probably plunk the sheet of laminate right down on target, but the rest of us poor mortals will have to use the old method of spreading brown paper over the tabletop. (Contact cement won't adhere to the paper unless it's cemented, too.)

Maneuver the laminate until it's *exactly* where it's supposed to be, then put one hand on top of the laminate and gradually let one corner of the table and laminate hold together. If you get this wrong, you will probably be able to unstick it, but once the whole edge is stuck, it's probably too late. Gradually pull out the paper "slip sheet" allowing more and more of the surfaces to adhere. After you're about halfway out with the paper, just pull it out all the way and press the rest together. Nothing is going to move the laminate once it's stuck that far.

Do the edges next, unless they're carved or molded, making sure that the top part is exactly right because there won't be any extra room with the top hanging over 1/8 inch. When done, go over the edges with a file, leaving a 45-degree edge all around. This looks better when both top and edges are done, but it also looks okay when just the top is laminated.

The pros use a router bit made especially for this purpose, and if you have a router and can get the bit, by all means use it for a nice, smooth edge (Fig. 11-14). You may be able to borrow or rent a tool from the dealer. If you're careful with the file, you'll do almost as well, however.

You may find it a lot easier to simply remove the entire tabletop and replace it with a plastic-laminate top already fabricated. Most metropolitan areas have shops that specialize in sink countertops and similar installations. They should be able to make a whole new tabletop for you, or sell you the particle-board core already covered with the laminate. You can then cut it to size with a jigsaw and just finish the edges.

MOSAIC TABLETOPS

The crowning glory of Roman and Byzantine architecture was often an intricate, colorful, and long-enduring **mosaic**. Intricate geometric patterns, pictorial fresco

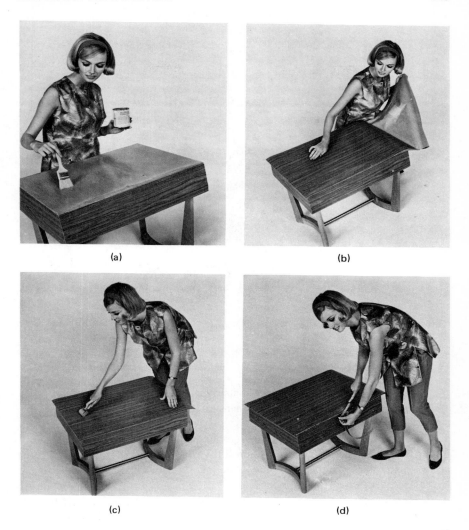

(a)

(b)

(c)

(d)

FIG. 11-13 • This sequence shows the basic technique of installing plastic laminates (even though the material shown here is a more flexible version of the usual types): (a) Contact adhesive is spread on both surfaces. (b) A slip sheet (brown paper is best) is placed between the glued surfaces and slowly withdrawn when the plastic is in the right position. (c) The surface is rolled to remove air bubbles and ensure a good bond. (d) A file is used to make neat, square edges. (*Courtesy of Wood Conversion Co.*)

designs, and sweeping murals were created from tiny pieces of glazed ceramic.

The do-it-yourselfer cannot hope to duplicate the great designs of those

FIG. 11-14 • A carbide-tipped trimming set is used to make professional edges on Formica and other plastic laminates. (*Courtesy of Black and Decker*)

golden days, but he can create a showpiece cocktail or outdoor snack table out of mosaic tiles. These tiles now come in a wide variety of shapes and sizes, although the most popular continue to be the 3/4-inch-square tiles that come in paper-backed sheets 12 by 12 inches.

Mosaic tiles can be laid over an old tabletop, or a new top can be constructed from 3/8-inch tempered hardboard or plywood. The paper-backed squares come in prearranged patterns that are quite attractive used as is, but you may wish to use a design of your own. In that event, you can either use the squares for a base, substituting other tiles for the ones you wish to change, or you can start from scratch with individual tiles directly onto the board. Patterns and suggested designs can be purchased from most mosaic tile dealers.

If you're lucky, you may not have to cut any tiles for a rectangular table. Round or other shapes will require some cutting, as will some rectangular tables. A tile-nipping pliers is the right tool for this and can also be purchased from the tile dealer. A round carbide sawblade is good for larger tiles.

Before you begin, you'll need an edge around the table, old or new. Use thin wood strips for this, wetting them to enable them to bend around round tables and other odd shapes. The strips should extend 1/8 inch above the old surface to allow the tiles to be set flush. An alternative way is to tile the edges of the table, in which case the edge tiles are set to extend 1/8 inch above the tabletop. Do edges first.

To lay the tiles, pour the special mosaic tile cement into a shallow mixing bowl. Trickle water into the bowl slowly and carefully, stirring gently all the time you're pouring to keep out air bubbles. Tap the bowl lightly on the table to bring any bubbles to the surface.

Pour the mix onto the surface to be worked and use a small trowel, a flat knife, or your hands to smooth it out as evenly as possible. Lay the tile into the cement quickly, pressing the sheet down firmly. Run the flat of your hand as firmly as you can over the paper-covered surface, working out to the edges with a circular movement. Keep rubbing until the entire surface is level, then wet the paper with a sponge.

Let the paper soak about 5 minutes, then peel it off carefully. If the paper doesn't come off easily, wet it some more and try again. Some tiles may be pulled up with the paper. If so, gently squeeze them back down again. Rub your hand around any depressed tile to force it up to level. If that doesn't work, carefully remove it and lay in a little more cement underneath.

Keep at this until entire surface is covered with tile. Cut any tiles that don't fit with the cutters. After each section is completed, cover the surface with a wet towel or newspapers so that the cement won't dry too fast.

When the above method is used, grouting should only be necessary when not enough cement was used underneath. The cement (grout, same thing) should ooze up between the tiles and fill the spaces. You may have to fill in edges, etc., and any other spots that aren't quite level.

Don't try to remove cement from tile surfaces until it is completely dry. A damp cloth should remove the fine film that sometimes covers the tile. Thicker patches can be removed with water and steel wool.

When the job is done, cover with a silicone sealer to protect the grout from discoloring. To keep it clean, apply every few years thereafter. No other maintenance is necessary (which is the beauty of this material).

ACRYLIC PLASTIC TABLETOPS

Acrylic plastic (Plexiglas and other brands) is generally used clear, although it also comes in attractive colored and smoky shades. This product can be used as a transparent protective cover for other materials, in which case it is cemented much like laminated plastics. The best use of acrylic plastics, however, is as a substitute for tops of smaller tables such as cocktail and end tables (Fig. 11-15). This material comes in thicknesses up to ¼ inch and can be sawed, drilled, and worked like wood. For the average use, a new top is cut from the new plastic,

FIG. 11-15 • Acrylic plastic can be used to replace small table tops or it can be placed over the existing surface, as with this desk writing area. Plexiglas was also used for the hobby case, desk lamp, pencil holder, and floor protection. (*Courtesy of Rohm and Haas Co.*)

sanded and smoothed on the edges as directed by the manufacturer, then glued or screwed to the old frame (Figs. 11-16 and 11-17). If screw holes are necessary, an ordinary hand or electric drill will do the job.

Although acrylic plastic can be scratched by hard use, it is impervious to alcohol, water, and other ordinary household hazards. It is ideally suited for modern furniture and can often be mixed with more traditional styles.

MARBLE, STONE, ETC., TABLETOPS

Marble, granite, and other stone tops are occasionally used in furniture restora-

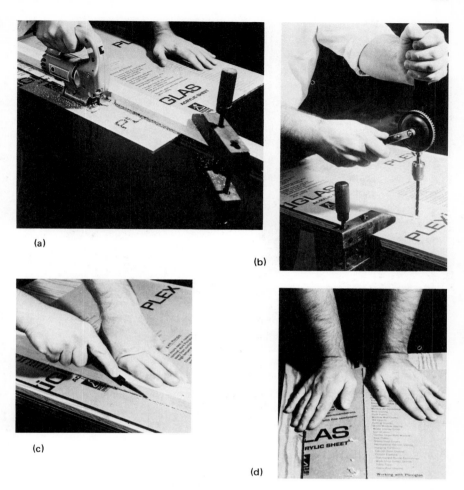

(a)

(b)

(c)

(d)

FIG. 11-16 • It is easy to work with Plexiglas acrylic plastic. It can be (a) sawed, (b) drilled, or (c–d) scribed and broken. You can also bend it on a straight line if heated to the proper temperature. (*Courtesy of Rohm and Haas Co.*)

tion. There is little that can be said about these natural materials except to make sure that the piece is cut to size by the dealer. This type of material is very difficult to cut without the proper specialized tools and skills.

To attach marble to a table frame, drill blind holes into the bottom with a masonry bit, fill the hole with polyester glue, and imbed bolts with threads out. Attach bolts through former screw holes in frame.

The only other limitation is your imagination. There is no reason, for

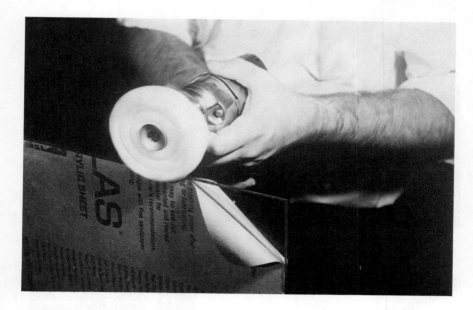

FIG. 11-17   •   For a transparent edge after sawing, sand with grits to 400 and follow by buffing with muslin wheel and fine compound. (*Courtesy of Rohm and Haas Co.*)

example, why you can't cover a table with anything you want as long as it can stand the wear it will get. Why not, for example, cover an old table with a butcher block, floor tile, indoor–outdoor carpeting, or anything else that strikes your fancy? Maybe it won't look so great, but it'll hold up. And unless you're in the antique business, who cares?

Using and Caring for Furniture

No matter how gorgeous it is, furniture is functional in concept rather than decorative. The decoration came later, sort of an added bonus. The best furniture, in fact, is an admirable marriage of the practical and the pretty.

But here we have a problem. If furniture were made simply to be admired, care and maintenance would be easy. Put it under glass and look at it—or eat it, maybe. Unfortunately, that lovely fabric is going to bear the brunt of greasy little fingers, and those spindly legs will have to hold up many hefty frames. That lovely finish will be host to the scrapings of plates and cuff buttons—not to mention the kids' toy trucks, with and without wheels.

So we have to give our furniture constant care to keep it from reverting to the derelict it was before you lavished your tender, loving care upon it. The best cure, as always, is an ounce or two—a pound, even—of prevention. So first listen to a couple of very bad no-no's.

─────── THINGS YOU SHOULDN'T DO ───────

1. The first thing you shouldn't do with furniture is expose it to extremes of cold and heat. This will result in bad things happening to the finish, the glue, the wood, and everything else. What, why, and how is not important. Just don't do it. It may ruin the piece so badly that it is unrestorable—and you know by now that furniture has to be in pretty rotten shape to be hopeless.

2. Probably the worst of the no-no's is to set a vase of flowers on a nice finish without some sort of barrier underneath it. A vase of flowers, if the flowers are to survive, will be filled with water, and invariably the vase will "sweat," causing little puddles of water to collect under and around the bottom. This is fatal for shellac and not very good for anything else, because it is a continuous process that will eventually spoil any finish.

3. Another bad idea is using water-based wax (meant for linoleum, vinyl, floors, etc.) on any kind of wood, including wood floors.

4. Neglect—doing nothing at all—is still another grievous no-no. A discussion of exactly what you should do to protect your furniture follows, but remember that almost any kind of action is better than doing nothing at all.

5. Letting foreign matter accumulate is another bad act. Clean up any spills, grease, etc., promptly (Fig. 12-1). Water, alcohol, or any other liquids will damage any finish if not wiped up promptly. The same holds true of other substances, particularly greasy ones.

6. This is going to insult your intelligence, but since everyone does something stupid once in awhile, here goes. Don't do dumb things like applying nail-polish remover over the end tables. Don't let the kids play with their chemistry set on the dining room table. There must be a hundred things like that which are mostly the result of not thinking. The next time you shuffle papers on your newly finished desk, for example, remember how hard you worked on it as you scrape the staples across the surface. Think!

─────── WOOD ───────

WAX VERSUS OIL

Read almost anything on this subject and your head begins to throb. One expert says use nothing but lemon oil; another tells you to use nothing but linseed oil, or some brand-name polish. It almost seems as though everybody owns some kind of wax or oil factory (or some stock, at least).

FIG. 12-1 • Always clean up spills and smudges as soon as possible.

When it comes right down to it, almost anything you use regularly on your furniture will be good for it. The key word is *regularly*. And it doesn't necessarily mean "frequently." It means at standard intervals. If you like the looks of furniture polish, fine. But you'll have to use it fairly often. How often depends on lots of things, primarily the recommendations of the manufacturer. Once a season is a very rough rule of thumb.

The various types of polishes are usually emulsions of mineral oil with maybe a little wax, lemon oil, or lanolin thrown in. Most are very good, but their chief benefit lies in the cleaning effect and the thin protective film that is left. Try a few different types out and see what looks and works best for you. But none of these ideas is as good as good wax.

We think wax is superior, if you use the right kind and apply it correctly. Not that it does any better job than regular oiling or polishing. It just lasts longer. The spray and liquid waxes are okay for routine cleaning and dusting, but if you want a surface that will last for months without needing anything but light dusting, paste wax is the thing—and the harder the better.

HOW TO WAX

Make sure that the wax you use contains a high percentage of carnauba wax, the hardest type commercially available, or candelilla wax, second best. You will have a difficult time finding which ingredients are in various products, so buy

FIG. 12-2 • Here's a trick to save wood surfaces from being scratched by ceramic or other rough materials. Put a bead of silicone rubber all along the offending areas. (*Courtesy of Dow Corning*)

the one that makes you rub the hardest. Many people in the know use automotive wax—Simonize or similar brand.

The other "secret" is to apply wax as thinly as possible. This doesn't mean to skimp; it does mean thorough application without thick build-up. Wax is only as good as the buffing job you do on it. The more you rub, the better it is, but the thicker the wax, the harder it is to buff. The best instrument for buffing is a lamb's-wool applicator over your ¼-inch drill. A chamois cloth is good, too, but pretty hard work.

How much wax to apply depends on what is under it. You don't really need any wax at all if your furniture has one of the new factory-sprayed lacquers. Occasional polishing is all that this type of finish needs. On the other end of the spectrum, a sealer finish requires several coats of wax—still very thin, regardless of the number of coats. Varnish, shellac, and other finishes usually benefit from just one or two thin coats of wax.

Wax should last at least 6 months, but if it starts to fade before then, the sheen can be revived by a rubdown with a soft, lintless cloth. When this fails, another coat of wax is in order. But be pecunious in the wax applications. Just so many coats can be applied before it starts to look overshiny. When the humidity is high, the wax may become sticky and pick up more dirt than usual.

When wax reaches the point where it's doing more harm than good, remove it entirely with liberal doses of mineral spirits or turpentine and start over.

THE RIGHT WAY TO POLISH

Would you believe that there are right and wrong ways to apply furniture polish? Well, the difference isn't all as vital as some "experts" would like to make you believe, but you do get better results if you apply it with a damp rag (helps clean off dirt) and keep folding the cloth when it gets dirty. It also works better if you polish with the grain.

There is a bewildering array of oil and/or wax emulsions that call themselves polishes. Most will do the job if applied in thin coats and used with generous servings of elbow grease. Some of these are really spray waxes or other mixtures, but it doesn't make too much difference what you use, as mentioned earlier, as long as you do what the manufacturer says—and at the proper intervals. No matter what you use, rub hard.

Tung oil, if you can find it, is one of those old-fashioned ingredients that we sort of favor. It gives a rich finish that's hard to duplicate. This and other good furniture polishes don't come cheap, but you can make your own "wonder polish" by mixing one part turpentine to one part boiled linseed oil. This mixture is ideal for lacquered or other finishes that are already highly polished and durable. The turpentine digs out the dirt and helps the oil to penetrate. The oil brightens and "feeds" the hungry wood fibers.

━━━━━━━━━━ PLASTICS ━━━━━━━━━━

In order to clean and care for any type of plastic, you should understand its characteristics (see Table 12-1). All plastics fall into two main groups.

Thermosetting plastics are set into a firm shape when they are manufactured. They may warp or crack but they do not become soft and pliable as they become warmer. Handles of cooking utensils, many plastic dishes, and laminated plastics are examples of thermosetting materials. They can be exposed to hot water and in general will take temperatures to about 300°F. They cannot tolerate direct contact with heat.

Thermoplastic synthetics become softer when heated and stiffer when cooled. This change takes place as often as the process is repeated. Many household articles, such as mixing bowls and measuring cups and spoons, are thermoplastic. Some of them are damaged when washed in dishwashers. Others can take the high temperature of washing and drying cycles.

In both groups of plastics are many that are resistant to breakage, scratching, staining, and chemical action. They can be washed with any of the cleaning agents used in water. Most are not damaged by acids and alcohol spilled on them, but some are damaged by chlorine bleaches.

Unless the label gives other information about a plastic article, these precautions are important:

- Wash with soap or other detergent, rinse, and dry off extra water at once. A damp cloth will often do the cleaning job.
- Avoid using abrasive powders and do not slide rough objects over the surface.
- Do not spill bleaches and drycleaning liquids on them. Wipe up at once any alcohol that is spilled.
- Handle rigid articles with care. They may break easily and may warp if they become too hot.

Most of the plastic materials used in furniture are a form of vinyl. If the fabric becomes dull and shabby looking, a liquid wax cleaner may restore some of its former beauty. Use sparingly, however. (See the table at the end of the chapter for the characteristics of various plastics.)

FIG. 12-3 • To renew and recolor old plastic, use an aerosol spray that is vinyl itself and becomes part of the plastic. (*Courtesy of Monroe B. Scharff and Co., Inc.*)

MARBLE

Marble is a lovely material that laid hidden in the earth for about 600 million years before it became your tabletop. Strong and durable as it is, its porous surface needs a lot more care and maintenance than most people realize. It should be covered with a protective coat of silicone-base wax or a suitable sealer such as "Tri-Seal" or both. Darker marble should have a coat of paste wax in addition. Make sure that any sealer you use is recommended for use on marble.

Scratches and etches are difficult to remove, but the best bet is to get the finest grade of abrasive paper available (try the hobby shop) and have at it with some fine oil. Polish the abraded spot afterward with jeweler's rouge or tin oxide, followed by a good buffing with your electric drill or chamois cloth.

Fresh stains should be removed promptly by rubbing lightly with a non-abrasive detergent. Stains that have set awhile are best removed with some laundry bleach or hydrogen peroxide with a drop of ammonia. Alcohol, naphtha, or acetone may also remove the stain, depending on what caused it. Tea and coffee are eradicated with bleach. Use naphtha (cleaning fluid) on grease and oil stains. Let the naphtha soak in a white blotter allowed to stand on the stain topped with cardboard and a heavy book or piece of glass.

If none of the above works, make a poultice out of naphtha and some fuller's earth. Cover the mixture with a damp cloth to retard drying.

To avoid difficult stain removal, follow regular maintenance procedures.

UPHOLSTERY CARE

At one time it was considered a big deal to have your furniture "Scotchgarded." Purists scoffed, of course, since it "covered up" the priceless fabric. Well, the purists were wrong. The fabric wasn't really "covered up," and the results prove that a protective film on your fine fabric will help preserve it considerably longer by keeping out a lot of harmful dirt and stains.

Today, you don't necessarily have to buy your fabrics preprotected. There are several brands you can buy and spray on yourself (including Scotchgard Fabric Protector). They are fairly expensive, but we think well worth it. Not only dirt and stains but water and other liquids are repelled by it—at least long enough for you to wipe them up without their soaking into the fabric. Tests by Consumers Union have backed up the efficacy of this type of product.

A common but frequently overlooked treatment for upholstery is frequent vacuuming. The longer dirt lays on a surface, the more it works its way deeper into the upholstery. *Use* all those fancy attachments—they work pretty well, believe it or not. If you don't have a vacuum or the fancy attachments, use a stiff whisk broom to keep dirt out of all those crevices. If you have any down pillows, by any chance, you'll *have* to whisk-broom them. The vacuum will pull out the feathers.

It helps to fluff up cushions and turn them over occasionally. Every once in awhile, remove the cushions entirely and take them outside for a breath of fresh air. If you're strong or have a muscleman around, take the whole piece outside during spring cleaning and let the breezes blow the stink out of it.

Spots should be removed from all upholstery fabrics as soon as possible. The cure for stains varies according to which of the many types of stains and the wide variety of fabrics are involved. Ordinary cleaning fluid is a good overall product but will not work on everything. Always test whatever it is you're using in an inconspicuous part of the same fabric to see how well it tests for colorfastness.

Probably the best all-around upholstery cleaner, one that takes care of most everyday dirt and grime, is a good upholstery shampoo, one that makes a thick, soapless lather. Apply it, let it stand for a few minutes (as directed), and whip it up into a lather. Then rub it down with a soft, clean brush and wipe it clean with a cloth or sponge. Let stand until thoroughly dry.

You can make your own shampoo by dissolving 6 tablespoons of white soap flakes like Ivory in 1 pint of boiling water. Add a couple of tablespoons of borax or a little ammonia to help soften the soap flakes. This mixture will take a little extra effort after application to get it into the proper lather. Let the foam, not the liquid, do the work.

Lipstick, fresh grease spots, and similar stains can often be absorbed into powders like fuller's earth, French chalk, talcum, or cornstarch. Mix the powders into a paste by adding cleaning fluid, naphtha, or carbon tetrachloride. The powders won't hurt the fabric, but the fluid might possibly, so test in an innocuous area as mentioned above.

A very handy little book on removing stains and everything else in the home is *How To Clean Everything* by Alma Chesnut Moore, originally published by Simon and Schuster, Inc., and available in paperback from Pocket Books, Inc.

If you can't remove the stain or just don't want to bother with it, there are professional cleaning services in most communities, some of whom will come to your home (for a fee, of course).

LEATHER

Leather takes less kindly to water than most other upholstery fabrics, so use as little of it as possible when cleaning it. Dust with an untreated cloth, clean with saddle or other mild soap, and follow directions, using as little water as possible. Wipe off soap with a minimally damp rag and dry as soon as possible with a soft cloth.

Another ingredient leather doesn't cotton to is wax. Never wax a leather chair and don't use mineral oil, which has a paraffin base.

What leather *does* cotton to are several oils, such as castor or neat's foot. One of these oils, lanolin, or other leather conditioner should be applied at least once a year, preferably every 6 months. This should keep the leather from cracking or drying out. Use a white petroleum jelly or very light conditioner for light-colored leather. Oils will darken the light colors too much.

Rub the oil or conditioner into the leather so that no residue remains to soil clothing. After thorough rubbing, wipe down with a clean, soft cloth.

METAL AND GLASS

Metal and glass don't need anything except an occasional dusting. When metal starts looking too bad, particularly outside stuff, a good coat or two of rust-resistant paint will bring it back to life. For touch-ups, be sure to use a primer over bare spots.

You can clean metal and glass with a waxy cleaner if you want. This does give the surface a little more sparkle and makes future fingermarks and spills easier to wipe off next time.

DUSTING

Routine maintenance of any type of furniture includes weekly dusting to remove specks of dirt and grime that eventually build up to an abrasive layer that erodes wax, varnish, shellac, oil, or whatever else is on top. Dust is no good for fabrics, either, and this is why regular vacuuming is important.

There are a lot of products sold heavily over television and elsewhere that are supposed to work wonders when you dust, and there is certainly nothing *wrong* with using them. They may possibly do some good. The thing to remember about dusting, though, is the type of cloth. You must use a clean, dry, hemmed cloth and you should rub good and hard. If you have a waxed surface, rub extra hard every month or so to bring out the original sheen. Never use an oily or treated cloth on a waxed surface. It only gums up the wax.

If the surface has been waxed previously, you can use a polish that contains wax but not oils, such as Pledge or Jubilee. A plain cloth is really all you need, though, as long as you rub hard enough.

THAT EXTRA SOMETHING

There are a lot of complex cures for spots and stains on furniture, some of which are given in Chapter 4. All the technical advice in the world, however, can't approach that old favorite—TLC—for effectiveness. If you really admire and respect—even "love"—furniture, you'll take the time and effort to care for it. And that is really the best advice anyone can offer.

TABLE 12-1 • Uses for and Characteristics of Common Plastics

Plastic	Typical household usage	Characteristics	Resistant to	Damaged by
Vinyl	Curtains, draperies, upholstery fabrics, counter, floor and wall coverings	Thermoplastic; in fabricated form is available in transparent, translucent, or opaque colors; as a coating on cloth or paper has a limited resistance to abrasion	Water, sunlight, weathering, dirt, acids, alcohols, most food stains	Boiling water, direct flame, moth repellents
Nylon	Curtains, draperies, upholstery, bouclés	Thermoplastic, but recent products not damaged by boiling water; range of colors, high tensile strength	Freezing temperatures, household chemicals, common solvents, oils, greases	Weathering, mineral oils, coffee, tea, certain vegetable and fruit juices
Laminated plastics	Countertops, tabletops, flooring	Thermosetting plastics such as phenolics, melamines, etc., may be used; produced in a wide range of colors or simulated veneers; light in weight; strong; durable	Boiling water, acids, alkalis, oils, common chemicals	Direct heat
Cellulosics, nitrates	Fabric coverings, lampshades	Thermoplastic; available in wide range of colors; take a lustrous finish; light in weight; tough; flammable	Weathering, household chemicals	Abrasion, heat, fire (flame)

238

Plastic	Typical household usage	Characteristics	Resistant to	Damaged by
Polyethylene	Kitchenware, flexible bowls, ice-cube trays	Thermoplastic; odorless, tasteless, flexible; lightweight; milky translucent in pastel colors	Chemicals, food acids, household solvents, freezing	Boiling water, abrasives
Polystyrenes	Picnic dishes, refrigerator storage boxes	Thermoplastic; available in wide range of brilliant colors, also in colorless transparent form; has metallic ring when tapped; nontoxic; heat resistance varies from 150 to 220° F	Ordinary chemicals	Cleaning fluid, acetones, citrus fruit, oils, boiling water, impact
Cellulose acetates	Measuring spoons, strainers, cups	Thermoplastic; colorful; may not be entirely odor- or taste-free		Boiling water, acetone, abrasives
Phenolics	Handles, knobs of cooking utensils, handles, frames of electric appliances	Thermosetting plastics; available in dark or mottled colors; good resistance to heat transmission; good electric insulators	Boiling water, impact, mild acids, solvents, oils	Flame, oven temperatures
Melamines	Tableware, plates	Thermosetting plastics; wide range of colors; odorless and tasteless; temperature range from −70 to 210°F	Light, acids, alkalis, boiling water, oils, household chemicals	Abrasives, flame, oven temperatures

239

Glossary

ABRASIVE—any material used for wearing away a surface by rubbing or friction. Sandpaper, steel wool, emery paper, silica, powdered pumice are the most common examples.

ACETATES—solvents for nitrocellulose. Various alcohols combined with acetic acid.

ACID STAIN—stains of an acid nature. Soluble in water. Water stains are often called acid stains.

ACRYLIC—a plastic resin used in latex paints and in certain fast-drying enamels and lacquers. Also a hard, clear plastic (Plexiglas).

ALKALI—a substance that neutralizes acids, such as lye, soda, lime, etc. Alkalis or strong alkaline solutions are highly destructive to paint films. Commonly found in uncured concrete, plaster, etc.

ALKYD RESIN—a synthetic resin made from chemicals. Today most solvent-thinned interior and exterior paints contain alkyd resins.

ALLIGATORING—a term used to describe a painted surface which has formed cracks, resembling the hide of the alligator.

ANHYDROUS—free of moisture.

ANILINE DYES—dyes made from coal tar or its derivatives.

ANNUAL GROWTH RING—the growth layer put on in a single growth year, including springwood and summerwood.

ANTIQUING—a furniture-finishing technique to give the appearance of age or wear. Also called highlighting, glazing, etc.

BACK—the side reverse to the face of a panel, or the poorer side of a panel in any grade of plywood that has a face and back.

BENDING, STEAM—the process of forming curved wood members by steaming or boiling the wood and bending it to a form.

BENZENE—a light-gravity petroleum distillate, "VM & P (Varnish Makers & Painters) Naphtha."

BENZOL—a coal-tar naphtha. A more powerful solvent than benzene. It is toxic and should be used with approved ventilation.

BINDER (Vehicle)—that portion of a paint or enamel which binds or cements the color pigment particles together in the dried film. Oils, resins, latex, and emulsions are examples of the most commonly used binders.

BIRD'S EYE—small localized areas in wood with the fibers indented and otherwise contorted to form small circular or elliptical figures remotely resembling birds' eyes on the tangential surface. Common in sugar maple and used for decorative purposes; rare in other hardwood species.

BLEACHING—the process of restoring wood to its original color (or making it lighter) by using oxalic acid or other bleaching compounds.

BLEACHING LACQUER—a sealing lacquer applied to light wood to prevent it from being darkened by filler. Usually a straight cotton solution. Has no bleaching action.

BLEEDING—discoloration caused by a soluble stain coming through a later coat.

BLISTERING—usually caused by applying paint to damp surfaces or surfaces into which moisture enters through some indirect source (poor joints, cracks, etc.). Moisture later tries to force its way through paint film and causes blister to form.

BLOOM—a deposit of foreign mattter on a finished surface. Usually composed of oil, smoke, or dust. Sometimes used for "hazing," as of shellac.

BLUEING—adding small amounts of blue pigments to white paints. This has the visual effect of making the finish look "whiter" to the eye. Nonyellowing white paints are usually blued.

BLUSH—a white to gray cast on lacquered surfaces. Usually caused by water trapped under the lacquer coat. Quite common in summer. Corrected by using a slower-drying thinner.

BODY (Consistency or Viscosity)—the thickness of a fluid.

BOILED LINSEED OIL—a misnomer, as it has not been "boiled." Instead, the drying time of raw oil is stepped up further by the addition of chemical driers. Never try to literally boil raw linseed oil.

BOW—the distortion in a board that deviates from flatness lengthwise but not across its face.

BRUSHABILITY—the ability or ease with which a paint, enamel, or varnish can be brushed on a surface under practical conditions.

BUFFING COMPOUND—a soft abrasive bonded in stick form with wax.

BURNING-IN—the process of patching with heated shellac and a knife.

BURNT SIENNA—made by roasting a raw pigment (sienna). Red-brown in color.

BURNT UMBER—roasted umber. Dark brown in color. Used by painters in making browns and tans.

CALCIUM CARBONATE—plain white chalk. Used as an extender for water-thinned paints and exterior colors.

CALKING COMPOUND—a pastelike material that is very sticky when applied yet dries on the surface and so may be painted. It remains pliable and elastic so can withstand the expansion and contraction of joints and cracks it is used to fill.

CAMBIUM—the one-cell-thick layer of tissue between the bark and wood that repeatedly subdivides to form new wood and bark cells.

CARBON BLACK—an intense black pigment made by burning natural gas.

CARNAUBA—the Brazilian palm tree that exudes a waxy residue of the same name used as a base in most good wax products.

CASEIN—a protein contained in milk used in making water-thinned paints and glues.

CASTOR OIL—a nondrying oil obtained from the castor bean. May be converted to a drying oil by chemical treatment to dehydrate it.

CATALYST—a chemical agent used in rather small amounts as an additive to activate a resin or chemical that produces a cured film.

CAUSTIC SODA—sodium hydroxide, lye. A white, crystalline substance of a very corrosive nature. Used mostly for cleaning metals.

CHALKING—powdering of a paint film.

CHECKING—the formation of short narrow cracks in the surface of a paint film.

CHINAWOOD OIL—*see* Tung Oil.

COLOR IN JAPAN—said of pigment colors ground and mixed with japan drier.

COLOR IN OIL—said of pigment colors ground and mixed in linseed oil.

COPAL—fossilized gum resins dug out of the ground. The hardest natural resins. A varnish made from copal gums is called a copal varnish.

CORE—also referred to as the "center." The innermost portion of plywood. It may consist of sawn lumber joined and glued, veneer, or wood composition board.

CRACKLE LACQUER—a special type of novelty lacquer producing a cracked top coat. The effect is produced by the rapid drying of the top coat over a slower-drying undercoat.

CROOK—the distortion in a board that deviates edgewise from a straight line from end to end of the board.

CROSSBAND (n.)—the layers of veneer whose grain direction is at right angles to that of the face plies, applied particularly to five-ply plywood and lumber core panels, and more generally to all layers between the core and the faces. Paired plies between the core and the faces having the same grain direction as the face are sometimes called "straight bands."

CROSSBAND (v.)—to place the grain of the layers of veneer at right angles in order to minimize swelling and shrinking.

CRYSTALLIZING LACQUER—a baking lacquer that produces a textured effect consisting of numerous small crystals.

CUP—the distortion in a board that deviates flatwise from a straight line across the width of the board.

DECAY—the decomposition of wood caused by fungi.

DENATURED ALCOHOL—a solvent for paint, shellac, etc. Made by denaturing grain alcohol by any of several approved formulas.

DRIERS—chemical compounds of various metals used to hasten the drying action of oils when added to paints, enamels, or varnishes.

DRYING OILS—oils that convert to solids when exposed to the oxygen in the air. The most common drying oils used in paints and varnishes are linseed, safflower, tung, soybean, and fish oil.

DURABILITY—as applied to wood, its lasting qualities or permanence in service with particular reference to decay. May be related directly to an exposure condition.

EARTH PIGMENTS—all pigments found in the earth. Umber, ochre, sienna, chalk, Van Dyke brown, barytes, and graphite are a few of the most common.

EDGE-GRAINED—*see* Grain: Edge-Grained Lumber.

EMULSION—a thick milk liquid formed by suspending fine particles (microscopic droplets) of an oil, resin, or other unmixable liquid in water.

EMULSION PAINT—a paint made by using an emulsion vehicle as binder for the pigment solids.

ENAMEL—a paint containing a rather high proportion of resin or varnish binder in comparison to the amount of pigment used. Usually produces glossy or semiglossy film.

EPOXY—a relatively new type of synthetic resin having very high resistance to most chemicals. In certain forms epoxy resins require addition of a catalyst to form a film.

EXTENDER—a pigment of low hiding power, used principally to "extend" or make paint go further and to bind together pigment particles of various shapes.

EXTERIOR—a term frequently applied to plywood, bonded with highly resistant adhesives, that is capable of withstanding prolonged exposure to severe service conditions without failure in the glue bonds.

FACE—the better side of a panel in any grade of plywood calling for a face and back; also either side of a panel where the grading rules draw no distinction between faces.

FIBER, WOOD—a comparatively long (1/25 or less to 1/3 inch), narrow, tapering, wood cell closed at both ends.

FIGURE—the desirable pattern produced in a wood surface by annual growth rings, rays, knots, deviations from regular grain such as interlocked and wavy grain, and irregular coloration.

FILLER—a composition material used to fill the pores and cracks in wood before applying paint, varnish, or enamel.

FISH OIL—the oil from marine animals (menhaden, sardines, whales, etc.)

FLAKING—a condition occuring when small pieces of paint film break off.

FLAT LACQUER—a lacquer that dries with a rubbed appearance.

FLAT PAINT—a category of interior paint formulated to produce a flat finish, without luster.

FLATTING AGENT—a metallic ingredient (aluminum, zinc, calcium, etc.) used in varnishes and lacquers to reduce the gloss or to give a finish a "rubbed" appearance.

FLOCK—shredded cloth fibers. Applied over a tacky substance to form a soft, clothlike finish.

FLOOR VARNISH—a type of varnish specially formulated to be used on floors. More resistance to foot traffic than other types of varnish.

FOSSIL RESIN—any of the natural resins obtained from the earth.

FRENCH POLISH—a shellac–linseed–oil combination applied with a cloth according to an old technique (see the text).

GLUE—a substance capable of holding materials together by surface attachment. (In woodworking it often means a substance capable of forming a strong bond with wood.)

GLUE LINE—the line visible on the edge of a plywood panel, indicating the layer of glue. Also applied to the layer of glue itself.

GRAIN—the direction, size, arrangement, appearance, or quality of the elements of wood or lumber:

CLOSE-GRAINED WOOD—wood with narrow, inconspicuous annual rings. The term is sometimes used to designate wood having small and closely spaced pores, but in this sense the term "fine-textured" is more often used.

COARSE-GRAINED WOOD—wood with wide conspicuous annual rings in which there is considerable difference between springwood and summerwood. The term is sometimes used to designate wood with large pores, such as oak, ash, chestnut, and walnut, but in this sense the term "coarse-textured" is more often used.

CROSS-GRAINED WOOD—wood in which the fibers deviate from a line parallel to the side of the piece. Cross-grain may be diagonal grain, spiral grain, or a combination.

CURLY-GRAINED WOOD—wood in which the fibers are distorted so that they have a curled appearance, as in "bird's-eye" wood. The areas showing curly grain may vary up to several inches in diameter.

DIAGONAL-GRAINED WOOD—wood in which the annual rings are at an angle with the axis of the piece as a result of sawing at an angle with the bark of the tree or log. A form of cross-grain.

EDGE-GRAINED LUMBER—lumber that has been quartersawed so that the wide surfaces extend approximately at right angles to the annual growth rings. Lumber is considered edge-grained when the rings form an angle of 45 to 90 degrees with the wide surface of the piece.

FLAT-GRAINED LUMBER—lumber that has been sawed so that the wide surfaces extend approximately parallel to the annual growth rings. Lumber is considered flat-grained when the annual growth rings make an angle of less than 45 degrees with the surface of the piece.

INTERLOCKED-GRAINED WOOD—wood in which the fibers are inclined in one direction in a number of rings of annual growth, then gradually reverse, and are inclined in an opposite direction in succeeding growth rings, then reverse again.

OPEN-GRAINED WOOD—common classification for woods with large pores, such as oak, ash, chestnut, and walnut. Also known as "coarse-textured."

SPIRAL-GRAINED WOOD—wood in which the fibers take a spiral course about the trunk of a tree instead of a normal vertical course. The spiral may extend in a right- or left-handed direction around the tree trunk. Spiral grain is a form of cross-grain.

STRAIGHT-GRAINED WOOD—wood in which the fibers run parallel to the axis of a piece.

VERTICAL-GRAINED LUMBER—another term for edge-grained lumber.

WAVY-GRAINED WOOD—wood in which the fibers collectively take the form of waves or undulations.

GRAIN RAISING—when water is applied to bare wood, the short surface fibers absorb water and stand up. This is grain raising. Liquids that do not raise the grain are called non-grain-raising (NGR).

GREEN—freshly sawed lumber or lumber that has received no intentional drying; unseasoned.

GUM—a natural, gummy material obtained from certain trees. They are *not* resins.

HARDBOARD—a manufactured material made of reconstituted wood, utilizing the tiny threadlike fibers to build up sheets or boards.

HARDWOOD—generally one of the botanical groups of trees that have broad leaves in contrast to the conifers or needle-bearing trees. The term has no reference to the actual hardness of the wood, although the wood from such trees is generally harder than the wood from softwood trees.

HEARTWOOD—the inner core of a woody stem composed of nonliving cells and usually differentiated from the outer enveloping layer (sapwood).

HIGH GLOSS FINISH—a category of interior paint or varnish formulated to produce a very lustrous glossy finish.

HOLIDAYS—areas of a surface missed by the refinisher. Also known as "skips."

INERT—inactive, a material to which the word "inert" is applied will not react chemically with other ingredients used with it in making paint, varnish, or enamel.

IRON OXIDE—a pigment available in red, brown, and yellow. It is sold under many names, such as jeweler's rouge, Venetian red, Indian red, mineral rouge, Spanish oxide, turkey red, and many others.

JACK FROST—a novelty lacquer that dries like frost on a windowpane.

JAPAN DRIER—varnish gum with a large proportion of metallic salts added for rapid drying. A japan drier for grinding with pigment colors should allow thinning with turpentine.

JEWELER'S ROUGE—*see* Iron Oxide.

KNOT—that portion of a branch or limb that has been surrounded by subsequent growth of the wood of the trunk or other portion of the tree. As a knot appears on the sawed surface, it is merely a section of the entire knot, its shape depending upon the direction of the cut.

KRAFT PAPER—a brownish paper made of sulfate pulp and used for wrapping paper, bags, containers, and various other products where strength is more important than color.

LAC—a natural resin secreted by the lac insect found in the Far East, and the only source of shellac.

LACQUER—a fast-drying finishing material containing an appreciable amount of nitrocellulose in combination with various gum resins and solvents.

LACQUER ENAMEL—clear lacquer with pigment added for color.

LAMPBLACK—a black pigment consisting of finely divided carbon.

LATEX—a dispersion emulsion of natural or synthetic rubber, or rubberlike resin in water.

LEVELING—the formation of a smooth film on either a horizontal or vertical surface by any means of application. A film that has good leveling characteristics is comparatively free of brushmarks.

LINSEED OIL—a vegetable oil, pressed from seeds of the flax plant. The raw material after heating and filtering is raw linseed oil. Heated to a higher temperature so as to admit a small amount of metallic drier, the oil becomes boiled linseed oil, even though it doesn't get that hot.

LIQUID FILLER—lacquer or varnish with finely divided inert pigments added.

LONG-OIL VARNISH—a varnish made with a relatively high proportion of oil to resin. They are generally slower drying, tougher, and more elastic than short-oil varnishes. Spar varnish is an excellent example of a long-oil varnish.

LUMBER—the product of the saw and planing mill, not further manufactured than by sawing, resawing, passing lengthwise through a standard planing machine, cross-cutting to length, and matching.

MASKING TAPE—a pressure-sensitive paper tape which, when properly placed around a surface to be painted, allows even cutoffs.

METAL PRIMER—first coater on metal. It is low in pigment but has great adhesive properties.

MILLWORK—generally, all building materials made of finished wood and manufactured in millwork plants and planing mills. Includes such items as inside and outside doors, window and door frames, blinds, porch work, mantels, panelwork, stairways, moldings, and interior trim. Does not include flooring, ceiling, or siding.

MINERAL SPIRITS—thinner with a petroleum base.

MOISTURE CONTENT—the percentage of water in lumber. Should be about 7 percent for furniture.

NAPHTHA—hydrocarbons suitable for use as paint thinners. Also called VM & P (Varnish Makers & Painters) Naphtha or Benzene.

NATURAL RESINS—obtained from the gummy exudations of trees. Damars and copals are the two main types of natural resins and are usually named after the locality in which they are found or the port from which they are shipped.

NEUTRAL OIL—a light-gravity mineral oil used in finishing rubbed work with pumice stone.

NITROCELLULOSE—raw cotton cellulose mixed with nitric and other acids. The basis for lacquers.

OCHRE—an earth pigment composed of yellow iron oxide.

OIL—a smooth, greasy, combustible material. Oils are classed as vegetable, animal, or mineral.

OIL COLORS—colors ground to a paste form in linseed oil.

OIL RUBBING—describes the process of rubbing a finished surface with oil and pumice or other mild abrasive. Neutral oil, paraffin oil, etc., are commonly used, also crude petroleum.

OIL-SOLUBLE—materials capable of being dissolved in oils, including linseed oil, turpentine, benzol, naphtha. Colored stains of this type are called oil yellow, oil red, etc.

OIL STAINS—oil-soluble colors in naphtha or similar solvent are oil stains of the penetrating type; oil-soluble colors in naphtha or turpentine but with pigment colors and a binder, such as linseed oil, are called pigment-oil stains. Wiping stains are pigment-oil stains.

OITICICA OIL—oil obtained from the oiticica nut, very similar to tung oil.

OLEO RESINOUS—any varnish made of oil and resin.

OPEN DEFECT—any irregularity such as a check, split, open joint, crack, knothole, or loose knot that interrupts the smooth continuity of wood veneer.

ORANGE PEEL—roughened appearance of a sprayed film caused by improper solvent balance. Happens with lacquer and enamel.

ORGANIC COLORS—pigments of animal, vegetable, or dyestuff origin (alizarine crimson and carmine).

OXIDIZE—to unite with oxygen.

PANEL—a sheet of plywood of any construction type.

PARTICLEBOARD—a composition board consisting of distinct particles of wood bonded together with a synthetic resin or other added binder.

PASTE FILLER—a filling material in paste form which is diluted with turpentine, naphtha, etc., before using. Usually refers to a filler for wood.

PEARLING LACQUER—fish scales (guanin) in suspension in a clear lacquer. In unmixed paste form, Pearl Essence.

PEELING—condition occurring when a paint film breaks away in comparatively large pieces. Usually due to applying paint on damp or greasy surfaces.

PENETRATING STAIN—stain color in oil or alcohol.

PERILLA OIL—a drying oil obtained from the seed of the perilla plant.

PIGMENT—finely ground mineral materials that are insoluble in oils, varnishes, lacquers, thinners, etc. They are used to impart color, opacity, and hiding power as well as other effects.

PLASTIC RESIN—a synthetic resin of very large molecular size having properties similar to a plastic.

PLASTIC WOOD—a mixture of groundwood and lacquer used to patch holes in wood surfaces. Trade name for wood dough.

PLASTICIZERS—a soft resin or oil added to or mixed in with hard resins that would otherwise be too brittle for practical use.

PLY—a single sheet of veneer, or several sheets laid with adjoining edges, that may or may not be glued, which form one layer in a piece of plywood.

PLYWOOD—a crossbanded assembly made of layers of veneer, or veneer in combination with a lumber core, particleboard core, or other type of composition material, or plies joined with an adhesive. Except for special construction, the grain of one or more plies is approximately at right angles to that of the other plies, and an odd number of plies is used.

POLYURETHANE RESIN—*see* Urethane Resin.

POLYVINYL ACETATE (PVA)—synthetic resins; have a high degree of stability, abrasion resistance, and durability. Usually used in latex form in paints.

POROUS SURFACE—any surface that will readily absorb a liquid such as water.

PRIMER—the "ground" or first coat.

PUMICE—a finely ground, soft stone abrasive used to obtain a satiny rubbed effect on varnished or enameled surfaces. 3F or 4F (the finest) is used on furniture.

PUTTY—a doughlike mixture of pigment (usually whiting) and linseed oil, sometimes mixed with white lead. Used to set glass in window frame, and to fill holes and cracks in wood.

PYROXYLIN—nitrocellulose.

QUARTERSAWED—*see* Grain: Edge-Grained Lumber.

RADIAL—coincident with a radius from the axis of the tree or log to the circumference. A radial section is a lengthwise section in a plane that extends from pith to bark.

RAW OIL—oil as received from the extracting process, and in its natural state.

RAYS, WOOD—strips of cells extending radially within a tree and varying in height from a few cells in some species to 4 or more inches in oak. The rays serve primarily to store food and transport it horizontally in the tree.

RED LEAD—a lead oxide used as a rust-inhibiting pigment, as well as a source of lead in driers.

REFINED SHELLAC—a grade of shellac from which the wax has been removed.

REMOVERS—liquid or paste compositions formulated to soften old paint or varnish coats and to aid in their removal by washing or scraping.

RESIN—a solid or semisolid material of vegetable or synthetic origin. The color ranges from yellow to amber to dark brown. Resin is usually transparent or translucent and is found in varying degrees of hardness. Soluble in alcohol but not in water.

RETARDERS—slow-drying solvents added to lacquer to slow or retard the drying time.

RING, ANNUAL—the annual growth layer as viewed on a cross section of a stem, branch, or root.

ROSIN—a relatively soft resin obtained from the exudations of pine trees. Wood rosin is obtained from stumps or from dead wood, while gum rosin is obtained from the living trees.

ROTARY CUT—veneer obtained by rotating a log against a cutting knife in such a way that a continuous sheet of veneer is unrolled spirally from the log.

ROTTENSTONE—a very fine limestone abrasive generally used after pumice to bring out a high gloss.

RUBBING COMPOUND—an abrasive mixture in paste form. Commonly used for rubbing lacquer surfaces. Supplied in various grades of fineness and in different types of mixing with water or mixing with naphtha.

RUBBING OIL—neutral, medium-heavy mineral oil used as a lubricant for pumice stone in rubbing varnish and lacquer.

RUBBING VARNISH—a hard-drying varnish that may be rubbed with an abrasive and water or oil to a uniform surface (almost all varnishes fall into this category).

RUNS—wrinkles in a paint film due to uneven flow. Also known as "sags."

SAFFLOWER OIL—a vegetable drying oil extracted from the seeds of the safflower plant. Normally grown in Nebraska, Colorado, and California.

SAGS—*see* Runs.

SANDING SEALER—a lacquer used as a seal coat over filler. It is usually given some filling action by the addition of a small amount of inert substances.

SAPWOOD—the living wood of pale color near the outside of the log. Under most conditions the sapwood is more susceptible to decay than heartwood.

SCARFING—the beveled cutting of the ends of two pieces of wood preparatory to forming a glued joint between them, called a scarf joint.

SEALER—a coat of shellac, paint, or other material used for the purpose of sealing the pores in a surface before top-coating.

SEASONING—removing moisture from greenwood to improve its serviceability.

> **AIR-DRIED**—dried by exposure to air, usually in a yard, without artificial heat.

> **KILN-DRIED**—dried in a kiln with the use of artificial heat.

SECOND GROWTH—timber that has grown after removal by cutting, fire, wind, or other agency, of all or large part of the previous stand.

SEMIGLOSS FINISH—a category of interior paint formulated to produce a slight luster.

SET—a paint film that has dried to the extent that it is firm is said to have "set."

SHELLAC—lac in flake form, suspended in an alcohol vehicle. (*See* Lac.) Natural shellac is orange and is whitened by bleaching.

SHORT-OIL VARNISH—a varnish with a relatively high proportion of resin to oil. Furniture and floor varnishes are usually short-oil varnishes. Produces a very hard surface that is resistant to wear and scuffing.

SIENNA—an earth pigment that is brownish yellow when raw, orange-red or reddish brown when burnt.

SILEX—a form of silica (quartz rock) used in making paste wood fibers and filler. It is transparent when combined with oil and is chemically inert and nonshrinking.

SILICONES—the oxide of silicon reduced to liquid form.

SKINNING—formation of a solid film on the exposed surface of paint or varnish in a container.

SLICING—the production of veneer by driving a half-log or flitch down against a pressure bar and knife while being held against a metal bedplate. The shearing action produces very smooth surfaces.

SOFTWOOD—wood derived from a coniferous tree, or the tree itself. The term has no reference to the actual hardness of the wood, although the wood from those trees *is* usually softer.

SOLVENT—any liquid capable of dissolving a certain material is said to be a solvent for that material.

SOYA OR SOYBEAN OIL—a vegetable oil extracted from soya beans. Particularly useful in finishing materials when combined in an alkyd resin.

SPACKLING COMPOUND—a finely ground mixture of powders which, when mixed with water, give a paste to be used in the repair of hairline cracks, nicks, and small holes in plaster or wood.

SPAR VARNISH—a very durable long-oil varnish formulated for resisting wear and tear on exterior surfaces, particularly boats and other marine surfaces. Formerly used on the spars of sailing ships, hence its name.

SPIRIT—sometimes used instead of "alcohol."

SPRINGWOOD—the portion of the annual growth ring that is formed during the early part of the season's growth. In most softwoods, and in ring-porous hardwoods, it is less dense and weaker mechanically than summerwood.

STAIN—coloring matter that is completely soluble in the liquid with which it is mixed. Differs from paint, lacquer, etc., where the coloring matter is finely divided pigments held in suspension and deposited on the surface of the work.

STEEL WOOL—fine strands of steel, used for rubbing varnished or lacquered surfaces, removing rust, etc. Comes in various grades. The more 0's in the designation, the finer the material.

STICK SHELLAC—shellac in solid stick form and in a wide variety of colors. Used for filling imperfections in wood.

STIPPLED FINISH—a textured finish obtained by special spraying equipment or by twisting and patting a piece of crumpled paper over the finish.

SUMMERWOOD—the portion of the annual growth ring that is formed after the springwood formation has ceased. In most softwoods and in ring-porous hardwoods, it is denser and stronger mechanically than springwood.

SURFACER—any finishing material used to build up a level surface (usually fillers).

SYNTHETIC—applies to any finishing material made wholly or in part from artificial resins.

TACK—a slight stickiness or tackiness on the surface of a paint or varnish film before it is completely set.

TACK CLOTH—a cloth impregnated with chemicals to provide a tackiness. Used for removing dust from surfaces to be finished.

TALL OIL—a drying oil obtained during the processing of pine-tree pulp.

TANGENTIAL—strictly, coincident with a tangent at the circumference of a tree or log, or parallel to such a tangent. In practice, however, it often means roughly coincident with a growth ring. A tangential section is a longitudinal section through a tree or limb and is perpendicular to a radius. Flat-grained and plainsawed lumber is sawed tangentially.

TEMPERA—water thinned or water-emulsion paint.

TEXTURE—a term often used interchangeably with grain. Sometimes used to combine the concepts of density and degree of contrast between springwood and summerwood.

THINNERS—volatile liquids used to regulate the consistency of paint and varnish.

THIXOTROPY—a condition wherein paint assumes a heavy body when undisturbed and a thin body when stirred or shaken.

TINT—a color diluted with white. Made by blending a full-strength color with white.

TITANIUM DIOXIDE—a compound of titanium, white in color. Used as a pigment in white and enamels and noted for its extreme hiding power and long-lasting whiteness.

TOLUOL—a coal-tar naphtha. Used as a diluent in the formulation of lacquer.

TONERS—pure dye colors ground into pigment and combined with a clear lacquer. Used to form a translucent base color in wood finishing, combining staining, and lacquering in one operation.

TUNG OIL—a drying oil obtained from the nut of the tung tree. Also known as Chinawood oil.

TURPENTINE—a colorless, volatile solvent obtained by distillation of the oleoresinous secretions found in pine trees, living and dead.

UMBER—an earth pigment of hydrated iron manganese ore. Ranges from olive shades in a raw condition to a dark rich brown in the burned state.

UNDERCOAT—any film below the top coat.

URETHANE (OR POLYURETHANE) RESIN—a synthetic resin formed by reaction of vegetable oils with certain uric acids.

VALUE—the lightness or darkness of a color.

VAN DYKE BROWN—a brown pigment which consists of decomposed vegetable matter that has almost become coal.

VARNISH—a liquid composition that is converted to a translucent or transparent solid film after being applied in a thin layer. Dries by oxidation of its vehicle.

VARNISH STAIN—varnish in which a stain has been dissolved.

VEGETABLE OIL—oils obtained from the seeds or nuts of vegetable growth. Such oils include linseed, soybean, hempseed, tung, perilla, and castor.

VEHICLE—the liquid portion of a varnish or paint. (*See* Binder.)

VENETIAN RED—a pigment consisting of calcium sulfate and red iron oxide.

VERMILION—sulfide of mercury used as a pigment.

VINYL—a synthetic resin resulting from the blending of copolymers or vinyl chloride and vinyl acetate.

VISCOSITY—the fluid thickness of an oil, varnish, paint, or enamel.

VOLATILE—said of a liquid that evaporates readily upon exposure to air.

WATER STAIN—colored dyes soluble in water.

WATER WHITE—transparent, like water. Used to describe any exceptionally clear lacquer or varnish.

WHITE LEAD—compounds of lead used as white pigments in many types of paint. Made in two types: basic lead carbonate and basic lead sulfate.

WHITING—calcium carbonate, limestone, or chalk used as pigments. Used principally for making putty and as an extender.

WOOD ALCOHOL—methyl alcohol, methanol. An alcohol obtained from the destructive distillation of wood.

XYLOL—an aromatic solvent produced from coal tar.

INDEX

Q

Quartersawed lumber, 13
Queen Anne period furniture, 66

R

Rabbeted joint, 82
Radial-arm saw, 40
Razor blades, 33
Reamalgamation, 118
Reed seat, 217
Resorcinol glue, 54
Ring removal, 113
Rope, 32
Rottenstone, 38
Router, 42
Rush seats, 48, 210

S

Sanding block, 34
Scraper, 36
Scratch awl, 35
Scratches, 113
Screw, 33, 104
Sealer coat, 142, 158
Seasoning lumber, 14
Seats, 199
Shaker style furniture, 73
Shears, 46
Shellac, 111, 150
    cutting chart, 166
    removing, 130
Sheraton, Thomas, 68
Slip seat, 199
Softwood, 10
Soybean glue, 53
Spindle-and-post chair, 207
Splattern, 186
Splint seat, 217

Split wood, 102
Spoke shave, 41
Springs, 172
Stains, 138
Staples, 45, 170
Steel wool, 37
Stencils, 194
Sticking drawer, 101
Stone tabletops, 226
Striping, 184
Stripping fabric, 169
Structural repair, 87
Styles of furniture, 61
"Surform" plane, 40
Synthetic-resin glue, 54

T

Tabletops, 221
Tack hammer, 45
Tape decoration, 198
Tissue paper finish, 198
Tools, 32
Tortoise-shell finish, 186
Traditional English furniture, 66
Trees, 10
Turpentine, 38
Tying springs, 173

U

Unfinished furniture, 147
Upholstery, 167
    care, 235
    tools, 45

V

Varnish, 112, 119, 152
    removal, 130